AF412167

Kierkegaard's Mirrors

Kierkegaard's Mirrors

Interest, Self, and Moral Vision

Patrick Stokes

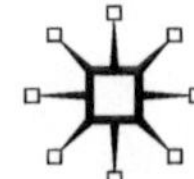

First published 2010 by
PALGRAVE MACMILLAN

Palgrave Macmillan in the UK is an imprint of Macmillan Publishers Limited, registered in England, company number 785998, of Houndmills, Basingstoke, Hampshire RG21 6XS.

Palgrave Macmillan in the US is a division of St Martin's Press LLC, 175 Fifth Avenue, New York, NY 10010.

Palgrave Macmillan is the global academic imprint of the above companies and has companies and representatives throughout the world.

Palgrave® and Macmillan® are registered trademarks in the United States, the United Kingdom, Europe and other countries.

ISBN-13: 978–0–230–24000–1 hardback

This book is printed on paper suitable for recycling and made from fully managed and sustained forest sources. Logging, pulping and manufacturing processes are expected to conform to the environmental regulations of the country of origin.

A catalogue record for this book is available from the British Library.

A catalog record for this book is available from the Library of Congress.

10 9 8 7 6 5 4 3 2 1
19 18 17 16 15 14 13 12 11 10

Printed and bound in Great Britain by
CPI Antony Rowe, Chippenham and Eastbourne

*To Jess, for her boundless love,
wisdom, patience, and faith.*

Contents

Acknowledgments

During my candidature at the University of Melbourne, Christopher Cordner provided guidance, encouragement, suggestions, and thoughtful discussion throughout the project that were invaluable both for developing the argument and placing it in a broader and richer context. I'm also grateful to Ian Weeks for his knowledgeable assistance and advice.

I spent two wonderfully productive periods at the Howard V. Hong and Edna H. Hong Kierkegaard Library at St. Olaf College, Minnesota: as a Summer Fellow in June 2002 (also partially funded by a grant from the Faculty of Arts at the University of Melbourne), and a Kierkegaard House Foundation Fellowship in July–December 2007. I can't do enough to express my gratitude to Gordon D. Marino, Cynthia Lund, the Foundation, and to the various staff and scholars at the library and the St Olaf community for these invaluable opportunities.

Final work on the manuscript took place under the auspices of a Danish Research Council for the Humanities Postdoctoral Fellowship at the Søren Kierkegaard Research Centre, University of Copenhagen. My deep thanks to Niels Jørgen Cappelørn, Bjarne Laurberg Olsen, and all my friends and colleagues at SKC for their help and support.

Julia Watkin provided advice and encouragement at several early stages of the project. Julia was always incredibly kind and helpful to me as she was to so many others; her passing in January 2005 robbed the Kierkegaard Studies community of one of its most loved and admired figures.

Chapters 2 and 3 were published as ' "Interest" in Kierkegaard's Structure of Consciousness' in *International Philosophical Quarterly*, 48:4 (December 2008) pp. 437–58, reprinted with kind permission of the publisher. Much of Chapters 6 and 7 were published as 'Kierkegaard's Mirrors: The Immediacy of Moral Vision' in *Inquiry* 50:1 (February 2007) pp. 70–94, reprinted by kind permission of Taylor & Francis Ltd (http://www.tandf.co.uk/journals). Most of Chapter 8 was published as 'Kierkegaardian Vision and the Concrete Other' in *Continental Philosophy Review* 39:4 (December 2006) pp. 393–413, reprinted with kind permission from Springer Science + Business Media. Abbreviations for primary sources used in the present work utilize the *International Kierkegaard*

Commentary series sigla, reproduced with the kind permission of Series Editor Robert L. Perkins and Mercer University Press.

This book has accumulated far too many intellectual and practical debts for me to ever reckon them all, but my special thanks to the following: William McDonald, Andrew Burgess, Robert Perkins, Sylvia Walsh, Marion Tapper, Douglas Adeney, Adam Buben, Søren Landkilde-hus, David Possen, John Lippitt, Anthony Rudd, John Davenport, James Giles, Kinya Masugata, Shin Fujieda, Nicole Saunders, Stephen Filmer, and various attendees at the 8th Australasian Philosophy Postgraduate Conference at the University of New England, September 2002, the 5th International Kierkegaard Conference, St Olaf College, June 2005, and the Kierkegaard and Asia Conference, University of Melbourne, December 2005.

Finally of course, my deepest thanks to my family and friends for their much-needed support, and, most of all, to my wife Jessica, without whose tireless help and unflagging encouragement this book would never have been possible.

Copenhagen
April 2009

Sigla

References to *Kierkegaard's Writings* (Princeton, NJ: Princeton University Press) and *Søren Kierkegaard's Journals and Papers* follow the sigla used in Mercer University Press' *International Kierkegaard Commentary* series:

CA   *The Concept of Anxiety* trans. Reidar Thomte in collaboration with Albert B. Anderson (1980)

CD   *Christian Discourses* and *The Crisis and a Crisis in the Life of an Actress* trans. Howard V. Hong and Edna H. Hong (1997)

CI   *The Concept of Irony* together with 'Notes on Schelling's Berlin Lectures' trans. Howard V. Hong and Edna H. Hong (1989)

CUP   *Concluding Unscientific Postscript to 'Philosophical Fragments'*, 2 vols., trans. Howard V. Hong and Edna H. Hong (1992)

EO, 1   *Either/Or* Volume One trans. Howard V. Hong and Edna H. Hong (1987)

EO, 2   *Either/Or* Volume Two trans. Howard V. Hong and Edna H. Hong (1995)

EUD   *Eighteen Upbuilding Discourses* trans. Howard V. Hong and Edna H. Hong (1990)

FSE   *For Self-Examination* and *Judge For Yourself!* trans. Howard V. Hong and Edna H. Hong (1990)

FT   *Fear and Trembling* and *Repetition* trans. Howard V. Hong and Edna H. Hong (1983)

JC   *Johannes Climacus or De omnibus dubitandum est.* See *Philosophical Fragments.*

JP   *Søren Kierkegaard's Journals and Papers*, 7 vols., ed. and trans. Howard V. Hong and Edna H. Hong, assisted by Gregor Malantschuk (Bloomington, IN, and London: Indiana University Press, 1967–78) (citiations give entry number rather than page number)

PC   *Practice in Christianity* trans. Howard V. Hong and Edna H. Hong (1991)

PF   *Philosophical Fragments* and *Johannes Climacus* trans. Howard V. Hong and Edna H. Hong (1985)

SLW   *Stages on Life's Way* trans. Howard V. Hong and Edna H. Hong (1988)

SUD   *The Sickness Unto Death* trans. Howard V. Hong and Edna H. Hong (1980)

UDVS   *Upbuilding Discourses in Various Spirits* trans. Howard V. Hong and Edna H. Hong (1993)

TM   *The Moment and Late Writings* trans. Howard V. Hong and Edna H. Hong (1998)

WL   *Works of Love* trans. Howard V. Hong and Edna H. Hong (1995)

The corresponding volume and page number in *Søren Kierkegaards Skrifter* (Copenhagen: Gads Forlag) has been provided wherever available:

SKS 1   *Af en endnu Levendes Papirer, Om Begrebet Ironi* ed. Niels Jørgen Cappelørn, Joakim Garff, Johnny Kondrup, and Finn Hauberg Mortensen (1997)

SKS 2   *Enten-Eller, Første del* ed. Niels Jørgen Cappelørn, Joakim Garff, Johnny Kondrup, and Finn Hauberg Mortensen (1997)

SKS 3   *Enten-Eller, Anden del* ed. Niels Jørgen Cappelørn, Joakim Garff, Johnny Kondrup, and Finn Hauberg Mortensen (1997)

SKS 4   *Gjentagelsen, Frygt og Bæven, Philosophiske Smuler, Begrebet Angest, Forord* ed. Niels Jørgen Cappelørn, Joakim Garff, Johnny Kondrup, and Finn Hauberg Mortensen (1997)

SKS 5   *Opbyggelige taler, 1843–44, Tre Taler ved tænkte Leiligheder* ed. Niels Jørgen Cappelørn, Joakim Garff, Jette Knudsen, Johnny Kondrup, and Finn Hauberg Mortensen (1998)

SKS 6   *Stadier paa Livets Vei* ed. Niels Jørgen Cappelørn, Joakim Garff, Jette Knudsen, Johnny Kondrup, and Finn Hauberg Mortensen (1999)

SKS 7   *Afsluttende uvidenskabelig Efterskrift* ed. Niels Jørgen Cappelørn, Joakim Garff, Jette Knudsen, and Johnny Kondrup (2002)

SKS 8   *En literair Anmeldelse og Opbyggelige Taler i forskjellig Aand* ed. Niels Jørgen Cappelørn, Joakim Garff, and Johnny Kondrup (2004)

SKS 9   *Kjærlighedens Gjerninger* ed. Niels Jørgen Cappelørn, Joakim Garff, and Johnny Kondrup (2004)

SKS 10   *Christlige Taler* ed. Niels Jørgen Cappelørn, Joakim Garff, and Johnny Kondrup (2004)

SKS 11   *Lilien paa Marken og Fuglen under Himlen, Tvende ethisk religieuse Smaa Afhandlinger, Sygdommen til Døden og 'Ypperstepræsten' – 'Tolderen' – 'Synderinden'* ed. Niels Jørgen

Cappelørn, Joakim Garff, Anne Mette Hansen, and Johnny Kondrup (2006)

SKS 12 *Indøvelse i Christendom, En opbyggelig Tale og To Taler ved Altergangen om Fredagen* ed. Niels Jørgen Cappelørn, Joakim Garff, Anne Mette Hansen, and Johnny Kondrup (2008)

SKS 18 *Journalerne EE, FF, GG, HH, JJ og KK* ed. Niels Jørgen Cappelørn, Joakim Garff, Jette Knudsen, and Johnny Kondrup (2001)

SKS 21 *Journalerne NB6-NB10* ed. Niels Jørgen Cappelørn, Joakim Garff, Jette Knudsen, and Johnny Kondrup (2003)

SKS 22 *Journalerne NB11-NB14* ed. Niels Jørgen Cappelørn, Joakim Garff, Jette Knudsen, and Johnny Kondrup (2005)

SKS 24 *Journalerne NB21-NB25* ed. Niels Jørgen Cappelørn, Joakim Garff, Anne Mette Hansen, and Johnny Kondrup (2007)

Where the relevant text has not yet appeared in SKS, I have cited *Søren Kierkegaards Samlede Værker* 2nd Edition. ed. A.B. Drachman, J.L. Heiberg, and H.O. Lange (Copenhagen: Gyldendalske Boghandel, 1901–06), indicated as 'SV2' followed by the volume and page number; and *Søren Kierkegaards Papirer*, ed. P. A. Heiberg, V. Kuhr, E. Torsting, Niels Thulstrup, and Niels Jørgen Cappelørn (Copenhagen: Gyldendal, 1909–48; 1968–70; 1975–78), designated '*Pap.*' and cited in the standard format: volume and tome number, entry category and number, and where appropriate page number and date e.g. (*Pap.* IV C 100, *n.d.* 1842–43).

Introduction

A thoughtless act

Let's begin, as Kierkegaard might begin, with a little thought-experiment.

On some indifferent evening, you and I sit in our homes in our respective slices of generic suburbia, watching inane television and grazing mindlessly on gloriously unhealthy snacks. You and I, let's say, are very similar – in fact, for the sake of argument, startlingly similar. We have near-identical backgrounds, temperaments, life experiences, moral commitments, political views, and religious beliefs. Beyond this, we have very similar *characters*. Now I don't, for a second, think it's possible to give anything like an exhaustive description of a person's character or personality.[1] Most elements of personality often can't be well-described *at all*; which is perhaps why we can learn more about a person's character from a few expressive actions than from extensive adjective-laden descriptions. But we know, I think, what it is to encounter two people with strikingly similar characters. Let's assume that's what an impartial observer would say about you and me.

Given how similar we are, one might reasonably expect that our motivational structures, our more-or-less settled patterns of seeing, caring, and responding to the world, will be correspondingly similar. When faced with the same state of affairs, we'd expect that we should, all things being equal, see the same features of the situation as salient, experience the same affective responses, and, at least most of the time, tend to act in ways that seem to express the same volitional responses to what we encounter.

At this moment, we also happen to be watching the same TV news program. The lead story tonight is about a massive humanitarian crisis abroad, perhaps an event like the Indian Ocean tsunami of December 2004. We are confronted with scenes of unimaginable human suffering. Involuntarily we let out sighs of profound sadness and pity at the fates of the people we see, and reel at the incomprehensible scale of the disaster. If asked later, we'd describe our mental state as a mixture of horror, pity, distress and an overwhelming sense that something should be done.

But here's where we part ways. I sit in my chair and ruminate on the horror of what I've seen and the urgency of addressing the problem. You leap from your chair and look up the phone number for the Red Cross, so you can call and find out what you can do to help – make a cash donation? Organize a food drive? Get on a plane and join the relief effort? In effect, you have acted, while I have continued to contemplate ineffectually without acting. Crucially, you didn't stop to think whether you are obliged to act, or whether you *should*. You didn't, in fact, stop to think *at all*.

So what's *missing* in my response that's present in yours? Successive models of moral psychology will struggle to accommodate this question. My response looks, superficially at least, like some form of *akrasia*, such as Plato flatly denied could exist and Aristotle attempted to explain away. However, the Aristotelian account of *akrasia* (usually translated, somewhat old-fashionedly, as 'incontinence') doesn't seem to have room for this situation. Clearly I'm not 'asleep or mad or drunk,' nor am I acting by virtue of some overpowering desire that is 'contrary to right reason.'[2] Nor does the distinction between knowledge we are using and knowledge we are not using (in the way that your knowledge that Moscow is in Russia was somehow 'inert' – not present to mind – until you read this sentence)[3] seem to help here.[4] As I've set up the example, you haven't had some thought to the effect that 'I can do something' or even 'I *should* do something' – you've simply moved immediately from a perception of the situation to the act of trying to help. True, your action expresses your *knowledge that you can* help, in the same way that my driving to the store expresses that I *know* how to drive a car. But just as I don't bring a series of cognitions about how to drive a car to mind as I do so ('turn the wheel slightly to the right, depress the accelerator...'), nor do you bring to mind some proposition about of yourself as an agent capable of acting in situations like this. At least, *you* don't, in this example. Perhaps a morally weaker person than you might have to remind themselves that they *can* act, but your action is so immediate there's simply no room for such a thought to occur.

Aristotle could still, perhaps, try to find room for us in another description of *akrasia*, wherein the *akrates'* action is governed by a practical syllogism which uses the universal premise but not the particular.[5] But if we try to cash out the cognitions we have had during this time in these syllogistic terms the result looks not merely artificial, but utterly implausible. The claim would here be that you have one premise more than I do, one further *thought* – while my thought stops at 'Someone should do something,' you think some further minor premise ('I'm someone' perhaps?) and so proceed to the conclusion that *you* should do something. I either don't realize I'm someone (and what could that possibly mean?) or am not 'using' that knowledge at the time in question. This just seems like a false description of your thought processes during this experience. You haven't thought 'I'm someone' or anything like it, and the way in which such a syllogism maps out our respective behaviors sounds very far removed from our lived moral experience.

If we sign up instead to the influential Humean view of moral psychology, in which desires act as our motivating principle while beliefs are motivationally inert, we are no better off. We have, on the scenario above, formed the same beliefs about the situation and, it seems, the same desire that something be done to alleviate the suffering we've seen. It seems wrong to say that your motivational set includes *one desire more* than mine: a desire that it be *you* who helps alleviate suffering.[6] That sort of desire doesn't seem to figure in your experience at all. Why, then, are our actions not the same? Shouldn't near-identical belief-plus-desire concatenations entail near-identical actions just as much as identical practical syllogisms? Of course we might object that the very fact that you did act and I did not demonstrates that for all our dispositional similarity, you nonetheless *must* have one more disposition that I must lack: a disposition to act generously in response to this type of situation.[7] If so, the very example is incoherently set up from the outset. But this move looks very much like a retreat into some form of behaviorism. It tries to explain the anomalous action in a way that assumes having a disposition *just is* repeatedly acting in a certain way: by definition, then, two people could not have the same dispositions and yet act differently. There's something plausible about this suggestion, but it asks us to pay an awfully steep price. What we wanted was some explanatory account that reconciles the inner mental and outer behavioral elements of the situation, and here we're being offered a 'reconciliation' that simply jettisons the 'inner' altogether (or at least analyses it away into entirely 'outer' terms, whereby dispositions *just are* patterns of behavior). If we are to retain any robust notion of interiority at all, this option can't be on the table.

One thing that seems to shipwreck the foregoing (admittedly sketchy) attempts to describe what's gone wrong in my response to the situation is that we're accustomed to thinking about moral cognition as a distinctively deliberative process. Without a deliberatively generated decision, we seem to have an action that is impelled rather than chosen, something morally akin to, to use Christine Korsgaard's example, a mother animal instinctively defending her cub: 'it is deeply impressive and lovely that she should do so, but it is not morality.'[8] Yet if deliberation has any role to play in the example I've sketched, it is at the point where you are deciding *how* to act, not *whether* to act; or more precisely, having decided to *help*, deliberation commences as a process for determining a more precise specification of the help-act(s) you will perform.[9] What neither of us did was deliberate about *whether* to help. For you, perhaps it's the case that helping presented itself as something like an Aristotelian final end, the sort of thing we cannot deliberate about;[10] you can (and did) deliberate about the means but not the end itself. As for me, I didn't even get to *that* point.

Strictly speaking, you didn't even *resolve* to act. You just acted, with such fluidity that we might describe your perception of the situation and practical response thereto as seamless. And crucially, your response is no less morally praiseworthy for being curiously 'empty' on the level of overt, reflective cognition directed toward action. It's automatic, but we'd baulk at calling it 'thoughtless.' In fact, it may well be the optimal moral response to this sort of situation. We might even think *less* of you, morally, had you paused to think 'Wait a moment. Before I give reign to my impulsive desire to help, I should take a minute to ensure that helping is, in fact, the morally correct response in this situation.' Compare our judgments of the person who sees someone drop $20 from their pocket and rushes to give it back to them, versus to the person who stops to consider whether they should give it back or not. Regardless of whether we want to cash this out in terms of the possession of virtues or stable dispositional states or having correct maxims or whatever, stopping to think seems to represent a moral *failure* on some level. This is not absolute of course – reflexively handing the $20 back to its ski-mask clad 'owner' who just happens to be running away from the bank carrying a shotgun and a bag hastily stuffed full of $20 notes would seem *culpably* thoughtless – but there is something compelling and familiar about the idea that unreflective actions are sometimes more morally valuable than reflective ones.

If we'd be uneasy describing your actions as 'thoughtless,' we'd have no such qualms about describing my response in these terms. For my part, I haven't had any distinct cognitions that might prevent me from getting out of my chair ('I don't want to get up,' 'I don't want to spend money,' 'It's not my problem,' 'Governments rather than individual citizens have a responsibility to fix this' and so on) just as you haven't had any equivalent thoughts that *impel* you to action. To that extent, my response has been just as reflectively 'empty' as yours. Yet my 'thoughtlessness' seems to be risible while yours is laudable. As noted above, it's not clear that I'm failing to 'use' some knowledge that you are using, or that I'm failing to make some inference that you've made successfully. If someone wanted to judge us by our motives, this would be tricky – there's no reflective content to our thoughts that a Kantian might be able to hang his affectively denuded hat upon, while if the Kantian were instead to look for 'pathological' motives he'll find that we both have precisely the same affective response to the situation operating over the course of the experience. Nor are we being judged according to some consequentialist standard. The judgments we pronounce upon our responses would be unchanged if it turned out that in fact (purely for the sake of argument!) giving money to aid agencies is ineffective, or less effective than other options or positively harmful.

Ultimately, it seems hard to know what to say about this situation at all. But here's one possible way of describing it that seems at least *prima facie* apt. In the situation I've described, I see the suffering of others as morally compelling. You see the suffering of others as morally compelling *you*. This sounds natural enough. Yet there's no difference in the thematic or conceptual content of our thoughts: your thoughts, like mine, were taken up entirely with the tragic circumstances unfolding before us. There is some noncognitive element in your apprehension of the situation that's missing from mine, even though our apprehensions are identical on the level of their cognitive and affective content. How can this be the case?

This isn't the only puzzling element of the situation. Yours is a 'selfless' act, as that term is usually used. But in another sense, insofar as your response instantiates your character and expresses your beliefs and attitudes, while mine *belies* my stated beliefs and professed feelings, your action is redolent with self while mine is indeed describable as *selfless* in a far from laudatory way. Your response expresses your subjectivity, while mine expresses a certain *abstraction* in my moral attunement to the world. Somehow, you are *in* your action in a way that I am not. Yet both responses to the situation are equally unreflective. Moreover, we can imagine someone who does exactly what you do, but does it in an 'automatic' way – perhaps through force of habit, which of course is no less expressive of settled dispositions – that is just as unreflective as your response, but still *selfless* in the way *my* response is. How can *this* be the case?

I think we can start to formulate answers to these questions if we articulate a new understanding of moral cognition in terms of normative moral *vision* rather than normative deliberation, good will, and so forth. That's not a particularly new claim – after all, Aristotelian *phronesis* is very largely a matter of perception – but I further claim that we already have available to us a rich, philosophically sophisticated and psychologically astute account of moral cognition that sees the *telos* of moral experience as the coinciding of vision and volition. This account is to be found, with the application of a little bit of exegetical elbow grease, in the work of a thinker who understood as perhaps few have that in the context of our moral lives 'It does not depend, then, merely upon what one sees, but what one sees depends upon how one sees; for all observation is not merely a receiving, a discovering, but also a bringing forth, and insofar as it is that, how the observer himself *is* indeed becomes decisive' (EUD, 59/SKS 5, 69).

What about Kierkegaard?

A century and a half now separates us from the final writings of Søren Kierkegaard. His philosophical reception, especially in the Anglophone world, was slow to get going, but there has been a veritable explosion of Kierkegaard' commentary in North America and Europe since the 1970s, marked by ever-increasing sophistication and insight.[11] Those who wish to come to grips with Kierkegaard's expansive, often dense, deliberately unsystematic, maddeningly fragmented, resolutely polyvocal writings, now have a vast and expanding repository of critical literature to guide them.

Yet it is easy to forget how young, in the scheme of things, this modern phase of Kierkegaard scholarship is, and how much remains to be done. It is perhaps a function of that relative youth that a crucial question has barely been asked, let alone answered: what are we to *do* with the Kierkegaard that our exegetical activity has uncovered? Or as Roger Poole asks, following Derrida, 'What, after all, today, for us, here, now, about Kierkegaard?'[12] To ask this question, as an increasing number of commentators are starting to do, is to move beyond self-contained explication of Kierkegaardian texts and bring them into dialogue with living questions and problems in moral philosophy, philosophy of mind, narrative theory, metaphysics of selfhood, philosophy of religion, theology, and even questions on the relation between science and faith. Readings developed by commentators such as M. Jamie Ferreira, John J. Davenport, C. Stephen Evans, Rick Anthony Furtak and others demonstrate that Kierkegaard's work has something to contribute to mainstream discussions in which his thought has hitherto been a stranger – or, at best, a 'continental' novelty, useful for providing pithy quotes and epigrams but otherwise not worthy of serious engagement.

Much of Kierkegaard's continuing relevance derives from his richly developed phenomenology of human experience. In assessments of Kierkegaard's place in the history of European thought, his influence on the development of twentieth-century Existentialism and strands of contemporary theology are usually foregrounded. This is only to be expected, but these emphases tend to obscure another crucial innovation in his work: the probing phenomenology of moral psychology.[13] In this, Kierkegaard is virtually unchallenged in nineteenth-century continental thought. Few philosophers have captured the variety and complexity of human psychology as the 'connoisseur of the human heart'[14] Kierkegaard, for few philosophers have enjoyed the mimetic leeway Kierkegaard's project gives him. Through the use of literary and indirect modes of communication, Kierkegaard presents a more fully developed description of moral experience than any other 'philosophical' writer of his era. Equally, though, his work is clearly still philosophical in character; his project allows him to conceptualize his descriptions of existence such that concepts, not empirical data, structure and develop his observations.

The results of this fusion of psychological acuity and dialectical rigor are impressive in their scope and thoroughness. *The Concept of Anxiety* deserves a hallowed place in the history of pre-Freudian psychology for its attempt to provide a conceptual schema for the origin and development of the phenomenon of anxiety. *Either/Or* provides a literary depiction in its first volume of what it dialectically dissects in its second – the dysfunctional psychology of the aesthete whose pursuit of pleasure and refusal to live under ethical qualifications conceal a fundamental despair. *The Sickness Unto Death* re-describes this phenomenon of despair under the assumption of a religiously qualified ontology of the self; a surprisingly broad variety of recognizable psychological phenomena are brought into this account.[15] These descriptions are the pay-off of the ontology: as Anthony Rudd puts it, 'If his descriptions are telling, if we can recognize ourselves in them, then the formidable-sounding theoretical framework which he assembles at the beginning of the work has justified itself by being put to work to produce perspicuous representations of aspects of human life.'[16] Perhaps not everyone *will* recognize the states of anxiety and despair described in these strange books; someone might charge that Kierkegaard (as Bertrand Russell accused Sartre of doing) is trying to elevate a rather idiosyncratic psychology into an ontology.[17] But if the pictures he paints of such phenomena *are* convincing then it's significant that these accounts are always structured by an underlying ontology that describes the symptoms of these maladies *in terms of* their diagnoses. The state of one in despair, for instance, is articulated in explicitly ontological terms; the ontology informs the symptomatology.

Kierkegaard therefore provides us with a valuable repository of psychological observation and a highly articulated philosophical anthropology and ontology underlying and supporting it. This means his phenomenology cannot be discussed in isolation from the conceptual premises that underlie it (which may bring into question whether Kierkegaard's method can be called 'phenomenology' at all, even apart from the usual complaints from strict Husserlians); yet one can still find insights that may stand even if other premises of the Kierkegaardian project are rejected. One cannot, for instance, discuss Kierkegaard's account of despair without attending to its religious presuppositions, yet a non-theist reader may still find Kierkegaard's account of the ontology of selfhood compelling even if, in fact, nothing answers to the name of God as it figures in that ontology. Or they may find his diagnoses of psychological phenomena as symptoms of an underlying ontological dysfunction valuable even if they cannot accept the ontology in its entirety. Yet the conceptual basis of Kierkegaard's psychology necessitates careful and rigorous explication of his texts. If Kierkegaard is to yield resources for contemporary discussions and debates, we must be clear about what Kierkegaard is saying before we attempt to transplant his ideas, piecemeal or in whole, into alien contexts that may rob them of their foundations.

Kierkegaard's psychological vocabulary

If the depth with which Kierkegaard pursues moral psychology is innovative, the rich and varied vocabulary he develops to specify and explore crucial aspects of the interior life (as seen from an ethico-religious viewpoint) is no less remarkable. Kierkegaard's moral psychology emphasizes the importance of terms such as passion, inwardness, decision, despair, anxiety, interest, concern, earnestness, repetition, inclosing reserve, and, most centrally, faith. Some of these terms are used in senses not appreciably different to their everyday usage, while others are given specialized application in Kierkegaard's work. Some terms belong entirely to an economy of interiority (such as *inderlighed*, 'inwardness,' and *angest*, 'anxiety'), while others cut across the internal/external divide (as with *alvor* 'earnestness, seriousness'). Significantly, none are straightforwardly the names of emotions, although all could be expected to have some sort of connection with emotional states.

However, if Kierkegaard's psychological vocabulary is varied, it is also to that same extent often ambiguous and inconsistent. Terms are used in different senses in different contexts, are often interchangeable, and are given only oblique explications rather than clear definitions. *Alvor* (earnestness) is an instructive example of this. Kierkegaard's pseudonym Vigilius Haufniensis declares that 'it would please me' if no definition of earnestness existed, because earnestness is 'so earnest a matter that even a definition of it becomes a frivolity' (CA, 147/SKS 4, 447). Yet within a short space he offers statements that appear to take the form of definitions, yet really only situate *alvor* in relation to other undefined terms such as *inderlighed*. This claim occurs in a work that purports to explicate the 'Concept of Anxiety,' yet which deliberately seems to resist giving a direct definition of what anxiety is. Kierkegaard does not – and, according to Haufniensis' claim, cannot – furnish us with a clear and precise definition of what he means when he uses these terms. To do so would be to approach them in the wrong way – or as Haufniensis would put it, we falsify the concept when we approach it in the wrong 'mood (CA, 14–15/SKS 4, 321–2; see Chapter 10 for more on this). The task of seeking and testing a definition of a concept such as earnestness or passion would make us mere spectators to concepts that essentially demand immediate participation, which would be incompatible with preoccupation with academic questions about the precise meanings of these terms. However, that no direct definition of these psychological states can be given does not mean they are not proper topics for conceptual exploration, which is precisely the task of works like *The Concept of Anxiety*. It certainly does not preclude *us* from seeking to understand precisely how these terms operate in Kierkegaard's account of moral psychology.

A path through interest

In the pages that follow, my task is decidedly, indeed unapologetically, exegetical in character. Our topic, or at least our guiding concept, will be Kierkegaard's use of the term *interesse* ('interest') and the related *bekymring* ('concern'). As such we will mine one of the few largely untouched patches of ground left to the Kierkegaardian exegete. In a sense, however, our topic is in reality a much broader one: the self-referentiality built into thought that is a central and crucial theme throughout Kierkegaard's work.[18] In some places Kierkegaard uses terms like 'interest' and 'concern' to pick out this self-reflexive element of thought; in other places, it remains implicit and unnamed. I hope to show that the role Kierkegaard's pseudonym Climacus gives to 'interest' in the structure of consciousness is echoed in the ontological structure of selfhood enunciated by another pseudonym, Anti-Climacus, and elsewhere in the texts attributed to both 'authors' and beyond. The identity of this self-reflexivity across different texts and contexts warrants us in extending the name 'interest' to cover all instances of it. Throughout, we will draw on insights from twentieth-century philosophers – notably Iris Murdoch, Bernard Williams and Ludwig Wittgenstein – in order both to throw light on the Kierkegaardian material and to point to modern contexts in which Kierkegaardian thought may yet prove useful.[19]

The approach of the book is thematic rather than chronological in character, although we'll note chronological factors where these are relevant to the development of the argument. This methodology is quite deliberate. One obvious way of explicating an author's use of a specific term would be to follow the authorship from beginning to end, noting each occurrence of the term and any changes in meaning and context that become apparent in each instance. Certain key terms in Kierkegaard would allow for such an approach; for instance, Alistair Hannay instructively notes the differences in 'despair' as it is used in the earlier *Either/Or* and the later *The Sickness Unto Death*.[20] The continuities between earlier and later usages allow us to narrow down on what Kierkegaard means by the term; the changes show how his sense of it develops over time.

With *interesse*, however, such a chronological approach will struggle to get off the ground. The term is explicitly used mostly in the Climacan writings and some journal entries from the early 1840s. By the late 1840s the term had more or less dropped out of currency, at least in its philosophically engaging senses (it remains both as a commonplace nonphilosophical term and in the form of the aesthetic category of *det interessant*, 'the interesting'). Such an approach would perhaps then issue in a finding that *interesse* is a minor term, and that whatever philosophical value it had for the Kierkegaard of the earlier 1840s, he comes to abandon it by the end of the decade.

Yet this is not the case. As will be shown, what is picked out by the use of *interesse* in the earlier works not only continues to play a role in the later texts, it is in fact crucial to the moral psychology of a cluster of works written in 1848 (*The Sickness Unto Death, Practice in Christianity*) and later (*For Self-Examination*). This can only become apparent, however, if we abandon a purely chronological approach in favor of one that seeks to uncover a foundational sense of *interesse* and then show how that sense ramifies through Kierkegaard's more conceptually or descriptively fully fleshed works. We move from the foundational ontology to the descriptions of cognition and imagination in concrete situations and consider how the structural features of the ontology express themselves in the experiences of actual selves.

Therefore, instead of following Kierkegaard's authorship and noting each occurrence of the term *interesse*, the present study reconstructs Kierkegaard's meaning beginning from its use in the schematic account of consciousness in *Johannes Climacus, or De Omnibus Dubitandum Est*. By isolating the meaning of *interesse* in this foundational context – an ontological description of the triadic structure of consciousness – we can identify the basic structural role it plays. This allows us then to look at whether the triadic structure of selfhood developed in *The Sickness Unto Death* requires a structural feature cognate to the role of *interesse* in consciousness. Once we have identified the structural role of *interesse* we can see how it operates on the psychological level, and how these elemental features of cognition play themselves out in the actual experience of moral life. What this thematic approach loses in chronological fidelity is therefore more than made up for by what it gains in conceptual insight.

What ultimately emerges from this investigation into *interesse* is a picture of something at the very heart of moral agency: an immediate self-referentiality built into vision that normatively defines what it is to perceive moral situations correctly. This is already to locate Kierkegaard within a stream of moral psychology, represented by such diverse figures as Murdoch, McDowell and Frankfurt, which emphasizes that our moral experience is of a world already saturated with value; we see things and people *as* loveable, precious, and irreplaceable.[21] These qualities are no less real or crucial features of morality for their being 'in the eye of the beholder,' as it were. But the Kierkegaardian innovation is the realization that the value-ladenness of the world has a relationship to the observer richer than mere dependence (as is the case with properties like color or tone, which depend upon the constitution and position of the observer). What *interesse* adds to the perceptualist picture of moral cognition is an articulation of the way we see the world *as claiming us*. For Kierkegaard, we do not simply see the world as valuable, but as personally, specifically obligating. Events and persons present a moral demand in themselves, but what Kierkegaard also realizes is that this demand addresses itself personally to the observer, and its normative character grasps us as individuals. As such, *interesse* is a term which emanates from the very structure of consciousness as a condition of all properly actualized moral agency: to see the world aright is to see it with interest in the new, highly specific sense of the word that Kierkegaard opens up.

Our inquiry falls into three parts. Part I deals with the structures of subjectivity, the mechanics of Kierkegaard's accounts of consciousness and selfhood and the role *interesse* plays therein. In Chapter 1, I home in on the specific sense of *interesse* to be developed here, both distinguishing it from Kierkegaard's aesthetic sense of 'the interesting' and showing how that aesthetic sense subtly prefigures the more 'developed' sense. We also consider the use of *interesse* in Kant and Hegel, to provide some insight into the broader philosophical context of Kierkegaard's use of the term. Chapters 2 and 3 begin the investigation of *interesse* at the structural level by considering its role in *Johannes Climacus, or De Omnibus Dubitandum Est*'s account of the ontology of consciousness. The central features of *interesse* that will ramify through Kierkegaard's entire moral psychology can already be discerned here in skeletal form. However, attention to the implications of Climacus' structuralizing of *interesse* in the account of consciousness reveals shortcomings in most contemporary interpretations of this term. Chapter 4 remains at the structural level, discussing the ontology of selfhood articulated in *The Sickness Unto Death*. Here, self-referential cognition is shown to have a structural role corresponding to its role in consciousness.

In Part II, we turn our attention to moral cognition and imagination and the interrelations of vision, volition, and action in Kierkegaard's thought. Chapter 5 continues the discussion of *Sickness* but turns its attention to that work's account of ethical imagination. Here the phenomenon of *interesse* is shown to play a crucial role in maintaining the relation between the concrete agent and their imaginatively posited possibilities necessary for agency. Chapter 6 continues to explore Kierkegaard's phenomenology of moral cognition, focusing on his frequent use of metaphors of self-recognition. To 'recognize oneself' in various representations expresses the apprehension of self-identity that is crucial for agency. This theme is continued in Chapter 7, which specifically examines Kierkegaard's use of mirror metaphors to draw out key features of his account of moral vision, such as immediacy, teleology, and self-referentiality (all of which are contained in Kierkegaard's use of *interesse*). Chapter 8 carries this discussion into perennial debates over whether Kierkegaard's account of self-reflexive moral vision effaces the other in their concrete particularity, reducing them to a mere cipher of duty. It argues that the non-thetic character of interest allows the other to stand simultaneously as distinctive other and moral demand.

Part III moves into questions of knowledge and meaning, and how the dialectic of knower and known in Kierkegaard centralizes the self-reflexivity we've by now come to know as *interesse*. Chapter 9 considers the discussion of 'concern' (*bekymring*) in the *Upbuilding Discourses*. In the face of misfortune and tragedy, we humans desperately seek meaning; but as Kierkegaard claims in both the *Discourses* and the *Concluding Unscientific Postscript*, the sort of meaning we seek involves 'concerned' knowledge, an understanding in which the subject is personally and essentially implicated. Chapter 10 looks more closely at the Climacan writings, arguing that despite some appearances to the contrary, the *Postscript* uses *interesse* in precisely the sense developed throughout the book. Here we see the teleological aspects of vision implicit in the account of moral cognition extended to knowledge, exploring Kierkegaard's use of locutions such as 'concerned knowledge' and the relationship between self-knowledge and knowledge *about* oneself.

In the Conclusion, I return to our thought-experiment developed above and suggest how Kierkegaard's concept of interest has equipped us with a powerful new grammar of moral vision, one that allows us to re-describe this situation in a new and compelling way.

A word about pseudonymity

Though this book seeks to synthesize disparate uses of *interesse* across the corpus into a single, coherent account of what the term means, Kierkegaard's technique of pseudonymity places important caveats on any such synthetic reading. The pseudonyms exist not to obscure authorship but to express distinct and often contradictory life-views, and accordingly the distinction between Kierkegaard's authorial voice and those of the pseudonyms must be taken seriously. Though Kierkegaard's position is often identical with that of certain pseudonyms, the distinction must still be maintained lest the deliberately polyvocal, multi-perspectival content of his authorship(s) be collapsed into a single 'Kierkegaardian' viewpoint. Poole has argued that Kierkegaard's earliest English-speaking proponents, such as Walter Lowrie, produced distorted readings of Kierkegaard precisely because of this project of 'blunt reading' that ignores pseudonymity.[22] Kierkegaard himself, under his own name, asks this favor of the reader: 'if it should occur to anyone to want to cite a single quotation from the [pseudonymous] books, that he will do me the service of citing the respective pseudonymous author's name, not mine' (CUP, 1:627/SKS 7, 571).

So far as possible, we will attempt to accede to Kierkegaard's request without thereby losing sight of the broader picture. In so doing, we take heed of Poole's warning, yet reject his evident contempt for those who 'are determined to talk "philosophy" with "Kierkegaard," whichever one of the strange many-colored costumes he may choose to turn up in.'[23] Attending sufficiently to pseudonymity does not mean that we cannot derive a useful pan-Kierkegaardian position from the pseudonymous and non-pseudonymous works (just as Kierkegaard, in the *Point of View*, retrospectively outlines a Kierkegaardian project that structures his entire authorship). In any case, it may well be illegitimate to want to *talk* philosophy with Kierkegaard, but to want to *do* philosophy with Kierkegaard is another matter altogether. Insofar as Kierkegaard implicitly licenses us to attribute to him the works published under his own name, we can also respectfully pass over suggestions, such as that made by Michael Strawser, that even the signed works are necessarily just as ironic and indirect as the pseudonymous texts.[24]

All translations of Kierkegaard's primary texts are my own; however I have generally stayed very close to those given in the Princeton University Press *Kierkegaard's Writings* and *Kierkegaard's Journals and Papers* series. Any traces of elegance the translations given here might still have is therefore entirely to the credit of Howard and Edna Hong and the other contributors to that series; the odium for any errors or clumsiness rests solely with me. All translations from Danish secondary texts are likewise mine unless otherwise specified.

Part I
Structures of Subjectivity

1

The Interesting and the Interested: Stages on a Concept's Way

Kierkegaard's rich psychological vocabulary, populated with evocative terms such as 'passion,' 'despair,' 'anxiety,' and so on, has excited extensive commentary. Yet one such term that has received relatively little attention in the course of English-language Kierkegaard scholarship (and only slightly more in Danish) has been the term *interesse*, universally translated as the English 'interest.' This lack of attention is understandable. In the pantheon of Kierkegaardian psychological descriptors, *interesse* appears to be a relatively minor entity compared to some of the other terms mentioned above. On the whole, Kierkegaard's interest in the term (and it's only fair to warn you that 'interest' puns like that are unavoidable from this point onward) is largely confined to the earlier phases of his authorship, occurring mostly in the journals around 1842–43 and the *Postscript*. The word *interesse* occurs around 165 times in the published works, which, given that (like its English counterpart) the word has ubiquitous, everyday uses, is hardly remarkable.[1]

Moreover, Kierkegaard uses the word in a variety of different ways which are heavily dependent on context and which also appear to alter somewhat as the authorship progresses.[2] This variety is at least in part a function of the word's frequency in everyday language. Even in modern English, 'interest' carries a plurality of meanings. 'He has an interest in all this' is, on its own, undecidably ambiguous. The sentence could be a description of the subject's psychological state, describing it as habitually disposed towards consideration of a specific topic. It is in this dispositional sense that we would say of a military history buff that 'he has an interest in military history.' The statement tells us something about the *preoccupations* of its subject. Alternatively, 'He has an interest in the outcome' could mean that the subject is in some way (materially, emotionally or otherwise) *invested* in the outcome; he stands to gain or lose something depending on what happens.[3] Both senses of the word are clearly related but differ markedly. In both cases, the outcome can be said to *matter* to the interested party in some way – but we would resist saying it will matter in the *same* way. This multiplicity of meanings is carried over into Kierkegaard's thought and fractured still further by the plurality of authorial voices in his works. As a result, several distinct meanings emerge, necessitating close attention to context to determine which is in play in any given passage. This interpretative work is made more urgent by the fact that Kierkegaard attaches different types of moral weight to the different senses.

This presents us with something of a problem, for the present investigation proposes to use Kierkegaard's use of the term *interesse* as a vehicle for exploring the role of self-referentiality in Kierkegaard's phenomenology of moral selfhood. Yet if it is used in multiple senses through Kierkegaard's work, we will first need to sift through Kierkegaard's uses of the term to identify the philosophically interesting sense(s) of *interesse* and distinguish it from other meanings the word has in Kierkegaard's writings. Like all of us, though, Kierkegaard doesn't work in a vacuum, and his use of *interesse* in a philosophical context doesn't spring from nowhere. It's therefore helpful to begin with a short consideration of the term's philosophical pedigree in the German Idealist thought that shaped Kierkegaard's philosophical context.

Interest before Kierkegaard

The charge that Kierkegaard did not use sufficiently rigorous, scholarly language attached to him as early as his magisterial dissertation defense in 1841, and, given the highly idiosyncratic nature of his works, it is easy to lose sight of the fact that as with any philosopher (or perhaps 'philosophical writer' might be a better description for Kierkegaard), his language is shaped by its context. The intellectual climate of Denmark in the first half of the nineteenth century was largely dominated by the distinctive philosophical vocabulary of German Idealism. While some of the crucial descriptors Kierkegaard uses in his moral psychology, such as *alvor* (earnestness), are quite distinct from their German-language analogues, others, most notably *angest* (anxiety, dread) are identical or nearly so. In the case of *angest*, this reinforces the sense that a clear genealogy can be given for the term, connecting Kierkegaard relatively unproblematically with Heideggerian *angest* and Sartrean *l'angoisse*. Additionally, it allows us to connect Kierkegaard's use of the term to those of earlier German-language writers.

Like *angest*, the word *interesse* is also identical in both Danish and German, and the categories of *interesse* and more particularly *det interessante* were both, as Carl Henrik Koch has shown, important in the work of both German and Danish authors leading into Kierkegaard's time.[4] In Schlegel's aesthetics, 'the interesting' stands as a key category of differentiation between classical and modern literature, a thought which is carried over into Heiberg's assertion that the Interesting is 'a modern concept, for which the old language does not even have a corresponding expression.'[5] F.C. Sibbern also discusses the interesting as an aesthetic category,[6] as a property of an object that sets the intellect or imagination in motion,[7] as does Johann August Eberhard.[8] Christian Garve also discusses *das Interessirende* at length, making the arresting claim that, in Koch's gloss, 'an interest in or for something is, in the final analysis, an interest for oneself.'[9] It's Schlegel, though, who goes the furthest in treating the interesting as a moral as well as aesthetic problem, developing a Kantian critique of the interesting as that which contingently and idiosyncratically delights the senses and sets thought in motion; modernity's pursuit of the interesting is therefore an orientation that is fundamentally selfish and amoral in its inability to admit of universalizability.[10] And this leads us to go back to Kant's use of the term in his moral thought, where *interesse* has a separate function from that of the aesthetic category of the interesting.

In the *Groundwork For The Metaphysics of Morals*, Kant uses *interesse* in an object-directed, dispositional sense, and sets it up as a possible (but ultimately failed) candidate for explaining moral action: 'An interest is that by which reason becomes practical i.e. becomes a cause determining the will.'[11] As with the *Critique of Judgment*'s account of interest as having a 'satisfaction' in an object's existence by which we experience *gratification* rather than merely *assenting* to its pleasantness,[12] Kant establishes interest as a contingent entity that mediates action and subject, and as such stands apart from the realm of considerations proper to morality. Any morality constructed upon, or justified by reference to, an interest or set of interests, will not be capable of sustaining the universality demanded by the form of moral judgments as laws.[13] These interests are altogether too contingent, too agent-specific, to furnish binding laws for all rational beings, and so can, at most, yield hypothetical imperatives, not categorical ones. This is the moral corollary of the Third Critique's claim that 'All interest presupposes or generates a want, and, as the determining ground of assent, it leaves the judgment about the object no longer free.'[14] It's worth noting that this is the sense that Schopenhauer, who ultimately extends Kant's claim that our satisfaction with what is beautiful is entirely *disinterested*[15] to commend a disinterested (and so hopefully will-less) comportment towards the entire phenomenal realm, uses *interesse*.[16]

Kant does, however, retain a different sense of *interesse* in which it operates as a key feature of legitimate moral cognition. While *interests* in their particularity cannot play any (determinative) role in the formulation of judgments of practical reason (because they cannot yield categorical imperatives), autonomous rational creatures take an *interest* in the categorically binding laws they give themselves:

> But why, then, ought I to subject myself to this principle [of the universalizability of maxims] and do so simply as a rational being [...]? I am willing to admit that no interest *impels* me to do so, for that would not give a categorical imperative; but I still must necessarily *take* an interest in it and have insight into how this comes about [17]

Moral action therefore requires that the agent experiences an interest in morality, but it must be a *pure* interest in which interest is experienced *immediately* in the moment in which reason uncovers will-determining law:

> Only such an interest is pure. But if it can determine the will only by means of another object of desire or on the presupposition of a special feeling of the subject, then reason takes only a mediate interest in the action, and [...] this latter interest would be only empirical and not pure rational interest.[18]

Earlier in the *Groundwork*, Kant sets up a parallel distinction between 'taking an interest' and 'acting from interest.' Taking an interest in an action here means acting according to principles of reason for their own sake, whereas acting from interest is adopting principles of reason insofar as they serve extraneous inclination: 'In the first case the action interests me, in the second, the object of the action (insofar as it is agreeable to me).'[19] Authentic moral agency therefore depends upon a certain orientation towards the representation of moral laws by the rational subject. Kant admits that we can never actually *explain* this subjective orientation, yet nonetheless insists it does occur and is central to morality.[20] Even here, in a moral system designed to expunge morality of all 'pathological' factors and explanations derived from human nature and particularity, a subjective experience bound up with moral thought becomes crucial to moral psychology. Kant's use of *interesse* is ultimately very different from Kierkegaard's, but in using the term to identify a subjective experience built into moral cognition (rather than being extraneous to it) and crucial to moral agency, he sets up a distinct resonance between the two.

Hegel's use of the term also occurs in the context of the motivational structures of the self. For Hegel, *interesse* is bound up with the particularity of individual will, and so shares some points of similarity with Kant's first sense noted above. However, in keeping with his notorious collapsing of interiority and exteriority, Hegel's use of the term operates more as an explanation of deliberate action than a distinct, 'inner' psychic state. Subjectivity only attains actuality through achieving 'objectivity,' that is, entering into causal relationships with the material world[21] – 'the individual human being *is* what the *deed* is.'[22] Consequently, rather than describing an interior state antecedent to action, *interesse* plays a role in explaining the specific way in which a particular individuality (which prior to action only exists in potential, for there is no substance to individuality prior to its expression in 'work') is instantiated *in* action. So 'the *interest* which the individual finds in something is the answer already given to the question, "whether he should act, and what should be done in a given case" '; interest and talent (a specific capacity that acts as a means) together are 'individuality itself, as an interfusion of being and action.'[23] In the *Philosophy of Right*, interest is equated with motive: motive is the 'moment of particularity' picked out by the agent's interest in an outcome. Importantly, even though interest is always connected with the agent's happiness or satisfaction of needs, an utterly unselfish action can still be interested, since, as Allen Wood notes, 'it derives from my awareness of the confirmation of my agency in a successful action.'[24] *Interesse* is thus central to the *particularity* of any specific act of agency – and, by extension, the instantiation of individuality in the world.

Interesse, then, is a term that, by the beginning of Kierkegaard's authorship in the 1840s, had considerable currency in the German Idealism that dominated Danish thought. Moreover, this usage went beyond the purely aesthetic category of 'the interesting' and played at least some sort of role within moral psychology. For both Kant and Hegel, though in different ways, interest was a key element in moral cognition (Kant) and action-theory (Hegel). The term is also already freighted with notions of subjectivity and particularity which will become central to Kierkegaard's employment of *interesse*. Yet within the small philosophical orbit of Golden-Age Denmark, in thrall to the intellectual currents of its southern neighbor, Kierkegaard seizes this venerable old German term and takes it in new and distinctive directions.

The interesting as aesthetic category

There are at least two primary senses in which Kierkegaard uses *interesse* in a way that attributes some philosophical import to the term, although the boundaries between these senses are often ambiguous and far from absolute. Indeed, as we will see shortly, there is a conflict *between* Kierkegaard's pseudonyms as to exactly where to locate the first sense in the aesthetic/ethical/religious 'stages' (*stadier*) that constitute the schema for his philosophical anthropology.

In *Either/Or*, the outset of Kierkegaard's authorship,[25] the *interesse* lexeme is closely related to the aesthetic category of *det Interessant*, 'the interesting,' which as we've just seen was in play in live discussions of aesthetics at the time. It's a category that has currency for Kierkegaard throughout his entire authorship, from the drafting of *Either/Or* in 1842 to the unpublished tenth issue of *The Moment*, written in July 1855 and ready for the printers at the time of Kierkegaard's death (TM, 335/SV2 XIV, 347). The aesthete 'author' of the first volume of *Either/Or* first uses this term in the context of literary criticism, showing under what aspects Don Giovanni in Mozart's eponymous opera comes under the category of the interesting. The interesting is here a description of those aspects of an artistic work which command our (non-moral) attention – what we find pleasurable or diverting. Yet the first half of *Either/Or* is not simply about aesthetics as they apply to art appreciation, but is concerned with the effort 'to live artistically' (EO, 1:292/SKS 2, 282), to live a life understood entirely in aesthetic categories. Such a project, we are told in the chapter 'The Rotation of Crops,' is actuated by the 'infinitely repulsive' power of boredom (EO, 1:285/SKS 2, 275).

In the desperate attempt to stave off boredom, the aesthete is compelled to find diversion in ever more aspects of life, that is, to find more and more things interesting. Understood as the counterpoint to the boring, the interesting becomes innately bound up with novelty, and the aesthete argues that a degree of control and refinement is necessary to maintain such novelty in life ('In arbitrariness lies the whole secret... it requires deep study to be arbitrary in such a way that a person does not run wild in it but himself has pleasure from it' [EO, 1:299/SKS 2, 288]). The 'rotation of crops' is a counsel of 'social prudence' whereby aesthetic selves are to avoid all long-term moral commitments, such as marriage, friendship, and participation in the life of the nation-state, for fear of boredom-inducing constraint and stability. Instead, the aesthete must cultivate an ability to be diverted by things of no consequence, for 'Each moment of life must not have so much meaning for someone that it would prevent him, at any moment he wishes, from forgetting about it' (EO, 1:293/SKS 2, 282).

The aesthete describes being obliged to listen to a boring lecture, and learning to overcome this boredom by allowing his attention to become absorbed in the lecturer's constant perspiration (EO, 1:299/SKS 2, 288). The capacity for aesthetic attention is therefore explicitly one which forecloses any attention to context by absorbing the viewer in trivia; the trivial has its interest entirely immanently and points to no larger domains of meaning or significance beyond itself. As such, trivia is comprised of discrete, diverting moments that are not brought into any broader register of significance and so never attain continuity. (This seems true when we consider the random, disconnected facts given in 'Did You Know?' lists or asked about in trivia quizzes.) The implications for the practical identity and coherence of a self so absorbed are obvious: it too will consist of discrete, unrelated observations, and apprehensions that never attain any interrelation. A self absorbed in trivia dissolves into multiplicity. The ability to forget past pleasures is also crucial in order to preserve novelty (EO, 1:292/SKS 2, 282), whatever the consequences for the conditions of personal identity, and accordingly moral agency. Through its refusal of any broader register of meaning, the interesting as a category can carry no moral weight – and insofar as the flight from boredom necessitates avoiding ethical commitment, it stands apart from ethical qualifications.

The final voice in the first volume of *Either/Or*, Johannes the Seducer, represents the demonic end-point of a highly refined, reflective aesthetic life-view. The Seducer has made love affairs into works of art, with every detail of the seduction calculated for effect and to elicit the maximum 'interest' from every aspect. The aesthete, as Kierkegaard explains in a preliminary sketch for 'The Seducer's Diary,' 'has wanted to exhaust the potentiality of the interesting' (EO, 1:500/*Pap.* III B 199:1 *n.d.* 1842), and to this end he manipulates the situation to extract every possible element of aesthetic interest from it. In a chilling final passage, the Seducer idly considers whether, next time, he could fool his victim into believing she had actually become bored with him, a deceit that 'could be a very interesting epilogue, which in and by itself could have psychological interest and besides that enrich one with many erotic observations' (EO, 1:445/SKS 2, 432). Again, by focusing his attention on independently engaging moments of observation, the aesthete evades any larger meanings that might be revealed by a consideration of his concrete relation to another person.

The Seducer, like the rotator of crops, seeks to avoid the 'weakness and habit' of ongoing relationships – and so, as soon as the seduction is complete, he abandons the object of the seduction, who ceases to be interesting once her resistance has fallen (EO, 1:445/SKS 2, 432). Once again, novelty is paramount and is threatened by any commitment that results in temporal duration. The character of Johannes the Seducer appears again in the later work *Stages on Life's Way*, where he insists that a forthcoming banquet be held in a purpose-built venue which is to be demolished as soon as festivities conclude, for 'there is nothing more nauseating than knowing that somewhere or other there is a setting that, in an immediate and impertinent way, wants to be an actuality' (SLW, 23/SKS 6, 28). Even the very persistence of objects, their ongoing continuity through time, offends the aesthete's sense for avoiding boredom through temporal fragmentation and atomization.

This sense of *interesse* places it firmly in the 'aesthetic' sphere which *Either/Or*, despite its deliberately open-ended, indirect, non-didactic structure, sets out to critique. In the second volume of *Either/Or* it is precisely this sense of interest, of the interesting as a function of a determination 'to comprehend all existence in aesthetic categories' (EO, 2:233/SKS 3, 223) that Judge William critiques. This would seem to foreclose the possibility of *interesse* and *det interessant* playing any more serious or central role in Kierkegaard's account of the development of full, ethico-religiously qualified selfhood. So when a commentator such as Julia Watkin claims that Kierkegaard's use of *interesse* is a *purely* aesthetic one, a polar opposite to earnestness (*alvor*), this seems intuitively plausible.[26]

However, even in *Either/Or*, there are already traces of a deeper element in the category of *det interessant* which gestures towards a more significant understanding of the term. Johannes the Seducer tells us:

> Therefore, a young girl should not be interesting either, for the interesting always contains a reflection upon oneself, just as for the same reason the interesting in art always gives insight into the artist as well [*det Interessante altid giver Kunstneren med*]. A young girl who wants to please by being interesting will, if anything, please herself.
>
> (EO, 1:339/SKS 2, 329)

This linkage of *det interessant* with self-reflection is worthy of note. The aesthetic is, in Kierkegaard's anthropology of the stages, a category of immediacy. The aesthetic in a person 'is that by which he immediately is what he is' (EO, 2:178/SKS 3, 173), a self who simply operates within the moods and dispositions it finds itself with as given. This does not mean that the aesthete has no capacity for reflection or complex thought. As John J. Davenport notes, the psychology of the aesthete exists on the plane of self-referentiality picked out by Harry Frankfurt's 'first-order preferences,' and these can be complex and highly articulated yet still 'lacking in the higher-order volitional movement of intrapersonal identification.'[27] Yet according to the Seducer, the attempt to make oneself interesting *does* involve a degree of self-reflection, of the sort that is a necessary (though not sufficient) condition for the attainment of Frankfurt's 'second-order volitions,' through identification with which the self achieves actuality.[28]

Here, Johannes the Seducer echoes and expands upon an insight found earlier in Romanticism's engagement with the category of the interesting, specifically in the work of Novalis: that the interesting involves an element of self-reflection.[29] Attempting to make oneself interesting is always a self-reflective action, both in the sense that one reflects upon what one *is* in trying to present an interesting self to the world, and in that one's 'interesting' self is itself a reflection of the attempt to *make oneself* interesting. This is always a conscious (and at least implicitly *self*-conscious) act, which already serves to raise it some of the way out of pure immediacy. Moreover, in trying to make myself interesting, I necessarily express what *I* believe the interesting to consist in. Hence the girl in the example 'pleases herself' in that in constructing an interesting self, she becomes interested in it. The notion that the interesting in art always retains something of the artist seems to belong to this last sense: the artwork tells us something about what sort of things engage an interested response from that artist.[30] The interesting seems to gesture beyond the object of interest towards the *relation* of interest in a way that other aesthetic categories, such as beauty, do not necessarily. It could be (contentiously) argued that beautiful objects do not depend upon their observers for their beauty, but what would it be to say an object is 'interesting' independent of any observer? The category of the interesting therefore implies the engaged observer, and does so in way that *discloses* something of the observer.

However, this self-reflection (like the self-reflection of the Aesthete himself, which, however penetrating, never penetrates into the ground of his own condition)[31] does not remove the interesting or interested person from aesthetic qualifications. The young girl who tries to make herself interesting (as seen through the essentialist and plainly misogynist eyes of Johannes the Seducer) does not thereby acquire any-thing beyond a new aesthetic determinant. The person absorbed in interest might acquire knowledge of what they find interesting, but this is as far as aesthetic interest can take them. *Det Interessant* thus remains an aesthetic category, even if it seems to involve an embryonic degree of self-reflection. The qualitative shift between the aesthetic and the ethical is not brought about by a merely quantitative increase in self-knowledge mediated through the category of the interesting.

Aesthetic interest as a border category

The category of the interesting is discussed again in *Fear and Trembling*, where the 'author' of that work, Johannes de silentio, raises its status somewhat. In that work, *det interessant* becomes a *confinium* (border ter-ritory) between the aesthetic and the ethical, 'the category of the turning point' (FT, 82–3/SKS 4, 173). The *confinia* are an often-overlooked fea-ture of the architectonic of the stages or spheres of existence as they are presented in *Concluding Unscientific Postscript*. They first appear in Kierkegaard's magisterial dissertation, where they are defined as 'a tran-sitional element [...] that properly belongs neither to the one nor to the other' (CI, 121/SKS 1, 173). They represent the categories of detach-ment from a sphere which precipitate (though do not necessitate) entry to another. This is plainly the sense de silentio has in mind for *det interessant* when he claims that a discourse which uses the category exegetically 'must constantly wander into the territory of ethics, while to be able to acquire significance it must grasp the problem with aes-thetic fervor and concupiscence' (FT, 83/SKS 4, 173). In the *Postscript*, Johannes Climacus claims that there are two *confinia*, irony and humor, which constitute transitional territory between the aesthetic and the ethical, and the ethical and the religious, respectively. Climacus, then, appears to contradict de silentio on this point, replacing the interesting with irony as the border category between the aesthetic and the ethical. Why, then, might de silentio take it that the interesting plays a similar role to irony?

Irony, as Andrew Cross has argued, operates as a category of transition from the aesthetic precisely because it constitutes 'the position of the person who has dissociated himself from his immediate nature but not yet achieved the partial reintegration with that nature that ethical self-choice involves.'[32] The ironic subject essentially takes nothing seriously, covertly maintaining an ironic distance from everything she says and does. Such a subject cuts itself off from immediate participation with the world 'in order to preserve itself in negative independence of everything' (CI, 257/SKS 1, 296).

Such a detachment is found in de silentio's attempts to delineate the boundaries of the aesthetic and the ethical. Silentio surveys the role of hiddenness through ancient and modern drama in an attempt 'to pursue hiddenness dialectically through aesthetics and ethics' (FT, 85/SKS 4, 175). In this context he argues that while a work of art requires a suspiciously artificial set of coincidences to bring about the sort of disclosure of the hidden it needs to be aesthetically interesting, the ethical demands immediate disclosure and does not look to the circumstances of life to provide the occasion (consider Wilde's *The Importance of Being Earnest* as an example of the subordination of ethical disclosure to aesthetic concealment). De silentio's discussion of the ethical demand for disclosure bespeaks an ethically motivated distrust of the literary *deus ex machina* plot devices which allow for the dramatically interesting concealments and revelations demanded by the aesthetic. While de silentio does not really take up a clearly proscriptive position here, he does delineate the differences between the aesthetic and ethical approaches to literature and so *occupies a position outside both*. In a limited sense, then, there is an element of ironic distancing from aesthetics *and* ethics in the process of tracing the contours of *det interessant*. Insofar as a discussion of the interesting is implicitly aware of the interest-generating mechanics of art, it has already taken up an agnostic position with regard to the interesting.[33] This detachment from the interesting is not automatic, however. In a journal entry, Kierkegaard claims that Constantine Constantius, 'author' of *Repetition*, is 'an ironist [who] battles the interesting but does not notice that he himself is caught in it' (JP, 3794/SKS 18, 195).

This distancing allows the competing demands of the ethical to come into view. De silentio argues that 'Socrates was the most interesting man who ever lived,' but was so precisely because of a vocation given to him by 'the god' (*Guden*), and he only achieves an interesting life through 'trouble and pain' (FT, 83/SKS 4, 173). Hence for 'anyone who thinks more earnestly about life' (FT, 83/SKS 4, 173), what is interesting about Socrates' life points beyond a merely aesthetic understanding towards an ethical one. As Gregor Malantschuk describes it, 'This point of view still lies in the aesthetic; but from here one can be led to what Socrates really represents, namely, the ethical's demand on the person.'[34]

The foregoing has shown that while there are distinct uses of the *interesse* morphemes that place these terms within the aesthetic sphere of existence, even within these uses there are tensions that pull away from the aesthetic towards the ethical. However, there is another sense of the word, distinct from the aesthetic sense (yet, as we have seen, subtly pre-figured in it) which plays a far more significant role in Kierkegaard's account of moral psychology. At the very conclusion of his book-length discussion of *det interessante* as an aesthetic category, Koch notes this dual sense: '*interesse* in the aesthetic sense is an expression for empti-ness and despair; *interesse* understood as an essential preoccupation is an expression for a striving in the direction of the individual.'[35] It's my claim that exploring this latter sense will bring into view the cen-tral place of self-reflexivity in Kierkegaard's picture of moral cognition. To get a grasp of this sense of *interesse* (and its allied terms), we will consider its place in the most foundational picture of the structures of cognition that Kierkegaard's writings contain: the schematic account of consciousness-as-interest developed in *Johannes Climacus*.

2
The Structure of Consciousness

For a thinker so centrally concerned with the irreducibility of human subjectivity, Kierkegaard and his pseudonyms devote relatively little time to the nature of consciousness – the key category in terms of which subjectivity is generally discussed in contemporary philosophy. Kierkegaard's only sustained treatment of the issue of consciousness occurs in a very short, unusually schematic section of the unfinished, unpublished *Johannes Climacus, or, De Omnibus Dubitandum Est*. This apparent lack of attention is perhaps surprising, as the pseudonyms who do the dialectical work of outlining the schematics of Kierkegaard's self-ontology make several claims that appear to centralize the role of consciousness in the development of selfhood. Indeed, in *The Sickness Unto Death*, the progression from what we might term 'basic' consciousness (something like mere sentience, and which, as we will see below, Kierkegaard claims hardly warrants the name 'consciousness' at all) to self-consciousness is coterminous with *becoming* a self:

> In general, consciousness, self-consciousness, is decisive in relation to the self. The more consciousness, the more self; the more consciousness, the more will; the more will, the more self. A person who has no will at all is not a self; but the more will he has, the more self-consciousness he has also.
>
> (SUD, 29/SKS 11, 145)

Anti-Climacus, 'author' of *Sickness*, here unequivocally equates consciousness with selfhood and volition. Of course we can't immediately ascribe Anti-Climacus' views to Kierkegaard himself, but this robust equation of consciousness *with* selfhood at least suggests that whatever role consciousness plays in broader Kierkegaardian thought will prove more than marginal. Elsewhere in the pseudonymous works, consciousness is innately tied up with Kierkegaard's account of the irreducible particularity of the self, and thus the entire issue of subjectivity:

> The most concrete content that consciousness can have is consciousness of itself, of the individual himself; not the pure self-consciousness, but the self-consciousness that is so concrete that no author, not even the most eloquent, not the one with the greatest powers of representation, has ever been able to describe a single one, although every single human being is such a one.
>
> (CA, 143/SKS 4, 443)

Again we see an apparent conflation of selfhood with self-consciousness. Consciousness is assigned a central place in the ontology of selfhood – and this only serves to make Kierkegaard's relative neglect of the topic all the more perplexing. These considerations alone give us reasons why a thorough discussion of Kierkegaardian moral psychology needs to take what Kierkegaard *does* say about the structure of consciousness into account.

Another reason for examining Kierkegaard's account of consciousness is that *Johannes Climacus'* outline of the structure of consciousness introduces many elements that occur in the more developed ontology of selfhood found in *The Sickness Unto Death* and elsewhere, but, in this context, relieved of some of their ethico-religious freight. The ontology contained in *Sickness* is an inherently theistic one, in which the self-progresses from unreflective activity to a form of self-relation that gestures – naturally but still resistibly, as we always have the option of the despair of defiance – towards the power that brought it into existence. So the self ultimately uncovers itself as established, derivative, and dependent upon the agency of a power outside itself.[1] A robustly religiously qualified, creaturely selfhood is the teleological end-state of this anthropology. It can therefore be claimed with some credibility that there is no religiously neutral ontology in Kierkegaard.[2]

However, the phenomenology of consciousness given in *Johannes Climacus*, which limits itself to the immediate structures of subjectivity, contains no reference towards an establishing power. While Anti-Climacus can claim that self-awareness points inexorably towards God (whether we choose to acknowledge it or not), *Johannes Climacus*, whether by design or an accident of its incompletion, demands no such God relation. Moreover, crucial aspects of the *Sickness* ontology, most notably the idea of selfhood as the 'third' that instantiates the relationship between dichotomous elements found within subjectivity, are presaged in this short account. Terms familiar from elsewhere in the Kierkegaardian corpus – ideality, contradiction, reflection – are here employed in a schema that, at face value at least, stands or falls independently of Kierkegaard's broader ethico-religious project. Most importantly for the present discussion, *Johannes Climacus* includes a short but fecund passage on consciousness as *interestedness*, including a teasing out of the etymology of *interesse* that locates the term at the very heart of existing subjectivity.

Immediacy and mediacy

Johannes Climacus is essentially an extended discussion of the nature of doubt, which seeks to reinstall doubt as an existential rather than merely intellectual problem. Far from the quickly discarded intellectual jumping-off point for 'modern [Post-Cartesian] philosophy,' doubt is, according to Climacus, fundamentally a personal and volitional matter.[3] Descartes' inquiry into doubt in the *Meditations* famously begins not with an impersonal, abstract consideration of the problems of epistemology, but with a first-person narrative in which it is the truth of *his* existence that is at issue: 'I am here, sitting by the fire, wearing a winter dressing gown, holding this piece of paper in my hands, and so on.'[4] Descartes progresses from a state of unreflective certainty to a state of doubt, arrived at precisely by calling into question the relation between the 'world' and his beliefs about it raising the possibility of noncorrelation between the sense-mediated realm of actuality and the contents of his beliefs, thoughts and assumptions. He thereby opens up a yawning gap between ideality and reality, and crucially, posits *himself* in relation to that gap, questioning *his* existence in the face of radical epistemic uncertainty. Yet as Anthony Rudd notes, despite this individual, first-person dimension to the inquiry of the *Meditations*, Descartes' doubt remains primarily an intellectual rather than personal exercise.[5] It's a 'blackboard doubt,' a skepticism we can profess in the comfort of the philosophy seminar room but which in no way informs the way we live our lives.

Yet in the incomplete second part of *Johannes Climacus*, Climacus begins by asking a question that appears even more impersonal than Descartes': 'How must existence be constituted in order for doubting to be possible?' (JC, 167/*Pap.* IV B 1, 144, *n.d.* 1842–43).[6] Climacus seeks 'to orient himself in consciousness such as it is in itself, as that which explains every specific consciousness, yet without being itself such a specific consciousness' (JC, 167-8/*Pap.* IV B 1, 145). Climacus sets out to locate the essential nature of consciousness as it *must* be for doubt to be possible. He speaks at this point of the 'consciousness of a child,' then tells us that this is, in fact, 'not at all qualified [as consciousness]' (JC, 168/*Pap.* IV B 1, 145). The same is presumably true of the consciousness of nonhuman animals, which Kierkegaard places in the same category in a draft of the work (JC, 252/*Pap.* IV B 14:3).[7] Infant and animal consciousness, it is claimed, are not instances of consciousness 'proper' because each 'has doubt outside of itself' – that is, it is 'immediate.'[8] The term 'immediacy' is employed in a bewildering range of contexts in Kierkegaard's work, but in the context of *Johannes Climacus* it carries the very basic sense of unmediated sense-data. Immediacy figures in this work as direct experience before it has been in any way assimilated *as* experience; it consists of sensory inputs, independently of how these data are interpreted or understood. Though this sense of 'immediacy' is so basic as to be incapable of carrying the pejorative connotations the term bears in the discussion of aesthetic selfhood, it nonetheless retains the essential characteristic of passivity. The immediate is that which is 'given' directly to the self by the self's sensory engagement with the world; it is that which the self, quite independently of its volition, *receives*. The immediate in consciousness is pure receptivity, that which is impressed upon the receiving self.

The structure of experience

In *Philosophical Fragments* Climacus makes a rather interesting claim about the nature of our experience of sensory data which distinguish between sense data *simpliciter* and the experience *of* an event:

> The same applies with respect to an event. The occurrence can be [*lader sig*] known immediately, but not at all *that* it has occurred; not even that it *is* occurring, even though it is occurring, as they say, right in front of one's nose.
>
> (PF, 81-82/SKS 4, 281. my emphases)

Climacus here opens up a distinction between our *reception of sense data* and our *experience of an event*. Although we experience an occurrence, we cannot experience it *as* an occurrence immediately. Our senses can give us the content of an event directly, but to experience that content *as* an event requires that certain cognitive conditions be met. We might see a light flashing sequentially, or feel a sensation of pain. But to unite the sense data which characterize the experience into awareness of the event *as* the event of a flashing light, or the experience of *being in pain*, as something occurring in time, requires the mediation of the data through consciousness. Just as Kant sought to show that our experience of a realm populated by discrete and enduring objects depends on the mediation of raw sensation through necessary categories of cognition, so Climacus argues that in order to have an experience, one needs to mediate the sense data in such a way that we understand the data as data *of* an experience.

Climacus consciousness, both in a general sense and as the consciousness of specific objects, is unthinkable without this mediation of immediacy. Raw sensibilia only becomes experience through the agency of consciousness, which serves to structure conceptually the raw products of sensation. In one sense, Climacus is still clearly beholden to the epistemological 'Myth of the Given' here. But while Climacus does take the concept of raw sensibilia seriously, he nonetheless holds, in a way that even an epistemologist like John McDowell might be broadly in sympathy with, that *experience* is not *prior to* our conceptualization but rather that experience *is* conceptualization; *all* our experience is always already conceptually structured. Hence Climacus declares it 'captious' to ask 'Which is first, immediacy or mediacy' (JC, 167/*Pap*. IV B 1, 146); hence the sense in which, as Harvey Ferguson notes, immediacy is 'a constructed and created category rather than an aspect of the naturally given world,' something that only emerges through reflective activity.[9] Yet crucially, Climacus insists that at least some sensibilia, by disclosing the limits of our conceptual resources (limits they have by virtue of their generality) refer us beyond our conceptual resources and thus gesture to our situation as 'Between' ideality and reality. Thus he insists – in a way that's in sympathy with McDowell's model of experience as being conceptual 'all the way out'[10] – on the reality of sense data and its ability to go beyond our concepts while reiterating that we have absolutely no nonconceptual access to it.

Like Kant, Climacus seeks to uncover the necessary structure of consciousness by working back from how consciousness is actually experienced. But Climacus is not interested in securing certainty through the derivation of necessary conditions for consciousness, as Kant seeks to do by postulating the Categories. He does not seek conditions for grounding the truth; rather, he seeks to show that the very *possibility* of 'truth' depends upon the existence of a consciousness in which untruth is equally essential, and in which doubt is a fundamental structural component. Climacus tells us that in immediacy there is no possibility of making distinctions, and therefore no possibility of a proposition's being either true or untrue:

> *Immediacy* is precisely *indeterminateness*. In immediacy there is no
> relation, for as soon as the relation is there, immediacy is cancelled.
> *Immediately, therefore, everything is true*, but this truth is in the next
> moment untruth, *for immediately everything is untrue*. If consciousness
> can remain in immediacy, then the question of truth is cancelled.
>
> (JC, 167/*Pap.* IV B 1, 145–6)

Immediacy is prior to all knowledge; the question of truth or falsehood (and by extension knowledge itself) is unthinkable unless immediate data are conceptualized. Hence there can be no question of claiming
immediacy is *prior to* mediation; such a claim cannot be intelligible, for
as soon as we speak of immediacy, we have passed over into mediated
experience:

> Which is first, immediacy or mediacy? That is a captious question [...]
> Cannot consciousness, then, remain in immediacy? That is a foolish
> question, for if it could do that, there would be no consciousness
> at all.
>
> (JC, 167/*Pap.* IV B 1, 146)

The thought here seems to be that neither immediacy nor mediacy can intelligibly exist independently, but are rather always already
present in any instantiation of consciousness. Just as for Kant 'Thoughts
without content are empty, intuitions without concepts are blind,'[11]
so too for Climacus. However, while Kant holds that this still licenses
us in carefully distinguishing the two (at least from a transcendental
perspective), Climacus returns us to their irreducible interdependence.
Consciousness, then, depends upon the cancellation of immediacy '[b]y
mediacy, which cancels immediacy by *pre*-supposing it' (JC, 167/*Pap.* IV
B 1, 146). Neither immediacy nor mediacy can be grasped without each
other, and they are only brought together in consciousness, in which
the immediate only exists as already mediated – but in this form the
immediate is, nonetheless, a necessary ground for the mediate. So consciousness, according to the formulation of *Johannes Climacus*, is the
'collision' of immediacy and mediacy, or, as he then puts it, the collision
of *reality* and *ideality*.

Trichotomous consciousness

For Climacus, to be conscious is to mediate the raw data of the world
through ideality, such that we can experience the data as experiences

rather than merely unconceptualized sequences of data (although to speak of 'sequences' is already to conceptualize the 'passing show' as being composed of discrete events). Immediacy must be mediated through its 'collision' with ideality/language/thought. The claim that Climacus makes here is not merely that consciousness is the place where thought is applied to raw sense-data (or, to put it into familiar, if contentious, terms, the place where sensibilia is conceptualized). He is claiming that consciousness is the 'site' where mutually exclusive elements touch, and where the categories of ideal thought engage with existence:

> Ideality and reality therefore collide; in which medium? In time? That is indeed an impossibility. In eternity? That is indeed an impossibility. In what then? In consciousness; there is the contradiction.
>
> (JC, 171/*Pap.* IV B 1, 150)

Consciousness is therefore distinct from our faculty for receiving sensory data – the sense in which an ant, for instance, might be said to be conscious. The Danish word for consciousness, *Bevisthed*, refers more explicitly to the 'awareness of awareness' or self-reflexivity of consciousness than its English or German equivalents.[12] Indeed, the unnamed editor of *Johannes Climacus* berates modern (German) philosophy for speaking of 'sense-consciousness,' 'perceiving consciousness,' 'understanding,' when 'it would be far preferable to call it "sense perception," "experience," for in consciousness there lies more' (JC, 169/*Pap.* IV B 1, 147).[13]

In that Climacus takes it that the conscious self experiences the world while the infant and the nonhuman animal do not, consciousness is radically different from bare sensibility, even if the transition from sensibility to consciousness in the infant is a gradual one. But we must be careful to understand what is meant by saying that 'in consciousness there is more.' It doesn't simply mean that consciousness simply 'adds' something (namely ideality) to animal sensibility or mere perception. As McDowell puts it, we don't have what animals have (nonconceptual content) *plus* something else (conceptualization), but instead have what animals have 'in a special form.'[14] We can see what this not-merely-additive 'more' consists in by considering the relation between consciousness and reflection. Climacus considers whether Consciousness is 'what usually was called *reflection*,' and comes to believe that it is not. Consciousness, we have seen, is the place in which the ideal and the actual are brought together in the relation of opposition.

Reflection, for Climacus (not necessarily for Kierkegaard, who uses both 'reflection' and 'reflexion' in a number of ways throughout his work),[15] is the interrelating of the ideal and real. The categories of reflection are, he notes:

> always *dichotomous*. For example: ideality and reality, soul and body, to know – the true, will – the good, love – the beautiful, God and the world etc. are categories of reflection. In reflection, they touch each other in such a way that a relation becomes possible.
>
> (JC, 169/*Pap.* IV B 1, 147)

Reflection, as the positing of duality, brings into being the *possibility* of a relation between the dual elements. In reflection, we bring two elements into opposition (here the actual and the ideal) and they *remain* in opposition. They aren't sublated into a homogenous, undifferentiated 'higher' category *a la* Hegel; rather they remain opposed, and it is *only* our reflection upon them which holds them together, by placing them in opposition in the medium of consciousness. As consciousness is generated by the opposition between ideality and reality, it follows that reflection is necessary for consciousness. To be conscious, we must posit the realms of the actual and the ideal and posit a relationship between them.

But – and here Climacus raises his standard against Idealism – reflection is *not the same thing* as consciousness, but is rather a necessary *but not sufficient* condition for the relation between the elements of a dichotomy to occur. Climacus defines the relationship between reflection and consciousness thus: 'Reflection is the *possibility of the relation*; consciousness is *the relation, the first form of which is contradiction*' (JC, 169/*Pap.* IV B 1, 147). Reflection is a human activity, and therefore reflection must occur within the context of human consciousness; without a consciousness to bring the elements into reflection there *is* no relation between them. Only a consciousness can reflect; only a consciousness can present the question of truth or falsehood to itself by encompassing actuality and ideality. As Gordon Marino notes, if reflection *could* occur outside of consciousness, actuality would fall out of the picture altogether: 'Existence (qua immediacy) is simply passed over into ideality and that is the end of it. In Kierkegaard's terms there is no "collision" between these two worlds apart, only a transition from the one into the other.'[16] Reflection is not prior to consciousness, but nor is merely an activity *of* consciousness – rather, 'reflection' is the abstract expression for an activity by which consciousness comes to be.

The transition from reflection to actualized consciousness does indeed add something to reflection, but the 'third' (*Tredie*) element that it introduces to the collision of ideality and reality is consciousness *as the collision itself*:

> The categories of consciousness, however, are *trichotomous*, which language also demonstrates; for when I say, *I* am conscious of *this sensory impression*, I am expressing a triad.
>
> (JC, 169/*Pap.* IV B 1, 148)

The triadic structure of this experience is clearer in Danish, where *'jeg bliver mig dette Sandseindtryk bevidst'* involves a bifurcation of the experiencing subject into object and subject (*jeg* and *mig*). Thus the object–subject schema involves a 'third' that is consciousness itself, but this 'third' implicitly references the experiencing subject. Thus in any experience at all there is a principle of self-identity already written into the experience, a sort of ownership of the experience and all that is in it. Of course, this ownership cannot be experienced as a sense of control over either ideality or reality – the world, after all, is given to us, and we are not free to posit any experience we chose. But nonetheless, the form of consciousness is such that it implicitly draws attention to the fact that it is *my* consciousness. This posits me as a third element in the relation, and so marks out a key structural feature of consciousness – its trichotomous nature – which crucially differentiates reflection and consciousness. Reflection is pure selfless abstraction; consciousness, by contrast, always points back towards the conscious self.

Reflection, doubt, resolution

It is this trichotomous nature of consciousness which makes comprehensible the nature of doubt. Doubt is not one of the two elements in reflection, but a relation *to* those elements which takes the form of contradiction. In doubt the subject relates the elements of ideality and reality, of the concrete and the abstract, by positing a noncorrelation between them, *and* positing itself in relation to the noncorrelation:

> If there were nothing but dichotomies, then there would be no doubt; for the possibility of doubt lies precisely in the third, which sets the two in relation to each other.
>
> (JC, 169/*Pap.* IV B 1, 148)

Dunning notes that there is an element of parody in Kierkegaard's use of the term 'Third' (*Tredie*, usually translated as 'third term' or 'third element' for the sake of clarity), at least as it is used in *The Concept of Irony*. Hegel uses the term to refer to that consciousness in which opposites are sublated; Dunning suggests that by referring to the self (and by implication himself) Kierkegaard is subtly mocking Hegel's habit of stepping back from the dialectical consciousness to write about 'our' relation to that consciousness.[17] Certainly, 'third' is 'Hegel's technical term for the consciousness that mediates the unfolding dialectic in thought,'[18] yet the Kierkegaardian 'third' is not an impersonal mediation to which we are to relate. Rather, it *is* us, standing in a position where we cannot mediate the elements before us but can only bring them into irresolvable collision.

The importance of this 'third' is shown by the claim that without it, reflection would not be able to stop itself. Systematic philosophy and logic give the impression of proceeding under their own power; a logical demonstration or a mathematical equation seems to 'unfold' before us as its internal terms manifest their full implications. Yet thoughts, even logical thoughts, do not take place independently in an impersonal 'thought space'; thoughts are thought, and hence thinking requires thinkers. Forgetting this fact leaves us with the problem that most exercises of human reason simply don't manage to confer the certainty of outcome secured by mathematics and pure logic. Our conclusions are always subject to reflective revision and uncertainty. The imperfection of human reason leaves us in a position where reflection, left to its own devices, would continue *ad infinitum* due to its inability to secure final and incorrigible certainties.

Climacus' denials that reflection could ever bring itself to a halt under its own power occur most commonly in relation to the (Hegelian) problem of how to begin the construction of a system of thought.[19] In the *Postscript*, he claims that the Hegelian System cannot begin with the immediate because the System necessarily comes *after* existence, and at any rate, 'the immediate never is, but is annulled [*ophævet*] when it is' (CUP, 1:112/SKS 7, 108). Consequently, the System must achieve its beginning through reflection. But 'Reflection has the notable quality that it is infinite,' meaning it 'cannot stop of its own accord, because in stopping itself it indeed uses itself' (CUP, 1:112/SKS 7, 109). C. Stephen Evans notes that Climacus here concurs with Donald Davidson in arguing that 'from the point of view of deliberation there is no way to bring the process to a close.'[20] We might, says Davidson, conclude that *p* is a better course of action than *q*, 'all things considered' – yet we don't, in fact, consider all things at all.[21] There is always the possibility that further reflection will alter our conclusions; maybe we've missed something, or made a mistake. *This* question, whether or not our conclusion might be subject to revision or not, is *itself* a question for reflection. So it is not in the nature of reflection to be able to resolve itself once and for all – it can only deliver conditional 'apparent' truths, not final certainties. Reflection, by its nature, continually undermines its own deliverances; or as Judge William rather memorably puts it:

> It has been correctly noted that reflection cannot be exhausted [*ikke lader sig udtømme*, lit. 'doesn't let itself be exhausted'], that it is infinite. Quite right, it cannot be exhausted in reflection, any more than someone, be he ever so hungry, can eat his own stomach, which is why one dares to look upon anyone who says he has done this, be he a systematic hero or a newsboy, as a Münchausen.
>
> (SLW, 161–2/SKS 6, 151)

Climacus wonders if 'perhaps' (and this 'perhaps' is, I think, redolent with Climacan irony) this infinity of reflection is what Hegel calls the 'spurious' infinity of endless iteration.[22] If it is, then it is significant, Climacus thinks, that 'spurious' (*schlechte*) is such a pejorative, ethically freighted term (CUP, 1:113/SKS 7, 109). To call reflection to a halt requires an *intervention*, and one that must occur from outside the objective content of reflection: 'reflection cannot be stopped objectively, and when it is stopped subjectively, it does not stop itself, but *it is the subject who stops it*' (CUP, 1:116/SKS 7, 112, my emphasis). For Climacus, to describe someone as being enmeshed in the 'spurious infinity' of reflection is to lay an ethical *charge* against them, a charge of 'not wanting to stop the infinity of reflection' (CUP, 1:113/SKS 7, 109).

To act requires resolution; it requires both that a conclusion be reached and that the possibility of further reflection be closed off. To act we have to actively *choose to cease deliberating* and make a decision. Only resolution, a 'leap,' can stop reflection (CUP, 1:113, 1:115/SKS 7, 109–10, 111). And if reflection can only be stopped by resolution, then it is always 'the subject who stops it' (CUP, 1:116/SKS 7, 112). Consequently, as Kierkegaard claims in his review of *Two Ages*, reflection can provide a refuge from our responsibility to act – we can use reflection (in the form of deliberation as a mental act) to defer action.[23] Such an evasion would not be so much a matter of making a conscious choice not to act, as of focusing on the question of what to do in such a way that the urgency which motivates the question in the first instance is elided –

in effect, taking *ourselves* out of the reflection, by trying (impossibly) to turn consciousness into pure, selfless reflection. This leaves Kierkegaard open to the accusation of irrationalism by denying that action can be determined by reason. However, Kierkegaard does not deny that we have reasons for making our decisions,[24] merely that the 'qualitative transition' – the 'leap' (*spring*) between reflection and belief, resolution and action – follows mechanically from those reasons. More is required. There must be a third term to impose itself upon reflection, to rein reflection in *as an activity for* an existing conscious being. In such a way reflection is placed into a subordinate relation to the concerns of the individual, and that we do this exposes our concern to *act*. To decide to break off reflection we have to be concerned about that which we reflect on and concerned to act in relation to it.[25]

This also has epistemological implications: to believe something to be true is to actively bring about a resolution which puts reflection at a rest it is incapable of producing by itself. Belief cannot emerge from the opposition of reflection unless the elements of the opposition are reflected upon by something that is necessarily always beyond the reflective process, something capable of calling that process to a halt in resolution. Doubt, therefore, can never be overcome by reflection, and becomes, as Climacus set out to show, not an intellectual problem but a personal one. In the experience of doubt I am referred back to the necessity of *choosing* to believe something; the Climacan account of consciousness 'points away from abstract doubt to the concrete doubter.'[26] Indeed, this irreducibly personal dimension of doubt is guaranteed by the categorical impossibility of commending doubt to any other person, 'for if the other person was not very slow, he might very well answer, "Thank you for this, but you must forgive me for now doubting the correctness of that statement"' (JC, 146/*Pap.* IV B 1, 128). The experience of doubt thus throws consciousness back upon itself: all of us find ourselves alone with a doubt that only we can overcome.

The limits of language

The way in which doubt points back to the conscious self also finds expression in the way language and the world interact in *Johannes Climacus*. Climacus refers to the content of immediacy as 'reality' (*realitet*), a term which subsequently acquires a relatively complex array of senses in Kierkegaard's published works (confusingly, Kierkegaard uses *realitet* and *virkelighed*, 'actuality,' interchangeably here, as opposed to the different senses the words have in other works).[27] Elsewhere, reality carries the sense of what *is* the world-in-itself. Equating immediately given sense data with a concrete external world seems to suggest uninterrogated realist assumptions are at work here,[28] although Climacus' point seems to be simply that sense data and whatever is taken to generate it belong on the immediate side of the ledger, without thereby making any ontological assertions. At any rate, whether or not we have access to an independent realm of things-in-themselves, such access can only come to us through experiences in the medium of consciousness, a medium which is structured such as to put actuality into immediate opposition to ideality. And ideality, we are told, is coterminous with language:

> Immediacy is reality, language is ideality, consciousness is contradiction [*Modsigelse*]. In the moment I make a statement about reality, the contradiction is there, for what I say is ideality.
>
> (JC, 168/*Pap.* IV B 1, 146)

This claimed contradiction depends upon skepticism about the ability of language to perfectly map onto the world. By virtue of the generalizing, abstracting character of language, which uses necessarily general concepts to describe the concrete and inexhaustibly specific stuff of the world, I implicitly generate a contradiction (or better, opposition – Kierkegaard is here not using *modsigelse* to pick out a relationship of strict logical contradiction)[29] between language and reality. This distinction between actuality and the statements we use to describe it brings these two elements into opposition and creates the possibility of truth or falsehood. Talking *about the world* opens up a breach between language and the 'stuff' that it conceptualizes, thus engendering the relationship of correspondence or reference that makes talk of truth or untruth possible. Such a relation cannot happen without the medium of consciousness with which to bring them into such a relation, and equally, consciousness only comes into being through the opposition:

> So long as this exchange takes place without mutual contact, consciousness exists only according to its possibility ... Reality is not consciousness, ideality no more so, and yet consciousness does not exist without both, and this contradiction is consciousness' coming-to-be and its essence.
>
> (JC, 168/*Pap.* IV B 1, 147)

Consciousness is fundamentally a contradiction, not in the sense of a logical impossibility but in the sense of being irreducibly composed of two irreconcilable elements. Consciousness both encompasses ideality/language and actuality, yet is not reducible to them. Thus the non-identity of language and the world becomes a problem at the very heart of consciousness itself, as the conscious self finds itself *involved* in the disjunction between ideality and reality, 'trapped between' concrete immediacy and the necessarily imperfect conceptualizations through which this is mediated.

We might ask an important question at this point: if all conscious experience is always mediated/conceptualized, why am I speaking of consciousness as trapped *between* immediacy and reality? Why can't we just say that we are *alienated* from the immediate? The answer, I think, is precisely the immediacy and 'closeness' with which the 'residue' left over from our imperfect conceptualizations imposes itself upon us. Most of the time – almost *all* of the time, in fact – the generality of the concepts by which we schematize the world presents no difficulty; the 'slippage' between our concepts and the world is rarely even noticeable and only occasionally problematic. Nonetheless there are many familiar examples of our inability to communicate because the immediate content of our experience resists conceptualization, not all as alien and unfamiliar as, for example, the experience of the Kantian 'sublime.' In a sense, the same conflict between language and reality occurs when we try to describe a particularly strange physiological feeling to a doctor, but we have a sufficiently rich public vocabulary to give the doctor a general sense of most of the sensations we feel. If I describe something rather unhelpfully as a 'singing pain,' a good doctor will be able to get a fair idea of the sort of thing I am describing by looking to the descriptions previous patients have given. My limited ability to describe what I feel will be only a minor impediment to a successful diagnosis. Similarly, as McDowell argues in reply to Gareth Evans, so long as we are equipped with the concept of a chromatic shade, the fact that our color concepts are necessarily more coarsely grained than the range of colors we experience should be no impediment to saying our experience of a new shade is conceptual in character. An unfamiliar color, according to McDowell, is no more an instance of 'non-conceptual content' than a familiar one, although the concept will, to a large extent, depend upon ostension ('*that* shade there').[30] Yet our very difficulty in describing what we experience ('it's like turquoise, but a bit darker, sort of greener, but ... ') throws us back to an awareness of our situatedness between language and the world, and the failure of correspondence is experienced as irreducibly *personal* in character. It is precisely *my* experience of a new shade or a strange physical sensation that eludes expression.

Similarly, Climacus' *Concluding Unscientific Postscript* is possessed of a far-reaching skepticism about the capacity of language to communicate the personal experience of the individual. Climacus is keenly aware that much of what is essential to the experience of the existing self, the 'actuality' of their existence, cannot be captured in the medium of language. Language constrains the data of immediate sensory experience into general forms, whereas the actuality of the existing individual, being 'the most concrete' for the individual, cannot be adequately expressed or made understandable to another human being. The apprehension of mortality provides a paradigm case of the inability of language to adequately convey the meaning and existential import of beliefs grasped with 'inwardness' (*inderlighed*, a nontechnical word which actually bears more connotations of 'fervor, sincerity, earnestness' than 'interiority').[31] My apprehension of the proposition 'I will die' is radically different when I understand the deeply personal meaning of this thought than when I simply utter it superficially (say, as the conclusion of a syllogism with the major premise 'all humans are mortal'). Yet in both cases the linguistic and conceptual content of the proposition remains unchanged. Language organizes the realm of particulars by slotting them into general categories; yet for myself, *I* am no such thing in general (CUP, 1:167/SKS 7, 155). We can try to convey the personal dimension of the inwardly appropriated proposition through emphasis ('*I* will die'), yet just stressing the *I* seems to leave the conceptual meaning unchanged, even if we can say I don't *understand* the concept unless I apprehend it with inwardness.[32]

Kierkegaard thus identifies crucial aspects of our interiority that cannot be 'captured' in language. This is a familiar thought – for instance, Hume struggled to capture linguistically the difference between an idea and a belief and was forced to appeal to immediate experience ('I scarce find any word that fully answers the case, but am oblig'd to have recourse to every one's feeling [...] An idea assented to *feels* different from a fictitious idea').[33] Nonetheless, Hume can at least gesture towards what he takes to be a common experience of interiority by using terms such as force, vivacity, firmness, and steadiness. These words are not provided as definitions, but merely as (fallible) pointers towards a phenomenon that, regardless of its ineffability, he takes it we can all recognize: 'Provided we agree about the thing, 'tis needless to dispute about the terms.'[34] Of course, if a reader did *not* agree about 'the thing,' Hume's task here would run aground precisely at this point, but then the possibility of communicative failure haunts *all* language in this way. Though we are talking about interior events that, strictly speaking, escape language, they are nonetheless capable of supporting meaning, and important meaning at that. These 'interior' events are thus not simply immediate sense data – in Hume's example, we *understand* that we believe something rather than simply passively receiving the 'feeling' of belief without ascribing meaning to this feeling – yet they are also not adequately expressible in language. In these experiences, the collision of immediacy and mediacy, actuality and ideality draws attention *back towards* individual consciousness as the site of the collision. The imperfect meeting of these elements brings consciousness itself into question, and this in an inescapably personal way.

This personal nature of the failure of language finds its strongest expression in Johannes de silentio's presentation of Abraham's situation in *Fear and Trembling*. In acting in such a way as to instantiate the inner certitude of his 'absolute relation to the absolute,' Abraham cannot articulate anything that, in human terms, might excuse him from culpability for attempting to kill Isaac.[35] The particularity of Abraham's experience escapes the inherently generalizing power of language to communicate it. There is something in the particular experience of this particular consciousness, some sense or feeling that resists conceptualization (so much so that even 'sense' and 'feeling' here seem fraught) and so cannot be made intelligible through the medium of language:

> When I, as I am speaking, in fact cannot make myself understandable, then I am not speaking, even if I talk uninterruptedly night and day. This is the case with Abraham. He can say everything; but one thing he cannot say, and yet if he cannot say that, that is, say it *in such a way that the other understands it*, then he is not speaking. The relieving element in speaking is that it translates me into the universal.
>
> (FT, 113/SKS 4, 201, my emphasis)

Abraham's inability to translate himself into the realm of public meanings that constitute the ethical *sittlicheit* render him, from the perspective of those meanings, insane or criminal. His inner certitude that God has called him to sacrifice his son on Mount Moriah comes into inescapable conflict with the meanings available to him through language. This conflict – between something immediate within him which provides certainty of something absurd and the mediating power of language – is precisely what demarcates Abraham's situation, and that of every 'Knight of Faith,' as an irreducibly personal one. Abraham's case is unique in that he is beyond generalized concepts because what he believes is inconsistent with the conceptual logic of public language (a loving God wants him to commit murder, God both will and will not require Isaac). Yet he nonetheless stands at the extreme point of a continuum that encompasses more prosaic experiences of being caught between language and actuality.

Finding ourselves in consciousness

As we have seen, Climacus places especial emphasis on the fact that the opposites that collide in experience do so in the 'medium' of consciousness. Experiences like doubt or language failure don't occur in the abstract or on paper: they always occur in the consciousness of an individual, in the here-and-now and with implications for *this* conscious self. A disjunction between thought and world 'on paper' has no such implications for selfhood, unless in reading about such a disparity the reader herself enters into doubt. In these experiences we find ourselves *between* ideality and reality in a way that gestures towards our own position, which becomes the locus of the problem. In doubt we necessarily relate ourselves as the doubter to the elements which, in their collision, make doubt possible. Climacus notes that in most languages doubt is etymologically related to the concept of 'doubleness' – in doubt we are 'in two minds' (JC, 169/*Pap.* IV B 1, 148). The duplexity of consciousness which emerges through the schism of ideal and real, thought and matter, belief and the world, is, Climacus notes, impossible for existing beings without a 'third' to posit the opposition – and that third is precisely the self. Thus in its engagement with existence the self is structurally compelled to posit itself in relation to the existence in which it finds itself.

'As soon as I as spirit become two, I am *eo ipso* three' (JC, 169/*Pap.* IV B 1, 148), because in pondering a relationship of non-identity I necessarily presuppose myself as the third element, as that which does the relating. We might understand the relation *itself* as the third, and the consciousness which posits that relation as a *fourth* element in consciousness, but it is clear Climacus does not want us to regard the relationship of contradiction, and we who observe that relationship, as being separate entities. We *are* the relation,[36] in that, by holding the opposing elements together, we supply the contradiction. Much in all as we may try to abstract ourselves from it, 'the abstracter is indeed an existing person, and as an existing person he is therefore in the dialectical element [in the triad], which he cannot mediate or merge' (CUP,

1:315/SKS 7, 287). The contradiction between ideality and reality only exists through and for the self that allows the contradiction to manifest itself in the medium of consciousness. We are the 'energizing force which is responsible for the collision.'[37] In a way we *own* the contradiction, even though we are not responsible for the contradiction in another sense – we allow the contradiction to come to exist by positing it in consciousness, but we ultimately did not make it the case that ideality and reality are different things.

Reflection, we have seen, is claimed to be the *possibility* of consciousness, just as consciousness is the actuality of reflection. For Climacus, this actuality of reflection in consciousness has another name as well:

> Reflection is the possibility of the relation. This can also be expressed thus: Reflection is *disinterested*. Consciousness, however, is the relation and thereby is the interest, a doubleness perfectly and with pregnant double meaning expressed in the word interest (*interesse* [being between]).
>
> (JC, 170/*Pap.* IV B 1, 148)

We are therefore *necessarily interested* in the experience of doubt. What, we now ask, might this mean?

3
Consciousness as Interest

In between being?

Climacus' identification of consciousness with *interesse* introduces a new, qualitatively thick (indeed, positively 'pregnant' with meaning according to Climacus) description into this otherwise dry and schematic account of consciousness. Characteristically, Climacus is not concerned with providing a clear definition of *interesse*, but he does flesh out its meaning by playing upon the Latin resonances of the word. Interest, he tells us, is a relation *inter-esse*, variously translated as 'between being,' 'being between,' even 'between us.' Just as 'consciousness,' in its extension as the actuality of reflection, is irreducibly existential, so too is *interesse*, with its connotations of immersion in being, understood as a descriptor of (or perhaps another name for) consciousness. In the *Postscript*, Climacus describes actuality (in the sense of the actuality of the existing individual) as 'an *inter-esse* between abstraction's hypothetical unity of thinking and being' (CUP, 1:314/SKS 7, 286). In other words, *interesse* is the emplacement between elements that can only be mediated into a comfortable unity in the abstract. In existence, no such mediation occurs, and so we find ourselves *being between* these irreconcilable elements.

Yet Climacus' choice of the term *interesse* is intended to express more than just the actuality of consciousness (which in any case would be adequately captured by the prior discussion of consciousness being the *actuality* of reflection). Elsewhere, Climacus speaks of 'being-in-between' (*mellemværelse*) as a property of 'imaginary constructions' (such as parables, which we'll be discussing in Chapter 7) as they are deployed in a project of indirect communication. The 'earnestness' found in an imaginary construction belongs essentially to its writer or speaker, not to the conceptual content of the construction itself. Should a hearer find earnestness in it, 'he does it essentially by himself, and this is precisely earnestness' (CUP, 1:264/SKS 7, 240). The imaginary construction works its effects on an irreducibly subjective level; it does not communicate any objective content 'didactically.' As such, it does not communicate the speaker to the hearer directly, but by virtue of its 'being-in-between' speaker and hearer it 'encourages the inwardness of the two *away from each other in inwardness*' (CUP, 1:264/SKS 7, 240). *Mellemværelse* as a property of objects of reflection – and thereby objects of consciousness – refers the contemplator back towards herself.

If we take it that the Danish *mellemværelse* and Latin *inter esse*, both literally 'between being,' are broadly equivalent in this sense, we must take it that the sense in which consciousness is interested is a sense in which objects of consciousness refer back towards the conscious being. Just as the imaginary construction leads both the constructor and the witness to the construction back into themselves, so the moments of intentional consciousness must, somehow, lead back towards the self. But how, phenomenally speaking, would this cash out?

Getting to grips with interest

In his discussion of Kierkegaardian ontology, John Elrod accedes to the Climacan claim that *interesse* is another name for consciousness in its aspect as the actuality of reflection: 'Consciousness cannot become the relationship of these dialectically opposing moments unless it is interested in them. Without interest, there can be no relation between the two.'[1] This is true so far as it goes, but it says nothing about the nature of interest, or why Climacus takes it that *interesse* picks out any interesting aspect(s) of consciousness. To justify a term as descriptively 'pregnant' as Climacus takes *interesse* to be, it would seem we need a somewhat fuller description of what the identification of consciousness with interest might mean. Accordingly, it would seem a useful strategy for Kierkegaard commentators to look to common psychological phenomena to fill out the term, looking for something within conscious experience that might correspond to the name.

The first avenue open to us in such a project is to understand interest in terms of the everyday uses of the word. Methodologically, this has much to recommend it, as Kierkegaard often uses words that look technical in translation but are actually common, nontechnical terms in Danish. It is this approach that Robert C. Roberts implicitly takes when he speaks of having a passion (as opposed to being *in* a passion)[2] as equivalent to having an interest.[3] Being interested, in this sense, is 'a pattern of caring…a concern, an enthusiasm,'[4] in short, a disposition directed towards specific objects and not others. This is the sense in which I can be said to be interested in the guitar, or football, or medieval history. Plainly, *this* sense does not fit the Climacan account of consciousness-as-interest. If 'interest' describes my 'pattern of caring' or 'enthusiasm' for, say, antique Arabian silverwork, then the predicate 'interested' will clearly not apply equally to my state of mind when watching an excruciatingly boring game of chess as when I am examining an exquisitely crafted Omani *khanjar* dagger. If we restrict interest to *this* sense, then we cannot make intelligible Climacus' identification of consciousness *in itself* as interest.

Nonetheless, Roberts is alone neither in seeing interest as essentially object-dependent and dispositional, nor in conflating interest with passion. With regard to the first, Westphal seems to regard interest (at least as it occurs in the *Postscript*) as an orientation we take towards specific kinds of objects:

> Climacus regularly identifies the interest of faith as *infinite, personal, passionate interest*. To call it infinite is to say that it is, in the language of Paul Tillich, one's ultimate concern, an interest superior to, and unconditioned by, all other interests.[5]

Though there undeniably *is* such an object-directed sense to be found within the *Postscript* (as will be discussed in Chapter 10), it cannot be reconciled with the Climacan account of consciousness-as-interest. Any interest that can be placed in a hierarchy of interests, even if given a position of superiority and unconditionality, implies a distinction between different states of consciousness corresponding to the different objects of those interests. Yet *Johannes Climacus* seeks to describe 'consciousness such as it is in itself, as that which explains every specific consciousness, yet without being itself such a specific consciousness' (JC, 167–8/*Pap*. IV B 1, 145). So 'interestedness' is something that could be posited of both states of rapturous engrossment and mind-numbing boredom.

Like Roberts, Westphal takes it that interest and passion (*lidenskab*) are broadly coterminous.[6] Considering its use in the *Postscript*, Edward J. Hughes likewise asserts that 'The term "interest" can be collapsed into an aspect of the term "passion,"'[7] while Evans also declares that 'interest' and 'consciousness' in *Johannes Climacus* correspond to 'passion' and 'existence,' respectively, in the later *Postscript*.[8] Evans takes his cues for the conflation of passion (*lidenskab*) and interest from the *Postscript*, where, as noted by Westphal above, 'interest' frequently occurs in conjunction with 'passion,' 'personal,' and 'infinite.' There is an undeniably – in fact, mathematically demonstrable – frequent textual contiguity between the terms *interesse* and *lidenskab*.[9] On this basis alone, it would be easy to conclude from *Postscript* that *lidenskab* and *interesse* are simply (or very nearly) synonymous, coupled together either for the sake of emphasis or perhaps to draw attention to the intentionality of the self's passion. (This second option would, however, seem unnecessary: passion is, in a sense, always intentional. If I am passionate, I am passionate *about something*, and to say of a person 'she is passionate' is simply to say 'she is passionate about many things or has a tendency to be passionate *about* things'). So it seems clear that a prominent reading of *interesse* among Kierkegaardians is that it is simply a synonym for passion. Yet this is, I think, a grave mistake.

The most immediate problem with this dominant interpretation is that the conflation of *lidenskab* and *interesse* does not fit easily into the schema of *Johannes Climacus*. Here, Climacus does not refer to consciousness as 'passionate,' and Evans' implicit claim – that this eccentric usage of *interesse* is superseded by *lidenskab* in the more developed *Postscript* – ignores the structural, schematic level on which *Johannes Climacus* operates. Consciousness-as-interestedness is a qualification of the *structure* of consciousness itself, rather than specific *states* of consciousness (however persistent or ephemeral they might be). The same objection seems to apply here as to the example of watching a boring game of chess. Can we claim that consciousness is, by its nature, *structurally* passionate, without doing pretty serious violence to the term 'passion' itself? Moreover, as we'll see in our discussion of infinitized feeling in Chapter 8, there are forms of passion which lack a crucial form of connection to the experience of the lived self, in ways that serve to distinguish interest and passion even further.

Yet the reading that conflates passion and interest isn't the only game in town: some commentators *have* sought to distinguish interest and passion. M. Jamie Ferreira and Gordon D. Marino both stress that passion and interest, though clearly very closely related, are *not* to be conflated. Marino stresses that, for the Climacus of *Johannes Climacus*, it is only by virtue of 'one's interest in his existence' that the relationship between reality and ideality is established.[10] As such, 'disinterest,' the hallmark of objectivity, removes the objective thinker from existence by dissolving his relationship to actuality. But this is not to suggest that 'abstracted man takes no interest in his abstractions'[11] – rather,

his attention is held by them in the manner of object-directed interest, which, as we have seen, can be described as (a) passion. Marino here
makes explicit that interest is fundamentally a relation to one*self* rather
than any external object. Of course, I do not spend all my conscious
hours (or, I hope, many of them) in contemplation of *myself*. So if 'interest' in this sense is taken to be a matter of object-directed disposition,
then like all such interests it fails the test of being an inherent aspect
of consciousness *as it is in itself*. Rather, interest must be some form of
self-referentiality that is implicit in *all* moments of consciousness, built
into the structure of consciousness itself.

Ferreira also locates interest in the contrast between subjectivity and
objectivity and equates it with what she elsewhere calls 'engagement.'[12]
Ferreira links the *Johannes Climacus* claim that interest, as consciousness,
constitutes the reality of the existing subject *qua* existing subject with
the *Postscript* claim that an infinite, passionate interest in one's eternal
happiness (*salighed*, variously translated as 'happiness' or 'blessedness')
is the *telos* of subjective thought. Thus the object-directed sense of
interest in *Postscript* that Westphal speaks of is brought into relation
with the more fundamental sense of interestedness as a characteristic of subjective thought. Importantly, Ferreira gets closer to the sense
in which interest must be fundamental to consciousness by linking
it to perception: 'What interests us is not what is absolutely other,
but what is *inter-esse*, between us, or more precisely, what is *seen-as*
between us.'[13] So interest is a characteristic of *vision*, a *seeing* of our
relationship to what we see. Interest here constitutes the nonneutral-
ity of the conscious subject, not simply in its reflection, but in its
apprehension.

Ferreira frames much of her discussion in terms of 'our prior invest-
ment of the world with particular values,' in the context of which
possibilities appear to us as already value-laden.[14] When we come to
make choices, we do not simply ascribe values to what we chose *ex
nihilo*. Rather, when we consider our options for choice, we already
acknowledge our attraction or sympathy with the choices we posit –
that is, we experience an existential relation between them and us.
We never choose from a totally neutral standpoint; rather, as Judge
William points out and Ferreira reiterates, we are already interested in
our choices before we choose. Choice, according to the model Ferreira
endorses, is simply 'becoming decisively interested. It is allowing one
interest or attraction to win out, to take precedence, i.e., to engage us
decisively,'[15] not so much a volitional selection as an act of 'affirmation'
or 'active recognition.'[16] Interest is thus built *into* conscious activity as

an *experience of relatedness* between the self and the objects and options it contemplates.

Like Ferreira, Myron B. Penner also attends to the irreducibly existential nature of *interesse*, as something that is inherently tied to subjectivity by virtue of its 'duplex situatedness.'[17] Interest is a product of the concrete, particular actuality of the existing subject which finds itself 'being between' the ideality and actuality, possibility and necessity, finitude and infinitude (and so on) that constitute it: 'Constitutional subjectivity is fundamentally characterized by the literal sense of 'being-between' definite states which in turn produces a teleological or intentional 'being-toward' that expresses the interested awareness of subjectivity.'[18]

Ferreira and Penner both emphasize here that in finding itself situated in the world, the self is 'interested' in that it is not neutral towards the objects of its consideration but already takes a position towards them. This reading makes Kierkegaardian interest sound decidedly close to Heideggerian 'concern' and 'care' (*sorge*), and indeed Penner notes the similarity at this point.[19] Mark C. Taylor also sees 'being in between' as crucial to *interesse*, which he understands as the actuality of the existing self: 'the "being between" actuality and potentiality is the exertion of the will, moved by interest, to realize possibilities.'[20] The being-between of *inter-esse* here is the insinuation of the self between thought and ideality (possibility being beyond the given and thus ideal). Yet as we noted above, the experience of finding oneself *between* thought and reality, as in doubt and language failure, refers us back to ourselves as caught between these two. This appears to be what Penner means by the intentional 'being-toward' produced by suspension between 'definite states,' yet it seems that this 'being toward' is precisely toward my own self.

Stuart Dalton also quite correctly notes that:

> [c]onsciousness is inter-ested because it finds itself always already between the ideality of language and the actuality of existence [...] Consciousness is inter-ested because it exists in the tension between ideality and actuality. The subject of consciousness fells the pull of both the real and the ideal. She cannot be indifferent to this tension, because she lives in it. The difference between the actual and the ideal structures all the contours of her experience.[21]

Yet as we have seen, we must be careful with our language here if we are to avoid the quadratic rather than trichotomous picture of consciousness: we don't just *live in* between ideality and actuality; we *are* the consciousness that constitutes the relation between them.

Non-thetic consciousness

All these readings I've cited here attempt to frame a discussion of interest in terms of its existential character, as an element of subjectivity innately tied to the actuality of the existing subject and its particularity. They emphasize *interesse* as a mode of engagement directed fundamentally at one's own existence. However, none seems to offer anything entirely adequate to Climacus' statement that consciousness *per se* is interested. In *Johannes Climacus*, interest enters the picture as a function of the way consciousness points back to the subject as caught up in the collision of ideality and concrete actuality; *interesse* is, in other words, the subjective correlate of the fact that insofar as reflection actually occurs, it necessarily occurs *for someone*. In light of our foregoing discussion of the nature of consciousness and the way 'being between' calls us to an awareness that all consciousness is consciousness *for us*, we are now in a position to define *interesse* as this *experience of self-referentiality in consciousness*. Consciousness contains a phenomenal property of referring back to my involvement, as conscious subject, in what I contemplate.

This thought about self-referential consciousness does not stop at the boundaries of the abandoned *Climacus* fragment. As late as 1848 Kierkegaard was (non-pseudonymously) reiterating that consciousness cannot be consciousness unless it contains within itself an implicit self-referentiality:

A knowledge that God is love is still not a consciousness of it. Consciousness, personal consciousness, requires that in my knowledge is, in addition, knowledge of myself and my relation to my knowledge. This is to believe, here to believe that God is love, and to believe that God is love is to love him.

(CD, 194/SKS 10, 204)

Consciousness (here defined, rather than qualified, as 'personal consciousness'), depends for its existence upon an inbuilt self-relation, without which perceptual consciousness is not consciousness in the strict sense. The same thought, though concerned with understanding rather than consciousness *per se*, also appears in *Works of Love*, where Kierkegaard puns on the term 'understanding' to bring out its relational aspect: 'at the base of all *understanding* lies first and foremost an *understanding* between the one who is to understand and that which is to be understood' (WL, 286/SKS 9, 284). Understanding is therefore *originally* self-relational, with this self-relation coded into the very structure of understanding, rather than a relation to oneself arising *after* one has comprehended the object to be understood.

However, it is important to qualify such a claim, for fidelity to the Climacan structure will prevent us from saying that interest is simply the *thought* that consciousness is consciousness-for-us or a form of characteristic self-reflection. It is certainly the case that we can be episodically conscious of our own consciousness – that is, we can reflect that our consciousness is *our* consciousness – and Climacus (and Kierkegaard generally) is very much aware of the dismal possibility of being self-reflective or inward 'for an hour on Sunday.' Yet such episodic awareness does not seem to be what Climacus means by his identification of consciousness with interestedness. By telling us that consciousness is interested, he does not seem to be saying that consciousness is frequently, or even preponderantly, concerned with its own status. As we saw above in relation to 'passions' and 'interests', such an object-directed sense of interest will not accord with the structural claims Climacus makes for consciousness in itself. To put it in a more modern nomenclature, Climacus is not a 'higher-order thought' theorist: he does not claim that our given mental state is conscious if and only if 'we have a roughly contemporaneous thought to the effect *that* we are in that very state.'[22]

Yet within the Climacan structure, there seems to be little room for locating *interesse* outside of the objects of consciousness. *Interesse* belongs properly to consciousness; it cannot, therefore, be part of either ideality or reality, but can only arise *within* the consciousness that brings these two into relation. If *interesse* cannot belong to either of these elements, then it seems natural to assign it to the *tredie*, the third element in consciousness necessitated by the interrelation of the other two. However, it is important that Climacus does not, in claiming that dichotomous selfhood is *eo ipso* trichotomous, thereby *revoke* the description of consciousness as *dichotomous* (just as, in *The Sickness Unto Death*, the statement that the person regarded as a synthesis between two polarities is 'still not a self' doesn't alter the fact that an achieved self still *is* a synthesis between two [SUD, 13/SKS 11, 129]). Rather he is saying that the duality essential to consciousness invokes the necessity of a third element, not a colliding element within consciousness, but the relation of collision itself which, in positing itself as the collision, actualizes consciousness.

The intentional content of consciousness is that object in which ideality and actuality meet. An intended object is, as we've seen, a mediated immediacy – that is, a unity, even if only a disjunctive, 'negative' unity, between immediacy and ideality. The 'third' of consciousness is not an element *within* this unity; rather it is the constitution of the relation of unity itself. It follows that *interesse*, understood as the awareness that this moment of consciousness is consciousness *for me*, cannot be an *object* of consciousness (except in episodic self-examination where we make a conscious effort to think about ourselves – that is, where consciousness intends *itself*). Unless we are constantly intending only ourselves, interest must be built into conscious experience without being what the experience is consciousness *of*. Climacus therefore would reject not only the 'higher order thought' theory, but higher order theories of consciousness altogether. There simply isn't room in this picture for any higher order thoughts or perceptions to get purchase on each moment of intentional consciousness.

This denial that consciousness can be constituted by thoughts or perceptions *about* being conscious connects Kierkegaard with key elements of the twentieth-century phenomenological tradition, in ways that have generally been under-attended to both by Kierkegaardians *and* by phenomenologists. What we are claiming here is that *interesse* amounts to a phenomenal property of 'for-me-ness,' a 'first-personal givenness' or 'primitive form of intrinsic self-reference'[23] built into consciousness itself – something that, according to Dan Zahavi, is posited by *every* major phenomenologist.[24] Husserl posited self-consciousness as a feature of subjectivity as such, while Heidegger spoke of a *Jemeinigkeit*, a sense of 'mineness,' and a claim that 'the self is present and implicated in all of its intentional comportments' prior to any thoughts it might have *about* itself.[25] Zahavi claims that all phenomenologists from Husserl onward have posited this property of for-me-ness as something not given by some form of reflection or observation *of* my conscious mental states, but built into each moment of consciousness: 'the feature that makes a mental state conscious is located within the state itself; it is an intrinsic property of those mental states that have it.'[26] If our discussion here is correct, however, the notion of immediate self-referentiality, of 'for-me-ness' as a constitutive feature of consciousness, actually goes back at least 60 years before Husserl hit upon it.

A standard motivation within the phenomenological tradition for positing this immediate self-consciousness is to avoid an infinite regress: if we needed thoughts *about* thoughts in order to be conscious, then we'd have to account for what makes *those* thoughts conscious, and so on. Again, Zahavi finds this argument operative in literally all major figures in phenomenology,[27] but probably the best-known version (and most instructive for our purposes) is Sartre's 'non-thetic consciousness' or 'non-positional self-consciousness': an self-awareness implicit *in* or attendant upon each moment of consciousness without forming part of its intentional, thetic content. For Sartre, consciousness must be accompanied by 'an immediate, noncognitive relation of the self to itself'[28] if it is to *be* consciousness; were I not conscious of being conscious in this way, I could not make my being conscious an object for subsequent reflection (leaving me incapable of answering questions like 'what were you conscious of just then?'); but I must be *pre-reflectively* so to avoid the infinite regress.

I think that precisely this non-thetic self-referentiality is at work in the Climacan account of consciousness as interestedness, and (as I'll seek to show throughout this book), in Kierkegaardian subjectivity in general. Westphal notes that the *Postscript*'s discussion of the necessity 'to think [the fact of my own mortality] into every moment of my life' (CUP, 1:167–68/SKS 7, 155–6) turns on precisely this sort of non-thetic consciousness, 'a mode of thinking that is not the thematizing of some knowable but the silent accomplice of all such thematizing.'[29] In the same way, consciousness that everything I am conscious of is *my* consciousness or is consciousness *for me* is not a theme, even a habitual one, of intentional consciousness, but is instead a non-reflective element of each moment of consciousness. All explicit thought-content is accompanied by an implicit, unthematized (but phenomenologically distinctive) sense that it is *I* thinking it. Again, this thought about implicit self-referentiality is not confined to the Climacan writings. The non-pseudonymous *Works of Love* also makes it manifest that the contemplator's relation to the object of consideration is contained *simultaneously* in the apprehension, rather than being added on in a temporally separable moment: 'it is something else to be so turned in thought that constantly at every moment remains conscious of oneself, conscious of one's own state during the thinking, or of what is happening in oneself during the thinking' (WL, 361/SKS 9, 355). There is only one way we can be 'conscious of our own state' at every moment, whatever we happen to be thinking: non-thetically.

This new interpretation of interest as part of the non-thetic background of consciousness will have important consequences for our reading of the way *interesse* operates in Kierkegaardian moral psychology generally. Most crucially, it removes any possibility of regarding interest as something that insinuates itself into thought diachronically. As will be developed in the following chapters, *interesse* as self-referentiality or a sense of 'involvement' is not (typically) a reflective moment that follows perception, as if the thoughts 'I see that *x*' and '*x* refers to/involves/makes demands of me' follow sequentially. Rather, my sense of involvement and implicatedness, my *interestedness*, is built non-thetically into perception *itself.* Ferreira, as we've noted, finds interest to be closely related to *vision*, and vision is, as we shall see, a particularly apt description for moral cognition, precisely because it captures a sense of non-reflective immediacy that is crucial to understanding Kierkegaard's moral psychology.

Interest as teleology

The claim that the proposition 'consciousness is interested' flows from the given structure of consciousness itself resonates, as we've noted, with twentieth-century phenomenological articulations of 'first-personal givenness' such as Sartre's claim for the necessity of non-thetic consciousness, and Heidegger's account of mineness (*jemeinigkeit*) and care (*sorge*, which, as we've seen, has been explicitly associated with Kierkegaardian *interesse*) as a fundamental determinant of *Dasein*. In both cases, the structure of the perceiving self, uncovered phenomeno-logically, necessitates these properties of consciousness if consciousness is to be possible *at all*. For Heidegger, the 'basic existential phenomenon' of care follows necessarily from the being of *Dasein* in that 'no sooner has *Dasein* expressed anything about itself to itself, than it has already interpreted itself as *care*.'[30] Like Kierkegaardian *interesse*, care is not to be identified with specific episodic states (Heidegger cites worry [*Besorgnis*] and carefreeness [*Sorglosigkeit*]) but is rather an ontological determi-nant of *Dasein*. It is not a specific attitude towards the self; rather, it is another name for the self's structure as being-ahead-of-itself-already-in-the-world.[31] Care lies 'before' (and so in) every attitude or comportment of *Dasein*;[32] as such, even indifference or unconcern are understood as forms of care.

It seems that we have also identified *interesse* as a necessarily present feature of consciousness at all times. To be conscious is to be interested; therefore, all consciousness always contains within it an implicit self-directedness. However, Kierkegaard differs from his phenomenologist descendants in claiming that we can, and in fact most of the time we *do*, fall into *disinterest*, a state where our thought seems to efface its own existential groundedness as *my* thought.[33] The Climacan writings are, in their function as a polemic against the all-encompassing 'objectivity' of speculative idealism, essentially diagnoses of disinterest in modern thought. Hegelian philosophy does not fail because of any internal contradictions or errors of thought;[34] rather it fails because the pursuit of a system of pure thought elides the relationship of this thought to the person thinking it. It is convicted not of being incorrect, but of being 'absent-minded.' By 'sinking all self-concern'[35] in abstract systems of thought, the objective, disinterested Hegelian thinker removes himself completely from his thought and never makes the (properly simultaneous) move of self-referentiality to consider how this thought concerns *him*. Malantschuk contends that Climacus is here arguing that disinterested knowledge, such as the knowledge of mathematics or metaphysics, 'belongs merely to the sphere of reflection, which brings two oppositions together, but has no concern with, or interest in, the knower.'[36] The objective thinker seeks to become pure reflection, something which, as we have seen, can never exist: reflection is only actualized in consciousness, which is always consciousness *for* someone. In effect, abstract, 'objective' thought actively seeks to elide the self in its concrete particularity from thought.

We have seen that Climacus takes interest to be an innate qualification of all consciousness. Yet he also clearly takes it that *disinterested* thought is not only possible, but can fill out the content of entire careers, indeed entire lives. This appears to be in conflict with his claim that consciousness *qua* consciousness is interested (seemingly equivalent to the phenomenologists' claim that all consciousness involves an implicit quality of first-personal givenness); the very possibility of disinterested consciousness calls this claim into question. If interest is *structurally* given as a determinant of consciousness, how can disinterest, the hallmark of the 'objective thinker' who is so ruthlessly parodied in the *Postscript*, be possible? (Unless, following Heidegger, we say that even disinterest is a form of interest – thus de-toothing Kierkegaard's entire critique).

The answer is that insofar as objective thought is still, nonetheless, being thought *by* someone, it is an *active elision* of something essential to thought, namely, its status as the activity of a thinking being. The objective thinker acts as if thought were something entirely disconnected from individual humans, but never, in fact, succeeds in translating herself into pure thought. As Nordentoft puts it, the individual is 'turned completely in the direction of his surroundings' and away from the self-concern that should properly be 'brought along' with such a movement.[37]

Thought remains an activity for existing beings. Therefore, seeking to be objective is not simply the non-presence of interest in thought; rather it is an attempt to evade the self-referentiality that, as we have seen, belongs properly *to* thought. Consciousness-as-interest establishes consciousness as structurally (non-thetically) self-referential; the attempt to expunge this self-referentiality from thought, as exemplified in the project of seeking to make oneself objective, is therefore a violation of a principle built into consciousness itself. To attempt to be disinterested is to run counter to the fact that consciousness always points towards the conscious self as that for which thought *is*. Conversely, to become a 'subjective thinker,' one who strives to ground all thought in the context of the 'task' (*opgave*) of being an existing human being, is to attend to this self-referentiality in thought, to be fully open to the sense of self-awareness or self-involvement generated by consciousness. The originary nature of *interesse* in consciousness makes interest *proper* to consciousness. In effect, interest provides a *telos* for consciousness: as such, where *interesse* is present in consciousness, thought, reflection and vision become teleologically qualified. Climacus explicitly links *interesse* and the teleological in the *Postscript*: 'as soon as I begin to want to make my thinking teleological in relation to something else, interest comes into play' (CUP, 1:319/SKS 7, 290). Thought only acquires a *telos* (other than the *telos* of immanence, the direction in which pure reason drags us unless we actively stop or direct it) when it seeks to reorient itself as a function of an existing thinker. As thought is infused with self-referentiality, so the conscious self becomes that to which all mental phenomena, and by extension all existence, is ultimately directed. The end to which all interested thought tends is the self. Seeking to be *disinterested*, by contrast, is an attempt to evade the self-involvement in thought essential to consciousness itself.

Imbuing *interesse* with teleological import in this way serves to accord it a regulative function. Thought that is pervaded by a non-thetic sense of self-involvement, in instantiating the teleology built into consciousness, is truer to the self's status as a concrete being that finds itself 'between' ideality and actuality than disinterested thought which never refers the content of thought back to the condition of the thinker. Interest stands as a 'reminder' that all thought is thought *for me*, that as I am thinking I am also existing, and my thinking is an act I undertake rather than the 'unfolding' of pure thought to which I am merely a passive spectator. Interest grounds consciousness in being by *immediately* (that is, non-diachronically) referring consciousness back to its own existence. And as we shall see, insofar as moral agency requires us to maintain an essential connection between the content of our thought and our own ethical condition as concrete beings in a realm of moral claims, the regulative function of *interesse* is not simply ontological or epistemological: it is crucially *ethical*.

The horribly dense and sometimes difficult discussion of these past two chapters has served to establish quite a remarkably substantive conclusion: that *interesse* is a non-thetic property of consciousness generated by the structure of consciousness-as-such, and therefore *proper to* consciousness in a way that carries teleological implications. Generated by the 'duplex situatedness' of human consciousness, that is, the self's finding itself 'being between' ideality and reality, interest directs us towards the here-and-now actuality of consciousness in an immediate way that is built into the very fabric of thought. We can also see now that what Climacus offers is already a much thicker concept than the bare property of 'first-personal-givenness' of the phenomenologists, even if it shares many of its key features such as non-theticallity. The property posited by Husserl, Heidegger and Sartre is a step beyond the purely formal 'mineness' of thoughts in Kant insofar it has distinctive *phenomenal* content, but that content is both somewhat thin and always present to the same degree. In effect, it's the default *feel* of all moments of subjectivity, a sort of omnipresent background hum, the property that answers to the intuition that there must be something-it-is-like-to-be-me. Many readers would perhaps find such an under-described property less than satisfying. Kierkegaardian interest, by contrast, seems to be far richer both conceptually and phenomenally: *interesse* is (at least ostensibly) defeasible, is teleologically normative, and insofar as interest and disinterest appear to be phenomenally distinguishable, it must be phenomenally 'thicker' than mere first-personal-givenness. Kierkegaard is often viewed as an ancestral figure in the thinking of figures like Heidegger and Sartre, but in this respect at least, Climacus seems to be far ahead of the later phenomenological tradition.

Proceeding from this basis, we can now seek to trace the operation of this immediate, non-thetic sense of 'involvement' or 'implication' through Kierkegaard's moral psychology. However, while we can now depart from the relatively Spartan schematics of *Johannes Climacus*, we must still explore the mechanics of Kierkegaard's other accounts of the ontology of selfhood, to show how interest operates in these accounts, and how this impacts upon the phenomena of moral cognition.

4
The Ontology of the Self

The sickness unto death: psychology and ontology

One reason *Johannes Climacus* has received relatively scant attention in Kierkegaard Studies has been its obvious brevity and schematic nature. As a treatment of the structure of consciousness, it is at once both full of resonance with other Kierkegaardian texts and tantalizingly incomplete. *Johannes Climacus* marks Kierkegaard's only substantial attempt to map out an ontology of consciousness as such. However, later in his writings, Kierkegaard does develop a sustained and complex account of the ontology of the *self*, most notably in *The Sickness Unto Death* and, to a lesser extent, in *The Concept of Anxiety*. These two works of depth psychology delve into specific psychological pathologies – respectively, Despair (*Fortvivelse*) and Anxiety (*Angest*) – and find these to be driven by structural features of the human self. Despair in particular turns out to be a 'sickness' that goes deeper than the merely dispositional level on which modern empirical psychology operates. Its occurrence expresses an underlying dysfunction on an ontological level, one that can in fact occur with no discernible psychological symptoms. (We saw above that Kierkegaard's psychology is, at heart, a 'clinical' one. Here, however, we can see the limits of that assessment, for what sense could empirical clinical psychology make of the notion of a completely asymptomatic mental illness?)

But to speak of a Kierkegaardian 'ontology,' of selfhood or anything else, already sounds suspiciously philosophical for a thinker like Kierkegaard. Defending his use of the term in relation to Kierkegaard, John Elrod claims that Kierkegaardian ontology involves a 'reading off' of key features of human experience, discerning 'universals' which, though not derived *a priori*, must nonetheless be structural givens if human experience is to be as it is.[1] If Elrod is right about this, then we should expect that, where Kierkegaard makes multiple attempts at articulating phenomena that point to such structural 'universals,' the different accounts will all yield recognizably cognate structures. In other words, insofar as his explanations of Consciousness, Despair, and Anxiety each points towards an underlying ontology, they should all reveal the *same* ontology. If we were talking about a systematic thinker, this point would scarcely need to be made; if multiple accounts of psychic phenomena all claimed to lead back to an underlying, universal structure of selfhood, but each account yielded incompatibly different structures, either the description of one or more phenomena, or the process by which ontological claims were derived from them, would immediately be called into question.

But Kierkegaard's thought, though programmatic, is not systematic. We cannot, therefore, simply assume a commonality between the structures enunciated in the *Johannes Climacus* fragment and the much later *Sickness Unto Death* (and, in less detail, *The Concept of Anxiety*). And as a consequence, we can't simply transpose terms from one ontology to another without first securing structural commonality between them. A term such as *interesse* might play a significant role in the structures of consciousness, as *Johannes Climacus* claims it does, but this does not, in and of itself, give us grounds to import the term into the ontology of selfhood described in *Sickness*. We therefore have to look at this ontology and the features it shares with *Johannes Climacus* to determine whether something in that structure fulfils the same role as *interesse* in the earlier work.

The Sickness Unto Death, a formidably dense work written from the persona of Anti-Climacus, 'a Christian on an extraordinarily high level' (JP, 6431/SKS 22, 128) who Kierkegaard considered higher than himself,[2] is unusual among the pseudonymous works for its directness and willingness to outline what appears to be an explicitly *philosophical* picture of what it is to be a self. The earlier reluctance to engage in 'didacticism' in the pseudonymous texts has been replaced by a desire to articulate an ontology of selfhood and then show that a number of (quite disparate) psychological phenomena arise from a dysfunction within this ontological constitution. As most of the first half of the text is taken up with this exercise in descriptive clinical psychology, Anti-Climacus outlines his ontological assumptions early in the book, in concentrated passages so obtuse and impenetrable they have sometimes been dismissed as a joke:

> The human being is spirit. But what is spirit? Spirit is the self. But what is the self? The self is a relation that relates itself to itself, or is that in the relation whereby the relation relates itself to itself; the self is not the relation, but is that the relation relates itself to itself. The human being is a synthesis of infinitude and finitude, of the temporal and eternal, of freedom and necessity, in short, a synthesis. A synthesis is a relation between two. Considered in this way, the human being is still not a self.
>
> (SUD, 13/SKS 11,129)

This *is* complex, and it is easy to read this oft-cited passage as an unsubtle parody of the grotesquely dense prose characteristic of the Hegelians. However, Anti-Climacus does develop an ontology that can be taken seriously,[3] and one that both mirrors and articulates the triadic structure of consciousness schematized in the *Johannes Climacus* fragment. As we shall see, Anti-Climacus' model of a process-driven self, generated by its own self-relation in holding together the elements of which it is comprised, depends upon the sort of immediate self-referentiality in thought which Climacus calls *interesse*.

Anti-Climacus holds that selfhood is not a stable 'given,' such that membership in the human race automatically confers the status of selfhood. Rather, selfhood is something to be attained, indeed something we are structurally *intended* to become but often do not: 'Every human being is primitively intended as a self, destined to become himself' (SUD, 33/SKS 11, 149). In fact, most of us never become 'conscious of being destined as spirit' (SUD, 26/SKS 11, 142) and so never become selves. In this non-substantivist conception of selfhood, the self is fundamentally a *task*, something we are supposed to become, not something we already find ourselves as being, and something we can easily cease to be: 'The greatest danger, that of losing oneself, can occur so quietly in the world as if it were nothing' (SUD, 33/SKS 11, 148).

To be human, then, is not already to be a self, but it *is* to be subject to a task to *become itself*. This formula, *to become yourself*, is one Kierkegaard uses elsewhere (in *Either/Or* for instance) and which would be used again by others.[4] *The Sickness Unto Death*, however, provides a sustained and detailed explication of what happens when a self *fails* to be what it is, the state Anti-Climacus describes as despair. In this work (unlike the more Hegelian sense of despair found in *Either/Or*), despair is presented to us as a specifically ontological dysfunction, a failure of the self to *be* in a thorough sense what it is. This dysfunction finds expression in a broad variety of psychological phenomena, and the first half of the book is given over to providing a typology of these phenomena and explaining them in terms of this underlying ontological malaise.[5]

The self-actualization that fails to occur when the self is in despair is essentially a matter of the correct internal relatedness of the elements of the self. The Anti-Climacan formula 'The self is a relation that relates itself to itself, or is that in the relation whereby the relation relates itself to itself; the self is not the relation, but is that the relation relates itself to itself' (SUD, 13/SKS 11, 129) makes it clear that selfhood emerges when the elements found within the human being are interrelated in a specifically *self-reflexive* way. But what *are* these elements, and what does their interrelation consist in?

The triadic model of selfhood

If selfhood is a state achieved by the 'correct' interrelation of 'the self to itself,' there must be some preexisting contents of the human individual (we need to be scrupulous in our use of the word 'self' here, even if Anti-Climacus is not) among which such a relation can take hold. For Anti-Climacus, the human being is a synthetic aggregate of oppositional elements: 'a synthesis of infinitude and finitude, of the temporal and eternal, of freedom and necessity, in short, a synthesis' (SUD, 13/SKS 11, 129). These polar dyads (which are never suggested to be exhaustive) pick out a series of descriptions under which human beings can be said to stand simultaneously. We are finite in our spatial and temporal extension, but have the concept of infinity, with the result that the boundlessness of our thought and our lived experience of finitude are thereby in tension. We are embedded in time and stuck in a present moment, but can transcend temporality in thought, allowing us to posit past and future, as well as timelessness and eternity. We can be correctly described as free and constrained in different respects at the same time. These descriptions therefore schematize the 'stuff' of human being such that to be a human individual is to be composed of a series of drastic internal tensions. We are not so much a network of integrated components as a conglomeration of oppositions – the active, self-aware holding-together of which, taken as a totality, answers to the name of 'self.'

There is already a clear congruency between this later, published ontology and the unfinished structure of consciousness articulated in the earlier *Johannes Climacus*. In both cases, the entities being considered (consciousness and selfhood) are, in the first instances, sites where opposites are brought together. Consciousness is the 'place' of collision for ideality and actuality, both of which are irreducible elements in the actuality of reflection (mediacy). The self, too, is a 'place' where polar opposites are brought together, apparently in some sort of 'synthesis.' But 'A synthesis is a relation between two,' and 'Considered in this way, the human being is still not a self' (SUD, 13/SKS 11,129). Just as the description of consciousness as a place of collision is inadequate without qualifying consciousness as 'interested,' so too a mere syncretion of polar opposites does not, in itself, constitute selfhood.

A second paragraph, just as forbidding as the first, describes what must be posited of this synthesis before it can be called a self:

> In the relation between two, the relation is the third as a negative unity, and the two relate themselves to the relation, and in the relation to the relation; thus the relation between the psychical and the physical is a relation that falls under the qualification of the psychical. If, however, this relation relates itself to itself, then this relation is the positive third, and this is the self.
>
> (SUD, 13/SKS 11, 129)

In *Johannes Climacus* we are told that when ideality and actuality are brought into opposition in reflection, the relation (of opposition) between them makes this dichotomy inherently *trichotomous*: 'As soon as I as spirit become two, I am *eo ipso* three' (JC, 169/*Pap.* IV B 1, 148). In *Sickness* too, the relation between the diametrically opposed elements that are found in the human being is constituted by a 'third' (*tredie*) which brings about the connection of the two elements in a way which constitutes an actual (rather than merely formal) relation of opposition. *This* Third is presented to us as Spirit (*Aand*) or, identically, the actualized Self (*Selvet*).

Anti-Climacus makes an important distinction between a purely *negative* unity, in which the elements of the dyad are held together simply by being two dialectically opposed elements which cannot be understood in isolation from each other.[6] Spirit is not simply the totality of a dialectical complex where the occupants of that complex cannot be understood except in terms of each other. Rather, spirit/self is a *positive* relationship, the 'positive third' (*det positive Tredie*) (SUD, 13/SKS 11, 129). This is obviously similar to the claims we saw earlier for the 'energizing' power of consciousness in generating the relationship between ideality and reality in reflection – the relation is not passive, nor does consciousness simply provide a ground on which to let reflection happen, but is an active, dynamic bringing together.

It is important to note at this point that the notion of 'third' as a positive power here does not commit Kierkegaard to any kind of substantivist conception of selfhood, whereby the self exists as an immaterial substance to which various accidentals accrete. Rather, as Mark C. Taylor has argued, Kierkegaard's understanding of selfhood follows Hegel's move away from substantivist understandings of the self (and empiricist accounts such as Hume's which, by retaining the concept of 'accidental' predicates, remain implicitly substantivist).[7] Kierkegaard's self is entirely a process-driven self,[8] and its sense of consolidation or unified identity will emerge entirely from its process of becoming. Indeed, the formulation that the self 'relates itself to itself,' essential to Kierkegaard's understanding of self, is actually Hegel's.[9]

Whereas *Johannes Climacus* speaks of the 'third' as 'interestedness,' in the Anti-Climacan ontology of selfhood, the quality of this relation between opposites that confers on it the status of selfhood is its positive, reflexive self-relation. 'the self is not the relation, but is that the relation relates itself to itself' (SUD, 13/SKS 11, 129). While there is an element of reflexivity inherent in the Danish *bevisthed*, and we have seen that the notion of self-reflexivity is central to what Kierkegaard means by *interesse* in *Johannes Climacus*, in *Sickness* the role of self-reflexivity is foregrounded altogether more explicitly. Just as consciousness is not consciousness if it is not implicitly consciousness *for* a consciousness, self is not self if it does not relate itself to itself in the act of relating the elements of selfhood.

To be Spirit, then – that is, to be self-conscious – is indeed a synthesis (just as being human is), but a synthesis of a very specific kind. Given Anti-Climacus' use of Hegelian terms, 'synthesis' might at first blush suggest a process of mediation, whereby the opposing terms are merged into a 'higher unity' that simultaneously preserves and nullifies their opposition. But it is clear that, whatever the Hegelian echoes within Anti-Climacus' ontology, this is not his intention. Rather, the opposites are maintained in an ongoing relationship of opposition. The self-relating relationship of the self does not resolve these oppositions; rather, it sustains their very tension by constituting the relation of opposition between them. And what makes this qualitatively different from merely immediately *being* composed of polar opposites (that is, being a human being *merely*) is self-reflexivity. Just as the defining characteristic of consciousness in *Johannes Climacus* was its non-thetic self-referentiality, so too here the condition for selfhood is precisely self-reflexivity. The 'self-relating relation' holds together the polar opposites that make up the human being, while *simultaneously* relating to *itself*.[10]

Importantly, there is no real sense of temporal priority at work in the *Sickness* account; the self does not relate the dyadic elements and *then* relate itself to this relation, but 'in the relation, relates itself to itself' – that is, simultaneously. This precludes the possibility that the relation of itself to itself can be straightforwardly a *reflective* relationship (as the relation between the dyads itself is). And corresponding to the claim I made in the last chapter that Climacus implicitly rejects 'higher order' theories of consciousness, the Anti-Climacan self does not achieve the status of selfhood by reflecting *upon* its own reflective activity, as if selfhood were instantiated by a type of second-order reflection. If that *were* the case, selfhood would only exist in moments of explicit self-reflection, as if being a self consisted in thinking thoughts *about* being a synthesis of opposed elements. It is clear, as I'll claim in the next chapter, that Anti-Climacus does not claim selfhood is only achieved by ceaseless thematic self-absorption. Selfhood is an *ethical* task for Anti-Climacus, and its ethical concretion involves acting in the world, not reflectively excusing oneself from it.

Equally, descriptions of spirit as 'the highest power or faculty within the self which controls and motivates its behavior'[11] should not lead us to think of spirit as a sort of higher order reflective subject that directs or controls the whole person. Such a self would either be continually oscillating between two registers of thought – what we might in other contexts call 'unreflective' and 'reflective' thought – or would be something thin and inherently mysterious, intervening in reflective activity, something like what Murdoch called the 'burrowing pinpoint of consciousness.'[12] Instead of such second-order reflection, a certain type of self-reflexive consciousness is in play here, one in which reflection contains within itself a decisively important self-relation that does not itself become the *object* of reflection. This looks very much like what, as we saw in the previous chapter, Westphal claims Climacus is searching for in his discussion of the thought of mortality: 'a mode of thinking that is not the thematizing of some knowable but the silent accomplice of all such thematizing.'[13] As we have seen, *interesse* is precisely such a necessarily non-thetic 'silent accomplice' to consciousness, an implicit self-reflexivity built into thought without being the conceptual *content* of thought. This, we saw, is necessary if we are to avoid two pernicious entailments of the identification of consciousness with interestedness: the idea that consciousness only exists in moments where it is reflecting on its own consciousness, and, arising from that, the infinite regress Sartre sought to avoid in his account of pre-reflective consciousness. It looks very much, then, like *interesse* – to reiterate, a non-thetic self-referentiality built into thought – plays the same decisive role in the constitution of selfhood as it does in the constitution of consciousness.

We have now seen that in both *Johannes Climacus* and *The Sickness Unto Death*, an immediate self-referentiality that is the non-thetic 'silent accomplice' of all thought is *the* defining characteristic of both consciousness and selfhood. The self is not thinking 'about' itself constantly, but in another sense, *all* its thought is about itself, because all thought is implicitly thought *for me*. It seems therefore entirely appropriate to use the Climacan term 'interest' and its cognates to describe this self-reflexivity as it occurs in *Sickness*. Does this mean that consciousness in the Climacan sense and selfhood are the same thing? The schematic nature of the *Climacus* fragment probably precludes us from making this identification completely, although Anti-Climacus himself does gesture towards it ('The more consciousness, the more self' [SUD, 29/SKS 11, 145]).

On the other hand, Anti-Climacus' ontology of selfhood explicitly contains a theological dimension that *Johannes Climacus* lacks. In *Sickness Unto Death*, we quickly learn that while self-relation may be a necessary condition of attaining selfhood, it is not sufficient, for the self must also relate itself to the 'power' which created it:

> Such a relation, that relates itself to itself, a self, must either have established itself or have been established by another [...] The human being's self is such a derived, established relation, a relation that relates itself to itself and in relating itself to itself relates itself to another.
>
> (SUD, 13–14/SKS 11, 130)

The self can, according to Anti-Climacus, only find 'rest' or 'equilibrium' when its self-relation also reflects itself in its relation to a transcendent ground of its being. By willing to be the self that it is, the self takes on an affirmative relation to the power which established it; conversely, by not willing to be itself (or by willing to be itself in only one aspect of its being) this self-defiance also 'reflects itself infinitely in the relation [of defiance] to the power that established it' (SUD, 14/SKS 11, 130). To avoid such defiance, the self-relation must become such that the self 'rests [or grounds] itself transparently' (SUD, 14/SKS 11, 130) in this power – and so authentic, actualized selfhood is necessarily selfhood 'before God.' Anti-Climacus thus writes from a religious viewpoint which colors his entire ontology, and which offers therefore only one possible interpretation of despair – it is sin – and only one possible, theistic, cure for it. His framework cannot entertain the notion of nihilism or a rejection of theism except as manifestations of despair rather than viable paths out of it.[14] If this theistic dimension *is* a feature of the earlier account of consciousness, it's hard to see where it is.

Nonetheless, what emerges from comparing these two texts is that *interesse* picks out a crucial structural feature of both Kierkegaard's understanding of consciousness and his concept of selfhood. This structural role is transferred, essentially intact, from the incomplete *Johannes Climacus* to the later, highly developed *Sickness Unto Death*. However, as we have noted, *Sickness* engages in ontology so as to better diagnose the psychopathology of despair, and it is therefore taken up largely with a description of various forms of psychological phenomena. These descriptions are structured by the ontology that has been articulated before them, but they also serve to illuminate how that ontology plays itself out in experience, how the self-relating mass of oppositions and tensions that is the subject experiences itself and its world. If the above account of the Anti-Climacan ontology of selfhood is correct, we should expect that *interesse* – immediate, non-thetic self-referentiality – should also be a feature of Anti-Climacan moral psychology more generally. In Part II, I intend to show just how important a feature of that psychology it truly is.

Part II
Moral Vision

5
Imagination and Agency

The dialectic of despair

As we've just seen, *The Sickness Unto Death* seeks to diagnose a surprisingly broad range of psychological phenomena in terms of the underlying ontological dysfunction of despair: the failure of the elements that compose selfhood to self-reflexively interrelate themselves correctly. In the forms of despair that Anti-Climacus describes, this typically takes the form of a self-relation skewed towards one element within selfhood to the exclusion of its opposite. The self can, in relating itself to itself, neglect or obscure elements within itself, and by not relating to itself in its totality, it thereby fails to actually relate to the synthetic being that it *is*. Thus regarded, despair is an attempt to evade the synthetic character of the self by only *identifying with* half of each oppositional dyad.[1] Accordingly, much of *Sickness* is taken up with discussion of despair in terms of the failure or exaggeration of one element in the mass of oppositions that make up the human being. Anti-Climacus, claiming as he does that despair can only be described dialectically (SUD, 30/SKS 11, 146), proceeds to articulate the varieties of despair in terms of what each *lacks*. Hence he claims that finitude's despair is to lack infinitude, possibility's despair is to lack necessity, and so forth.

One of the most interesting of these discussions of the species of despair is that devoted to the despair of infinitization, the despair which lacks finitude. Like all forms of despair, the self afflicted with this despair is not the self it is in the full sense; it loses itself in infinitude and escapes from its particularity as a concrete individual. There are, so we are told, three modes of this despairing infinitization: (1) infinitized knowing, (2) infinitized feeling, and (3) infinitized willing. Each is significant for the purposes of explicating what interest means in the context of the

Anti-Climacan account of selfhood, but for the moment, our discussion will come to concentrate on infinitized willing, where the self's failure to be fully what it is expresses itself in its *agency*.

The self suffering from infinitude's despair is rendered 'fantastic' (*phantastiske*), a state in which their knowing, willing, or feeling becomes fundamentally detached from their lived reality:

> The fantastic is generally that which leads a human being out into the infinite in such a way that it only leads him away from himself and thereby prevents him from coming back to himself.
>
> (SUD, 31/SKS 11, 147)

The fantastic self is carried away into the infinite in such a way that it becomes further and further removed from the concrete, actual being that it is. Its feeling, knowing and willing (SUD, 31–32/SKS 11, 147–8) all become directed towards the unreal in a way that excludes the actual. It follows that to avoid this form of despair (without denying the infinite half of the finite/infinite dyad altogether, which would also be a form of despair), we would have to be led out into the infinite in such a way that we *do* come back to ourselves. Our infinitization must somehow remain 'grounded' in the real without our losing our character as simultaneously infinite and finite; we must enter the infinite in such a way that we return to our finite, limited, situated reality. This apparently paradoxical demand can only be actualized, it will be shown, via a self-referentiality built into the imaginative process itself – that is, *interesse*.

Imagination and infinitization

Central to Anti-Climacus' account of infinitization is imagination (*phantasie*), which in a somewhat Kantian way[2] he takes to be not merely one mental capacity among others, but *the* basis for all other mental activity:

> Imagination is in general the medium of infinitizing; it is not a capacity like the other capacities [feeling, knowing and willing] – if one wishes to speak in those terms, it is the capacity *instar omnium* [for all capacities].
>
> (SUD, 30–31/ SKS 11, 147)

As commentators such as David J. Gouwens and M. Jamie Ferreira have shown, Kierkegaard's account of imagination is rich, multifaceted and polyvocal,[3] and frequently ambivalent (for one thing, Gouwens claims he regards imagination as both a state *and* an activity).[4]

Moreover, Kierkegaard and his various pseudonyms offer different assessments of the ethical value of imagination. There are times when Kierkegaard seems to regard the imaginative capacity as a rather unfortunate impediment to the realization of one's ethico-religious duties in concrete existence, while in other places he treats imagination as necessary *condition* of ethical engagement.

A similar tension with respect to the ethical value of imagination can be found in the work of Iris Murdoch, who identifies 'personal fantasy' as 'the chief enemy of excellence in morality (and also in art) [...] the tissue of self-aggrandising and consoling wishes and dreams which prevents one from seeing what is there outside one.'[5] Yet Murdoch also acknowledges the necessity of imagination for moral agency and its essential role in moral life. This leads her to draw a crucial distinction between 'fantasy' and 'imagination,' with 'fantasy the strong cunning enemy of the discerning, intelligent, more truly inventive power of the imagination.'[6] Without the capacity to envisage morally compelling alternatives to the present state of affairs, we cannot act as moral agents at all. 'I can only choose within the world I can *see*, in the moral sense of "see" which implies that clear vision is a result of moral imagination and moral effort.'[7] Moreover, ethical imagination[8] is needed not just to posit alternatives to how things are, but to understand the *current* state of affairs *differently*, seeing things from another's point of view, perhaps, or understanding a person under different qualifications.[9] In attempting to look upon someone more justly or lovingly, we look at them as, for instance, 'delightfully youthful' instead of 'tiresomely juvenile.'[10] This moral value of this imaginatively mediated shift in vision also goes beyond reimagining the present to encompass the positing of future possibilities as well.

More recently, Catriona Mackenzie has noted that 'imaginative projection' is both a source of self-insight (for instance, by rehearsing how we would react in projected situations) and a threat to precisely that self-knowledge: 'it can be a source of emotional irrationality, an indulgence in wishful thinking, or an aid in self-deception, leading us to make decisions that we regret [...] we feel as though we were carried away by the cogency of the imagining and, in being carried away, failed to notice evidence to which we ought to have been attentive and which might have given us pause to reflect on the reliability of our imaginings.'[11] Kierkegaard, across his corpus, is very much alive to the conflict between imagination as both a threat to moral life and as a crucial component of it: self-delusion and thoughtless reverie are ever-present dangers, but the capacity of love to 'hide a multitude of sins' (a recurring topic in

Kierkegaard's religious ethics) will also depend heavily on this capacity for imaginative redescription.[12] Paralleling Murdoch's distinction between 'fantasy' and 'imagination,' it's interesting to note in passing that while Anti-Climacus uses the term *phantasie*, in the discourses on love Kierkegaard often uses *indbildningskraft* – both mean 'imagination,' but the latter term does not resonate with *phantastiske* in the same way.

While his attitudes towards imagination may be ambivalent, Kierkegaard consistently understands imagination as the ability of thought to go beyond the given data of immediacy and posit what *is not*: not there, not yet, no longer, never was. Thus imagination, as with the ideal in the account of consciousness in *Johannes Climacus*, acts as a sort of negation of the immediately given, a positing of possibility over against the actual. Despite the connotations of the word *phantasie*, Anti-Climacus draws a picture of imagination which initially strips imagination of any 'fantastical' connotations. The definition of imagination as 'the capacity *instar omnium*' operates on a very fundamental level: imagination is not just an activity of thought but thought's very condition of possibility. Moreover, imagination is intimately bound up with the very ontological possibility of selfhood as well:

> The self is reflection, and the imagination is reflection, is the self's representation, which is the self's possibility. The imagination is the possibility of all reflection, and the intensity of this medium is the possibility of the self's intensity.
>
> (SUD, 31/SKS, 11, 147)

Imagination is here presented as both identical with reflection *and* the possibility of reflection – something so central to reflection it is both a necessary *condition* of reflection and an alternative name for it. The transcendent nature of reflection, its going beyond the given, is only possible insofar as the reflector is an imaginative being.

But if the self is to avoid despair the imagination must remain 'grounded' in reality; it must somehow relate itself back to the situation of the existing self. So for Anti-Climacus, the appropriate use of imagination is one which does, indeed, look very much like 'ethical imagination' in the Murdochian sense, in which we posit morally desirable states of affairs in opposition to present circumstances:

> Insofar as the self, as a synthesis of finitude and infinitude, is established, is κατα δυναμιν [potential], in order to become itself [*at vorde*] it reflects itself in the medium of imagination, and thereby the

infinite possibility shows itself. The self is κατα δυναμιν [potentially] just as much possible as it is necessary, for it is indeed itself, it is necessary, but it must become itself.

(SUD, 35/SKS 11, 151)

Here Anti-Climacus makes it clear that any actualization of the self is dependent upon the subject's ability to posit another, ideal self which it is to become. Gouwens notes that imagination plays much the same role in Judge William's moral psychology in *Either/Or*.[13] However, this Murdochian notion of ethical imagination as a mechanism for redescribing the present or positing future courses of action does not, on the face of it, seem to contain within itself the sort of tensions which Anti-Climacus emphasizes. Anti-Climacus presents ethical imagination in terms of a holding together of two polar opposites: the infinity of possibilities opened up by imaginative activity, and the limitedness of the concrete, particular facts of the individual's existence. This tension constantly threatens to tear us loose from our moorings: the despair of infinitude is an imaginatively driven loss of grounding in reality, where *phantasie* devolves and drags us away from the realm of action altogether. For Anti-Climacus, then, successful ethical imagination cannot be *merely* a going-beyond of the immediate, but a going-beyond that is simultaneously a coming-back to concrete actuality.

What is posited in imagination has the specific qualification of becoming *possibility*, and this already adds something to the content of imaginative thought. What we imagine is not simply an inert piece of representational imagery or conceptual construct, but instead something that bears a distinct modal relationship to the world and the imagining subject, a relationship of potentiality. Johannes Climacus make this same point in the *Postscript*:

When I think something I want to do, but have not yet done, then this thought, however precise it is, however much it may be called a *thought actuality*, is a possibility. Conversely, when I think something that someone else has done, therefore think an actuality, then I take this given actuality out of actuality and place it over in possibility.

(CUP, 1:321/SKS 7, 292)

What we imagine takes on a specific phenomenal character, that of *possibility*, and this character calls out beyond the immediate 'stuff' of imaginative construction towards actuality. It adopts an orientation towards the real in the mode of potentiality. For Anti-Climacus, the possibility of the despair of infinitization turns upon whether imagination maintains its 'ties' with being in this sense. Yet here we already seem to be granting to imagination capacities beyond itself, if we understand imagination as an activity of negating the given by positing what is not. How can imagination, as an 'infinitizing' negation of the actual, retain its connection *to* the actual? To answer this question, it is perhaps instructive to begin by looking at the opposite 'uses' of imagination. What does a 'reality-connected' act of imagination look like, and what does its opposite look like?

Imagination and reality

The notion of two contrasting forms of imagination, one of which retains a real relation to our existence the other does not, is a theme familiar from Sartre. In *Being and Nothingness*, the being of 'negative facts' is discerned by the ability to 'negate' (transcend) the given 'plenitude' of sense data and posit the nonbeing of beings. Sartre's well-worn example is stepping into a café and seeing that my friend Pierre is not there; although one cannot *see* any appearance or object that corresponds to the absence of Pierre, nonetheless we can experience his absence. However, Sartre posits an important difference between the actual *experience* of absence and the merely frivolous positing of absence:

> It is an objective fact at present that I have *discovered* this [Pierre's] absence [...] by contrast, judgments which I can make subsequently to amuse myself, such as, 'Wellington is not in this cafe, Paul Valéry is no longer here, etc' – these have a purely abstract meaning; they are pure applications of the principle of negation without real or efficacious foundation, and they never succeed in establishing a *real* relation between the cafe and Wellington or Valéry. Here the relation 'is not' is merely *thought*.[14]

How are these two imaginative exercises different? On the one hand, both are, strictly speaking, transcendences of what is given towards an imaginary realm; both go *beyond* the experienced world. Yet the latter example of absence has an inescapable air of triviality about it; this absence has force only rhetorically or playfully, *not* ontologically. My imaginative activity stands in a direct relationship with my experience of the world, and it can be employed both to elucidate how the world stands for me (by disclosing the absence of a person who is actually not there) or I can use it in a way which does not 'connect' with my lived experience at all. The absence of Pierre is the lived experience of an actual event; the absence of Wellington is a mere daydream. Their equivalence as products of a negative activity on the part of an existing consciousness is only apparent on a formal, abstract level.

For Sartre, the determinative factor is simply human projects and their attendant expectations: I *expect* to see Pierre in the café whereas I plainly don't expect to see Wellington. Although Kierkegaard does not have the same conception of human projects as Sartre (even though Kierkegaard does indeed regard a self as *en opgave*, a task), he does seem to hold to a similar distinction between uses of imagination which relate to our concrete existence and uses which do not. Ferreira discerns two competing conceptions of the ethical import of imaginative activity which are illuminating in this context.[15] In *The Concept of Anxiety*, the imaginative process of envisaging possibility is read in a way that the 'author', Vigilius Haufniensis, takes to run contrary to the popular conception of the 'lightness' of possibility:

> Possibility is therefore the weightiest of all categories [...] in possibility all things are equally possible, and the one who has truly been brought up by possibility has grasped the terrible judt as well as the joyful [...] he knows better than a child knows his ABCs that he can demand absolutely nothing of life and that the terrible, perdition and annihilation live next door to every person.
>
> (CA, 156/SKS 4, 455)

The realm of the possible has metaphoric 'weight' precisely because in possibility, anything, even the most devastating of fates, is possible.[16] By contrast, according to Haufniensis, what passes for 'light' possibility is 'rather a mendacious invention that human depravity has painted up,' 'a possibility that was so beautiful, so enchanting, while at the foundation of this possibility lay, at most, a little youthful giddiness, of which they ought rather be ashamed' (CA, 156/SKS 4, 455).

Haufniensis here identifies two completely different uses of the faculty of imagination: one that will yield a terrifying realm of possibilities and another that is merely a tool for creating pleasure. *Either/Or*'s A takes this second approach further, explicitly endorsing the use of possibility as a form of pure entertainment: 'Pleasure disappoints, possibility does not. And what wine is so sparkling, what so fragrant, what so intoxicating!' (EO, 1:41/SKS 2, 50). Like intoxication, possibility is here no more than a diverting mental state which transports the self into a state of rapture. Indeed, in *Either/Or*, it is clear that part of the value of possibility for the aesthete is precisely that it takes the subject away from the 'heavy' realm of actuality – heavy because it makes demands, contains commitments, and so on.

There is a sense in which the 'heavy' sense of possibility maintains its modal relation to concrete reality, by presenting itself as something that *can be* or *should be* actualized, whereas the 'light' sense of possibility is nothing but escape from our concretion. Imaginatively posited scenarios, in the first case, call out beyond imagination into the concrete realm which we inhabit. In the playfulness of idle fancy, however, we may well posit possibilities for ourselves, but we never *find ourselves* in them. Thus the 'heavy' sense of actuality in *Either/Or* and the 'heavy' sense of possibility in *The Concept of Anxiety* are aligned in that both make demands upon the individual that a disconnected, playful exercise of the imagination does not. Haufniensis' claim that possibility is 'heavier' than actuality can be reconciled with this claim by noting that while actuality places demands upon the individual, its demanding character is presumably circumscribed precisely by being concrete and hence finite. Possibility, being infinite, makes infinite demands.[17]

So our imaginative capacity can pull us in two incompatible directions. On the one hand, it can posit possibilities *for us*, which presage or demand actualization and are thus intimately bound up with our being as existing individuals. Some of these possibilities further present themselves to us as *tasks*,[18] possibilities which are 'related to the self as a morally binding authority.'[19] On the other hand, imagination can take us completely beyond our existence and into a realm of sheer reverie. That's certainly a pleasant place to be, but it remains essentially unconnected from *our* existence. From an ethically or religiously qualified outlook, such a use of imagination can only be interpreted as an evasion of our responsibilities in the concrete realm.

It is clear that this sort of distinction is at work in Anti-Climacus' account. However, his definition of imagination as 'infinitizing reflection' – that is, reflection which opens up the unlimited realm of possibility[20] – creates difficulties for this sort of reading. When we reflect imaginatively, our reflection is no longer limited by the interplay of concrete sense data and the concepts which imperfectly map that data, as in *Johannes Climacus*. Reflection may now range over a field of possibilities which has no limit. This leads us to an important corollary: imagination, like reflection, has nothing within itself which can stop itself.

Transcending ethical vision

As we've seen, the reflective process can continue *ad infinitum* under its own steam; even the most apparently decisive conclusions of reflection become only objects of reflection themselves. Reflection can only be halted by an active, volitional 'closing-off' of reflection on the part of the reflecting being. In much the same way, imagination seems to have nothing within itself as a mental activity whereby it can call itself to rest. This is especially the case when imagination is presented explicitly as an 'infinitizing' power, a capacity to open up infinite possibilities. It is not limited by the given; rather, it is the ability to infinitely transcend the given – or simply negate it. As such there is nothing inherent in the concept of imagination-as-infinitizing-reflection that can bring it back to reality under its own power. The natural tendency of unimpeded *phantasie* will be to render us *phantastiske*. We therefore seem to be at the mercy of imagination as a power destined to drag us away from the concrete.

Yet in lived experience we do, every day, translate our imaginative activity into action. That we do so implies a grounding of imaginative activity in actuality, such that our imagined possibilities present themselves as possibilities *for us to actualize*, and a relation between the imagined and the actual is thereby maintained in imaginative activity. Gouwens claims that Judge William in *Either/Or* sets up a model of ethical imagination (reflection upon one's actuality in order to idealize it) whereby '[r]eflection on the actual self is an anchor for the infinitizing movement of the imagination.'[21] But the question remains: how is such an anchoring even possible? How can imaginative contemplation itself remain 'grounded' and yet remain imaginative?

There is nothing in the idea of imagination itself that should call us back to the fact that we are existing beings who are imagining – indeed, if imagination is essentially a negation of the world we should not expect to find some mechanism internal to imagination to reaffirm the concrete. Even if we consider imagination as internal 'visualizing' (leaving aside Rylean objections to such a description), the images we posit, in and of themselves, have no inbuilt reference to *me* as the imagining subject. Bernard Williams has argued that visualization should not be thought of as 'thinking myself seeing,' as if, in visualizing myself engaged in some activity, I necessarily suppose myself as a spectator in the world I visualize.[22] Just as the point of view of a movie camera is not supposed to represent the point of view of a person standing in the scene, so my imaginative representation of myself does not, in the structure of the imagery itself, require or presuppose that my empirical self is in the imagined world.

Of course, Williams notes, I *can* place myself-as-spectator in the imagery in specific imaginative projects such as where I 'imagine myself walking through the Medici Apartments,' visualizing how the world would look through my eyes as I walk around.[23] Yet just as we might watch a movie scene shot from the point of view of a character and yet clearly not *be* that character, what mechanism, even in the Medici Apartments example, would compel us to relate that image back to ourselves as a concrete being engaged in the *activity of* visualizing ourselves walking? Nothing in the representation *itself* refers us back to the imagining self. Our memories, too, might appear in what Parfit, following Peacocke, calls the 'first person mode of presentation' (broadly, the memory is visually structured from a specific viewpoint which corresponds to that of the subject in an actual experience), yet this in no way implies that this is the viewpoint of the person doing the remembering.[24]

We do, of course, import much of ourselves as we actually are into our imaginative activity, as Williams also notes: 'It is, for instance, relative to my real wants, ambitions and character that the imagined happenings are, to me in them, satisfying or upsetting.'[25] My imagined self is pleased or distressed by the events occurring to it in the fantasy world according to a certain concordance between the imagined self and the psychological dispositions of the empirical self on which it is modeled. Note, however, that there is an important disconnection between my imagined self reacting in a particular way, and my 'actual' self reacting to the image. If I imagine myself winning the lottery, I visualize my imagined self reacting with great pleasure, yet I may find the actual imaginative experience *itself* unpleasant. Far from partaking in the pleasure of winning vast wealth, which so delights my *imagined* self, I may experience this daydream as bitter and miserable, precisely because I am *in fact* very unlikely to ever become rich. The entire imaginative episode is pervaded by something from outside itself, and it is *this*, and not anything proper to the image *as such*, which gives it its decisive meaning for the empirical me. This essential meaning cannot be discerned from the image itself.

And this failure of the visualized scenario to refer back *in itself* to the actual imaginer holds even if my *reason* for visualizing the Medici Apartments in the first place is directly connected to my real-life situation (perhaps I expect or plan to go there tomorrow, or I am trying to decide whether to make such a visit). I may posit attractive or compelling courses of possible action which are intimately related to my concrete situation, but that does not, *in and of itself*, bring me back to my concretion. There is no reason why I cannot simply continue to imagine these possibilities, maybe even imagine them as possibilities *to be actualized*, without enacting them or bringing them about. One may envision oneself in what Anti-Climacus calls the 'mirror of possibility' and yet not come to make the essential connection between the ideal self thus posited and the self which does the positing:

> Already in relation to seeing one*self* in a mirror it is necessary to recognize [*kjender*] oneself, for if one does not, then one does not see one*self* but only a human being.
>
> (SUD, 37/SKS 11, 152)

I might have compelling visions of what to do, even what I *must* do, without breaking away from the vision in order to enact it. Where it is *moral* agency specifically that is at issue we might regard a person who acts in this way as morally weak or akratic in some sense, and we might find this makes it harder to understand or empathize with, but it is not too taxing to imagine what such an existence might be like. I might long entertain the thought of starting a charitable foundation for poor children but somehow never get around to it, despite ample time and opportunity. Assuming I'm not secretly averse to parting with the time and money, it seems I simply don't take the idea *seriously* in the sense of seeing it as something to actualize, though if you were to ask me I'd insist I was quite intent on carrying the plan out 'someday.' More prosaically, we've probably all had the experience of planning how we'd confront someone over their behavior, often for moral reasons ('You really shouldn't talk to people like that,' 'I think you should stop deliberately humiliating your children in that way,' 'About your habit of taking other people's food from the fridge...') but, just as often, not following through with it. Sometimes we seriously want to carry these plans out and are frustrated by extrinsic factors such as shyness or fear of repercussions. At other times, as Mackenzie puts it, the cogency (in Wollheim's term) of our imaginative representation, its ability to impact upon the subject affectively, causes us to slip into the imaginative perspective of some radically different (perhaps more assertive and forthright) person that we'd *like* to be; the subject eventually comes to 'dismiss the imagining as fantasy' as a result of 'her own realization that she has effected this transmutation and that the point of view of the imagining is only notionally hers.'[26] But sometimes, too, we *don't* make this move of dismissal, and nor is it clear that we've slipped into imaginatively occupying a viewpoint that is too factually or causally remote from our current situation to be viewable as *us*. These are the cases where we might think we're utterly serious about taking the course of action we imaginatively picture, when in fact we're really just playing with the idea. We don't fully *inhabit* the (quite realizable) possibilities we imaginatively assent to.

Stripping this thought of its moral dimensions, it resolves into the Kierkegaardian point that thought and being are distinct, and so 'To *think* a possibility is not to *be* the one who has accomplished that possibility by translating it into actuality.'[27] An object of imagination, no matter how closely its contents align with my existence and cohere with my moral commitments, remains simply an object of imagination. Thus to relate imagination back to my concretion is to transcend imagination in order to incorporate it into lived experience, into the project of living a human life. Ferreira's two moves of transcendence at work here: an imaginative transcendence of the given, and a 'transcending of imaginative vision itself, as mere vision' that 'issues in a doing rather than merely a vision.'[28] But as we've seen, imagination *itself* cannot make this second move. There's an attractively simple folk-psychology we might appeal to here: the self imagines possibilities, and then chooses whether or not to incorporate these into its life, using imagination as a springboard to action – and while this is correct, speaking in this way may suggest a picture which is at odds with what Anti-Climacus intends in his discussion of imagination.

Earlier we saw that while reflection cannot stop itself, and must be halted by an act of will, this does not mean it is stopped by something that imposes itself from without such as an unreflective, non-rational impulse or passion. Rather, it's only when reflection contains an implicit, non-thematic awareness of *itself* as reflection *for* a concrete, conscious subject that deliberation can be halted. A parallel point crops up when considering how we 'transcend' ethical imagination. Just as we must stop reflecting in order to act, or to make a beginning, it seems natural to say that we need to cease imaginative activity in order to act upon the possibilities we have posited. Speaking this may lead us to believe we have solved the problem of how imagination can maintain an essential connection with reality. If we conceive of the self as *first* imagining a possibility and *then* choosing to put it into effect, we no longer have to account for the problem of how an essentially negative activity can relate itself back to actuality. Imagination simply throws up a series of pictures, and the self – a rational, deliberative, decisive self – selects which of these pictures it will enact.[29] This seems like a natural fit for Ferreira's two moments of transcendence, or Gouwens' 'twofold' ethical movement, in which the self imaginatively entertains possibilities and then 'takes this picture of the possible self which the imagination has presented, and makes it a goal of action.'[30]

Outlining Kierkegaard's understanding of ethical imagination in this way implies a temporal priority in which imagination is operative in the first moment of ethical deliberation (positing possibilities) but not the second (decision). Yet Anti-Climacus does not want to circumscribe imagination in this way; he takes it that feeling, willing, and knowing are all, at base, dependent upon imagination. Imagination pervades *all* psychic activity; and if this is so, we cannot say that imagination comes *first*. Fidelity to Anti-Climacus' insistence that imagination is inseparable from reflection and *active at the same moment* as resolution, will compel us to avoid the picture of a reflective self which first imagines possibilities and *then* chooses deliberatively from the options it has imagined.

So if we take Anti-Climacus' conception of the imagination as 'capacity *instar omnium*' into account, we must be careful that positing the necessary 'transcendence' of moral imagination doesn't commit us to an ontology whereby some other (non-imaginative) mental faculty or state actively calls off or directs the imaginative process. Spirit, as we've seen, is not a sort of second-order consciousness directing the activity of reflection and imagination according to some independent will. The idea of the self or spirit calling a halt to imagination or reflection evokes the image of a sort of meta-person (perhaps something like the long-exorcised 'homunculus' of cognitive science),[31] a fully formed rational being interfering with the reflective affairs of the 'surface' consciousness. We can easily fall into picturing the self as a sort of arbitrator, listening intently to reflection and interrupting every so often to issue a dictate that then becomes the self's resolution or volition. There is, however, nothing in Kierkegaard's ontology that should lead us to this conclusion and much to speak against it. Such a 'meta-person' would either have to have its *own* reflection (thus engendering an infinite regress), or, as intimated above, would have to be essentially nonrational. This would deliver us into a (somewhat caricatured) existentialist account of agency whereby a totally free, unfettered, irrational will periodically intrudes upon the rational and reflective activity of mind, and it is this will that constitutes the true *self*. Despite his emphasis on freedom and personal volition, Kierkegaard's account of moral agency is far richer, and involves far more interplay between volitional and non-volitional aspects of the self, than such a bare existentialist conception would allow. It's worth noting here that Murdoch extends 'existentialist' in this sense to cover not only the likes of Sartre, but Hampshire, Hare and Ayer as well, seeing in all of them 'the identification of the true person with the empty choosing will, and the corresponding emphasis upon the idea of movement rather than vision.'[32]

The idea that the self calls imagination to halt and *then* chooses whether to act upon it or not implies that this move is reflective in character (a claim Elrod makes more or less explicitly).[33] But this introduces a temporality which is at odds with the tenor of Anti-Climacan (and Kierkegaardian) thought. Anti-Climacus' description of the imaginative activity of the self when not in despair does not contain any hint of a 'stepping back' from imagination; rather there is a paradoxical holding together of the infinite (the imagined) and the particular (concrete actuality). His description of willing, for example, makes it clear that imagination isn't merely set aside, but is maintained at the same time as the appropriation of the concrete. To avoid despair, the self must:

> continually become proportionately concrete to the same degree that it is abstract, so that the more it is infinitized in purpose and resolve, the more personally present and contemporary it becomes in the small part of the task that can be carried out at once, so that in being infinitized it comes back to itself in the most rigorous sense, so that when furthest away from itself (when it is most infinitized in purpose and resolve), it is in the same moment[34] personally closest to carrying out the infinitely small part of the work that can be accomplished this very day, this very hour, this very moment.
>
> (SUD, 32/SKS 11,148)

So, frustratingly, the question survives: how can this infinitizing power come back to itself? If we reject the 'meta-self' ontology sketched above, as I think we must, there remains something paradoxical about the idea of imagination which can lead us out into possibility (that is, what is absolutely *not*) and at the same time lead us back to ourselves in our concrete particularity. The trick here[35] is to hold the concrete and the ideal together in tension, so that there is a genuine relation achieved between the ideal vision and the realm of actuality. As we have seen, *Sickness* is built around the idea that the self is composed of polar opposites, held in tension; what emerges from the discussion of infinitizing despair is that this holding in tension is centrally dependent upon imagination. To keep the infinite in view when only the concrete is given, in such a way as to understand the concrete *in* the infinite; to keep a broad moral imperative in view while attending to the small details of the particular; these achievements are essentially imaginative in character. If we consider only the concrete, we lose sight of the ideal, and if we simply ruminate on the ideal, we lose contact with the actual. Only by considering one and imagining the other *at the same time* can a true relation be brought about between them, a relation of tension which allows genuine moral action to occur. The ideal picture of possibility and the apprehension of concrete actuality are both kept present to ourselves *at once*, bringing them into a relation in which their distance from one another is both emphasized and made productive.

This unity of the actual and imaginary is a feature of any morally qualified grasp of a given situation. In other words, the transcendence of moral vision as mere vision, to reiterate Ferreira's formulation, must actually occur from *within* that vision if, as Ferreira herself claims, the maintenance of tension (without which we cannot experience or live the paradoxical) is an essentially imaginative activity.[36] Anti-Climacus sees imagination as being bound up with ethical thought, being active both in the positing of possibility *and* the apprehension of concrete particularity. Ethical imagination is not therefore a precursor to action, something we do *before* we act, but is a way of apprehending possibility and actuality *simultaneously* – that is, ethical imagination is a faculty for *seeing possibility in the world*.

Imagination and interest

We therefore emerge with a picture of human motivation in which the self imagines its possibilities and keeps them imaginatively present to itself at the same time as it enacts them in the world. We don't shift back and forth between two competing registers of possibility and actuality; rather, we apprehend actuality as permeated by possibility, in a way which seems to push us irresistibly towards metaphors of *vision*. We *see* the present as permeated by imagined ideals and goals; the possible transfigures the actual, investing the here-and-now with a richer, forward-projecting realm of meaning. We see both what *is* and *what could be* in the same unified apprehension.

But we've also seen that it's possible to imagine possibilities, even ones intimately related to my actual concrete situation, and yet not experience them as possibilities *for me*. Some imagined possibilities have a property of phenomenal *connection* with the self that I am now, while others do not. In the cases of mere detached reverie or of the playful positing of what is not, I maintain a neutrality towards what is imagined, a neutrality that disappears when something presents itself as *a possibility for me* in the phenomenally rich sense. As ethical imagination involves no reflective 'stepping back' of the sort we've been discussing, this first-personal modal relation cannot be something added to imagined possibility subsequently by reflection. Rather, we must find this relationship of 'possible-for-me' *immediately* in what we imagine, *experiencing* it as being innately bound up with our self as it exists such that we can see it as a live possibility. When we look into Anti-Climacus' 'mirror of possibility,' we have to see what we imagine as being *us* in a real sense, even though it is an *us* which we have yet to become. We must see the selves we posit as standing in an essential relationship to our *being*, an existential connection between possibility and actuality in which we *live* the connection.

We could, if we wish to draw upon Kierkegaard's vocabulary, describe this experience of relationship to what we imaginatively posit as passionate (*lidenskabelig*) imagination. Ferreira understands passion as 'the exercise of imagination attaining subjectivity – in understanding oppositions together in the "contradiction" of existence, in striving to unite finite and infinite, in becoming who we are.'[37] In the *Postscript*, *lidenskab* also plays a role in the self's holding itself together in the medium of imagination: 'In passion the existing subject is infinitized in the eternity of the imagination, and yet he is also most definitely himself' (CUP, 1:197/SKS 7, 181).

Importantly, *lidenskab* is neither a quality of reflection nor imagination; it is a state associated with the experience of reflection or imagination under certain conditions but not contained *a priori* within reflection itself (for we can reflect or imagine dispassionately). And yet, passion is nonetheless decisive for the nature and meaning of these activities. Dispassionate and passionate reflection on, say, whether one is in love would be qualitatively vastly different activities, even if the *questions* asked in each case are identical. Picture an anxious bride on the morning of her wedding, suddenly gripped by a profound uncertainty that finds expression in the question 'do I *really* love him?' Now imagine a psychologist who finds herself able to regard her own life in a mode of professional observation, dispassionately reflecting on exactly the same question about her current relationship. In both cases they ask the same question and perhaps even look at the same sort of evidence (introspectibilia, past behaviors, and so on) in order to come up with an answer. Yet these are, clearly, radically different enquiries, not by virtue of their content, but because of the affective qualities overlaid on the experience. The psychologist is arguably missing something pretty basic; as we'll discuss in Part III, there are certain forms of knowledge that one cannot reasonably be affectively indifferent to, and surely knowledge of whether or not I am in love is of that type. But we can still imagine a person asking the question dispassionately – though as Climacus tells us, a lover without passion is 'a mediocre fellow' (PF, 37/SKS 4, 243).

Lidenskab therefore seems to share important structural features with the type of self-relatedness experienced in imagination, a self-relatedness neither given in the imagined content (even in William's Medici Apartments example) nor present in all experiences of imagination (as evinced by flights of pure fantasy). Certainly, *lidenskab* is crucial in the attaining of subjectivity and thus self-actualization (although there are a number of inconsistencies and variations in the way Kierkegaard actually uses the term, which calls us to exercise caution when using it).[38] But *lidenskab* as such does not seem to contain the same notion of a self-referential, existential connection between the self and that which it represents to itself in imagination. The despair of 'infinitized feeling,' as we'll see in Chapter 8, implies that passion, like imagination, can become disconnected from lived reality for want of self-referential 'groundedness.' Though *Lidenskab* gestures towards the pathos central to the Anti-Climacan account of selfhood, something more precise is needed to identify the specific mode of thought which can constitute the relationship between actuality and imagination.

What appears to be needed to constitute the relation of 'my possibility' between that which is imaginatively posited and the imagining self is an experience whereby the self immediately understands its representations as *its own*, as having significance for the existing, actual self in the here-and-now. As this must be immediate, this import to the subject must be experienced as being embedded in what is imagined, even though the imagining self is nowhere in the content of what is imagined. In short, what's needed is a property of non-thetic self-referentiality that is part of the imaginative experience itself: what we need here is *interesse*.

Interesse is a relationship *inter-esse*, between beings. In the case of the possible selves we envisage in the act of imagining our possibilities, there is an actual, existential relationship between us and our possibilities, in that we are our possibilities and yet not yet them:

> But the mirror of possibility is no ordinary mirror; it must be used with the utmost caution. For in the highest sense, it is valid to say that this mirror is untrue. That a self appears to be such and such in the possibility of itself is only a half-truth; for in the possibility of itself the self is still far from or is only half of itself.
>
> (SUD, 37/SKS 11, 152)

Anti-Climacus here refers to what Ferreira calls the paradoxical 'not yet, but already' character of our imaginatively projected possibilities, implicit in any transition from one world-view to another (because we cannot shift from one such perspective to another without already being in some sense in the second perspective).[39] He shares this awareness with Climacus, who assigns to possibility the paradoxical ontological status of 'a being that nevertheless is non-being' (PF, 74/SKS 4, 274). While we are not the ideal self we posit, there still exists a phenomenal sense in which we are, in fact, co-identical with the selves we imagine. In effect, we find *ourselves* in what we imagine in a very real sense when that imagination is interested. In a disinterested contemplation of the ideal self, I would not find *myself* in the same way; I would instead posit the ideal self as an object for 'objective' contemplation rather than immediately experiencing it as something crucially related to my life as I live it here and now.

The claim of the ideal

To posit an ideal with genuine interest is to find *within the vision itself* an immediate, decisive phenomenal sense of self-involvement. The experience described here is one of being directly *claimed* by the imagined image. Such an experience of being *claimed* by what we imagine is presented throughout Kierkegaard's moral phenomenology as having the distinct qualities of immediate unity (the self apprehends its 'claimedness' in the same moment as it apprehends the ideal; there is no temporal 'lag')[40] and immediate self-reference we've been discussing here. In his own voice, Kierkegaard claims that 'apart from all its other good characteristics, the good, the truly great and noble, also has the quality that it does not allow the observer to be indifferent. It is as if it extracts a pledge from the person who has once seen it' (EUD, 359/SKS 5, 345-6). But in *Practice in Christianity*, it is Anti-Climacus once again who gives a developed example of the phenomenology of being claimed in this way, in this case by a moral exemplar:

> We shall now imagine a youth; with his imagination he conceives one or another image of perfection (ideal). Perhaps it is a deliverance of history, and thus from a time past; therefore it has been actual, has had the actuality of being. Or perhaps it is formed by the imagination itself, so it has no relation to or determination by time and place, but has only thought-actuality. To this image (since, for the youth, it exists only in the imagination, that is, in the imagination's infinite distance from actuality, is the image of complete perfection, not the image of striving and suffering perfection) the youth is now

drawn by his imagination, or his imagination draws the image to him. He falls in love with this image, or this image becomes his love, his inspiration, for him his more perfect (more ideal) self.

(PC, 186–7/SKS 12, 186)

The youth has posited (or received) an ideal which he takes on board as an ideal for himself. Note, however, the form of his engagement with this ideal is through being *drawn to* the image (or having imagination draw the image to him, which does not seem to make a significant difference here). There is a clear sense in this passage of the efficacy of the ideal in the youth's life being a relation brought about by the youth finding *within the image itself* that which makes it so. He doesn't import meaning into the image but instead finds the image *itself* imparts meaning. In falling in love *with the image*, and finding inspiration in it over time, the youth keeps coming back to the image to make present to himself what is significant in it. The image is not merely an illustration of some moral meaning; it is no mere memory-aid. It is a 'live' conveyor of meaning.

But this meaning is one that involves the youth directly and personally. The youth takes this image on board as an *ideal* – that is, a possibility which presents itself specifically as *to be actualized* – 'through the imagination he is always at home with this image, which he desires to resemble' (PC, 189/SKS 12, 188). This in no way dilutes the image's current non-actuality, not least because of the limitations of imagery itself: the youth can only picture the *ideal*, not the suffering which attends attempting to fulfill it (because this of course is clearly a religious ideal, an *imitatio Christi*); even if he *does* picture the suffering, it is still only *idealized* suffering (PC, 188/SKS 12, 187–8). Anti-Climacus regards these limitations on our imaginative capacities as essential for reality to be 'structured' correctly and meaningfully (PC, 188/SKS 12, 188). Yet this ultimately detracts neither from the power of the image to captivate, nor from the fact that the image presents itself as a *demand*, as essentially related to the imaginer.

The self finds that their ideal is not commensurate with actuality. Of course, *any* ideal is an expression of how the world is *not*, but the picture is doubly complicated here by the assertion that the suffering involved in the attempt to actualize the ideal cannot be included in the ideal itself. In a sense, the youth 'has let himself be enticed by his imagination to go out too far, so he has become overwrought and ridiculous, and does not fit into actuality' (PC, 189/SKS 12, 189). We have heard this language before. This being dragged out of actuality by imagination is precisely the despair of infinitization we've been discussing. Here the youth's 'conceitedly [taking the ideal] in vain as a dream' (PC, 190/SKS 12, 189) is a function of the infinitizing character of imagination, which, as 'the capacity for perfecting (idealizing)' (PC, 192/SKS 12, 191) is always pulling against actuality. Again, the cure for this form of despair is a reengagement with reality in which the actual and the ideal are held together *simultaneously*:

> the earnestness in life is to *will* to be, to *will* to express the perfection (ideality) in actuality's everydayness, to *will* it, so that one does not, to one's own ruin, once and for all busily draw a line over it, or conceitedly take it in vain as a dream – oh, a tragic lack of earnestness in both cases! – but humbly will it in actuality.
>
> (PC, 190/SKS 12, 189)

Anti-Climacus takes it that there will be a development in the youth's understanding of life, whereby suffering increases and finally the youth comes to understand that there will be no end to suffering – an understanding which was kept from him by Governance because it would have crushed him had he realized at the outset. But throughout this development the simultaneity of imagination and actualization remains unchanged, even if the *understanding* whereby the ideal that is enacted changes over time. Moreover, the youth is 'transformed in likeness to this image, which imprints or impresses itself on all his thought and on his every single utterance' (PC, 189/SKS 12, 188). The youth attains the simultaneity of the ideal and the concrete even with respect to his thought and speech, even if, as in this case, the image itself (by virtue of being an image of that which is beyond idealization)[41] is such that it will tend to deceive him.

In cases like the youth's ideal, there is a clear sense in which the image presents itself to the subject as *making demands in and of itself*, rather than appearing as a neutrality from which demands can be reflectively deduced. The image appears as something essentially connected to the observer in and of itself; *interesse*, the immediate apprehension of self-relatedness, is built into our experience of the image. Yet this sense of self-involvement, of being personally claimed, is at the same time not given by the content of the image itself: the youth isn't *himself* directly pictured in his image of the exemplar. Nor is his own relation to the image reflectively deduced; we simply either experience ourselves as claimed by the image, or we do not. *Interesse* supervenes upon our imaginative experience in ways which, though not altering the content of what is imagined, determine whether that content retains a relation to actuality or fails to do so.

True to his method of clarifying the nature of normative mental states by describing their opposite, Anti-Climacus illustrates what a *dis*interested positing of an imaginative ideal would look like in his discussion of admiration. The youth, who aspires to actualize (by imitating) the ideal he cherishes, is counterposed to the figure of the admirer, whose relation to the ideal never becomes self-reflexive. The admirer 'keeps himself personally detached' from the object of his admiration, and 'consciously or unconsciously does not discover that what is admired contains a requirement upon him, to be or at least to strive to be what is admired' (PC, 241/SKS 12, 234). Except where circumstances beyond my control make it impossible for me to try to emulate the object of my admiration – for instance, if I admire another's good fortune or natural talents or beauty (PC, 241/SKS 12, 234-5) – that which I admire issues a demand that I am to try to resemble it. If I admire an ethical exemplar, such as the model of perfect goodness that the youth posits, then insofar as the ethical is the universally human, the exemplar exercises a claim upon me: 'I am to resemble him, and *immediately begin* my striving to resemble him' (PC, 242/SKS 12, 235, emphasis added).

Ultimately, whereas 'earnestness' (*alvor*) in relation to an imaginative ideal is necessary if that ideal is to be instantiated in my concrete actuality, admiration is actually a strategy for *avoiding* the responsibility conferred by an ideal, 'a cunning that seeks evasion and excuse' (PC, 242/SKS 12, 235). The admirer acknowledges, in a sense, the normativity that the exemplar represents while never seeking to relate that normative demand back to her own life. She never goes beyond the mere spectator relation of a theater-goer to the action of a play (PC, 244/SKS 12, 237) – using, as we've seen, the power of imagination to drag us out of actuality and into a diversionary realm of detached, impotent possibility. The object of admiration is kept at a *merely* imaginative distance from the concrete actuality of the admirer who, by keeping herself out of her contemplation of what she admires, never allows it to attain an actual relation to her lived reality. What is missing in mere admiration of the ethical exemplar is precisely an experience of *immediate self-referentiality* as expressed in Anti-Climacus' description of the imitator's apprehension of the exemplar:

> I straight away begin to think about myself, simply and solely to think about myself. When I become aware of the other person, this unselfish, magnanimous person, I immediately come to say to

myself: Are you now such as he is? I forget him completely in favor of myself [*jeg glemmer ganske ham over mig selv*].

(PC, 242/SKS 12, 235)

Now, this sounds very much as if Anti-Climacus is claiming that the demand given in the exemplar causes the self to ignore the exemplar and concentrate on itself: a shift from one intentional object to another. However, while the 'other person vanishes more and more as he is assimilated into me' (PC 242–3/SKS 12, 236), insofar as the other remains an ideal to be actualized, 'a requirement upon my life, like a sting in my soul that propels me forward' (PC, 242/SKS 12, 236), they remain imaginatively present in the simultaneity of ideal and actual that Anti-Climacus presents in *Sickness*. In the apprehension of the ideal, the imitator experiences an immediate self-referentiality that infuses the perception of the admired one in a way that is missing in the mere admirer's apprehension of *exactly the same exemplar*. Both are looking at the same object, both discern the same salient features and declare these to be admirable, but one observer's perception is supervened upon by *interesse* while the other's is not. Both are looking at the same thing, but one's vision is self-reflexive while the other's is not.

We've now seen that Kierkegaard's phenomenology of moral imagination in the Anti-Climacan writings clearly depends upon self-referential cognition. In later chapters, we will return to Anti-Climacus' claim that the despair of infinitization expresses itself also in a subject's feeling and knowing. For now, however, I'd like to draw out the role played by *self-recognition* in Kierkegaard's moral psychology, the experience of seeing ourselves – and claims upon us – in the world as we encounter it.

6
Self-Recognition

The fragile man of immediacy

As we've just seen, self-referentiality plays a crucial regulatory role in Kierkegaard's picture of moral imagination (at least in the Anti-Climacan writings), in that it tethers our otherwise flighty imagination to the reality of our lived experience. Central to this is an experience of *identifying* oneself with an ideal self posited in imaginative moral contemplation. So it should come as no surprise, then, that Kierkegaard's writings contain a persistent concern with *self-recognition* as a key description of moral imagination. The ability to experience oneself as essentially involved in the subject matter of contemplation turns crucially on an ability to *see* oneself in what one imagines, apprehending ourselves under ethical and religious determinants. In Kierkegaardian moral psychology, the Socratic 'know thyself' becomes an injunction to *see yourself* in idealistic self-presentations, and the conditions of possibility for this sort of self-recognition are thereby brought into issue.

The necessary conditions for self-recognition in imaginative activity are an important topic in *The Sickness Unto Death*. Insofar as despair is a form of maladjusted comportment or orientation toward oneself, one element that has to be present in any form of despair (minimally in the 'lower' forms of despair, where a largely unconscious self is basically unaware of being in despair) is an *awareness of what one is*. A self-reflexive account of selfhood, such as Kierkegaard offers, requires at least some degree of self-knowledge.[1] Anti-Climacus tells us that when selfhood is properly constituted, all knowledge becomes *self*-knowledge (SUD, 31/SKS 11, 147); and further, escape from *fortvivelse* is only possible for a self which has uncovered its creaturely, dependent, derived nature by 'rest[ing] transparently in the power that established it' (SUD, 14/SKS 11,

130), a claim that implies knowledge of what the subject is and how it came to be. Attaining the sort of teleologically satisfied state envisioned by Anti-Climacus is therefore dependent upon *understanding* what one is, as well as *relating* oneself correctly to oneself.

Such self-knowledge requires a degree of reflection which is unavailable to the 'man of immediacy,' the self unreflectively consumed by worldly affairs and the minutiae of civil life. Such a self understands itself purely by the qualifications applied to it in the world:

> For the man of immediacy does not know [*kjender*] himself, he quite literally knows himself by the clothes he wears, he identifies having a self (and here again is the infinitely comical) by the outward.
>
> (SUD, 53/SKS 11, 168)

Anti-Climacus here faults the 'man of immediacy' for failing to see himself for what he *actually is*. He defines himself – that is, he *represents* himself to himself – as the sum total of his social relations: well-respected in the community, addressed as 'He Himself' by his servants and 'His Honor' downtown. 'In Christendom he is a Christian,' 'in the very same sense as in [...] Holland [he would be] a Hollander' (SUD, 56/SKS 11, 171). Yet to see this register of external qualifications as a comprehensive account of what one is, is a mistake; indeed, 'there is hardly a more ludicrous mistake, for a self is precisely infinitely distinct from an externality' (SUD, 53/SKS 11, 168). Elsewhere Kierkegaard claims that such a self 'does not exist; his innermost being has been consumed and depithed [...] he has himself become what was coveted: a title regarded as a human being' (CD, 58/SKS 10, 67). The self, as we have seen, is a self-reflexive self-relation that relates to itself and (simultaneously) to its context; in this reflective moment 'begins the act of separation wherein the self becomes aware of itself as essentially different from the environment and the outward and from their influence upon it' (SUD, 54/SKS 11, 169). To fail to posit oneself as 'infinitely distinct' from the social environment, even if inextricably bound up in it, is to not have a self at all.

This absence of selfhood in the 'man of immediacy' finds expression in concerns over self-recognition in his imaginative self-representations. The self composed of externalities finds itself, when confronted by threshold cases which question its survival outside the confines of the world in and through which it defines itself, in a crisis of self-recognition:

The question of immortality has often occupied him, and more than once he has asked the priest whether there is such an immortality, whether one would actually recognize himself again; something that must surely be of very particular interest to him, since he has no self.

(SUD, 56/SKS 11, 171)

Immortality provides this subject with a challenge to its very understanding of what it is. Life after death provides a model of continued survival beyond all earthly contexts and determinants; this troubles the 'man of immediacy' precisely because it poses the problem of individual, personal existence beyond or outside of those factors that he takes to make him who he is. Recognizing himself in any imaginary representation of the afterlife becomes problematic because, without an understanding of any self beyond external categories, there is nothing he could 'hang' personal identity on when confronted by a post-death existence. In fairness to the person of immediacy, there are (though presumably the busy man of affairs Anti-Climacus describes doesn't know this) serious problems posed by posthumous survival for psychological theories of personal identity.[2] But the person of immediacy has such an external, context-dependent – and therefore vulnerable – sense of personal identity that even if posthumous psychological survival preserved personal identity in the strict logical sense (such that selves could be 'reidentified' after death as being identical with antemortem persons) it would be extremely hard for *him* to reidentify himself in the afterlife. If he only knows himself by his titles, the prerogatives of his job, his designer-label suits and expensive haircuts, what could he possibly make of the idea of *him*self, the person he is now, existing in a 'world' without titles, jobs, suits or even embodiment? There is an element of caricature here of course, but the caricature of the person of immediacy serves, like the example of immortality, as an extreme and conceptually clean example of something familiar in a more localized and diluted way. Consider the career-minded person who experiences a crisis of identity after retirement, or the husband who experiences something similar after a divorce; these greater or lesser volatilizations of identity sit on a continuum of which the man of immediacy's concern for posthumous reidentification constitutes the extreme end.

Also brought into relief by the concept of immortality is the eternality that Kierkegaard takes to be inherent in the self, that within the self which, try as it might, it cannot get *rid* of (SUD, 17/SKS 11, 133). To consider 'eternal life' is therefore to contemplate the 'eternal' sense of the self as that which sustains the continuity of personal identity in this life and the next. But the socially constituted self *has* no concept of itself beyond temporal, finite determinants; as such, there is nothing transcending these determinants which it could recognize as being itself. For this reason, Kierkegaard uses the example of wondering whether we will be able to recognize ourselves and others in the afterlife as emblematic of a mode of thinking which, by concentrating on the form and content of posthumous survival, misses the essential *meaning* of such claimed survival. Such questions as whether we shall know each other in heaven are, according to the discourse on immortality in *Christian Discourses*, an attempt to evade the implications of immortality as judgment. The contemplator distracts herself with questions of what immortality will be like, whether its existence is logically demonstrable – and in doing so, escapes consideration of how she should live if she is in fact immortal and careening towards the judgment of immortality. This intellectual curiosity is in stark contrast to the reaction impending judgment *should* have on us: 'it is only all too certain, fear it!' (CD, 205/SKS 10, 214). These transcendent concerns for the self are simply outside the narrow round of questions the immediate self allows itself to consider; in worrying over relatively trivial, superficial questions about the nature of the afterlife it escapes the self-evaluation and responsibility that such an afterlife should occasion.[3]

Anti-Climacus provides another crisis of recognition for the 'man of immediacy,' occasioned this time by conscious despair over oneself. In despairing over oneself, the self wants to do away with itself, a form of despair which can be brought about by failure in the external world. The loss of those things through which the immediate self knows herself – rank, social esteem, wealth, propriety etc – volatilize the self and leave it wanting to be rid of itself, or to become someone else. Here too the conditions for self-recognition are made central to an appreciation of what the self is:

> When the whole externality has now completely changed for the person of immediacy, and he has despaired, he goes one step further; he thinks something like this, it becomes his wish: What if I became someone else, got myself a new self. Well, what if he did become someone else – I wonder whether he would recognize himself again?
> (SUD, 53/SKS 11, 169)

It is notoriously difficult, when dealing with 'science fiction' scenarios like this, to pin personal identity down. Yet the phenomena Kierkegaard describes here – wanting to become someone else – are more familiar and prosaic than, say, the body-swaps described by figures from Locke[4] to Williams,[5] or personal fission as famously discussed by Wiggins,[6] Parfit,[7] and many others. To become 'another self' here is simply to swap one set of external qualifications for another, to take on the 'life' of someone else. The familiar desire to *be* a particular person who is, say, famous or wealthy is usually, if it is interrogated at all, likely to resolve into a desire to have the same material circumstances. This carries, in itself, no particularly troubling implications with respect to individual identity conditions. Even a desire to have had some or all of the same experiences as another generally will amount to a desire for *my* having experienced the same events or activities as *they* have. For the immediate self, though, according to Anti-Climacus, there *is* no 'deeper' self that could be transferred from the old circumstances into the new such as would be a necessary condition of continuous identity. In the progression from rags to riches, the person progressing *ceases to exist* unless they have some deeper understanding of selfhood, some sense of his self which transcends his immediate outward situation.[8]

This claim looks badly overdrawn, but it is in fact entailed by the relational character of Anti-Climacan selfhood, according to which it is only through the self's active self-relation that the discrete moments of the psychological person are brought into relation. Lacking such self-relation, the subject's only remaining continuity is found in unreflective psychological dispositions and volatile, contingent externalities – what Anti-Climacus in fact calls *sinful* continuity (SUD, 105–06/SKS 11, 217–18). Certainly, this self has *some* sort of persistence, but the identity conditions it can cite for itself are too shallow and too extrinsic to carry the robust and sustainable individuation necessary for authentic selfhood. If it is so fragile and vulnerable to changes in its outward circumstances, even relatively trivial ones, we'd have deep reservations about calling it a self at all.

The trials of the drunken peasant

To illustrate this 'infinitely comical' volatility of immediate selfhood, Kierkegaard deploys one of his characteristic parables, bringing the problems of self-recognition for immediately constituted selves into sharp comic relief:

> The tale is told of a peasant, who came barefooted into the capital, and who had enough money that he could buy himself a pair of stockings and shoes with enough left over to drink his fill – it's said that as he drunkenly tried to find his way home, he ended up lying

in the middle of the road and fell asleep. Then a carriage drove up, and the driver shouted to him to move, or else he would drive over his legs. The drunken peasant woke up, looked at his legs and, when he did not recognize them because of the shoes and stockings, said: 'So let him drive, they are not my legs.'

(SUD, 53/SKS 11, 169)

The presentation of the Peasant story initially serves, on one level, to reiterate the point that a person is more than simply a collection of appearances, and that conflating selfhood with externalities will render that self 'infinitely comical.' To only know yourself by your outward circumstances is not simply an error, it is an error so ludicrous as to be laughable. But there are a number of other features of this charming vignette (it's always been one of my favorites among Kierkegaard's parables) that are relevant to Kierkegaard's project as well, and which serve to illustrate the role of vision and *interesse* in apprehending oneself in one's concrete moral situation.

Firstly, this is a failure of *vision*, not of deliberation or epistemic reasoning. The peasant reacts to the coachman's warning immediately, but what is lacking in the peasant's response is not something that would normally be supplied by deliberation, even longer or more rigorous deliberation. Hence the standard against which we judge the peasant here is not simply one of intelligence or powers of deduction.[9] Rather, the peasant fails to do what we would expect of him: to grasp his situation *immediately* and get out of the way. He should not have to *think* about what these stocking-clad objects in front of him are; rather, he should just see that they are his, or more generally, he should *see that he is in danger*.

Non-reflectivity is crucial here. For Kierkegaard, as we have seen, doubt, *contra* post-Cartesian philosophers, cannot be called to a halt by anything internal to it. A drunken peasant with a philosophical bent or uncommon intellectual acuity would not secure reasons for moving his legs by reflecting on whether the legs before him were his or not. Most likely, he would be lost to an inescapable skepticism as to whether there were legs there at all. Jamie Lorentzen treats this parable as a 'comic representation of a person lacking fundamental self-knowledge.'[10] This is obviously true so far as it goes, but the 'knowledge' involved here seems to be of a very specific kind. The peasant's failure to *know* that these are his legs before him seems radically different to a failure to know, say, the melting temperature of lead, or even something as personally central as his age or his mother's name. His epistemic relation between himself and his legs is such that we may start to question whether 'knowledge' is the correct name for this relation at all.

Our response to Anti-Climacus' parable is that the peasant should immediately see the legs as his, without any sort of inquiry into the status and provenance of the legs before him. His failure is adequately expressed in saying he 'failed to recognize his own legs'; such a description does not need to be analyzed into any more basic terms, nor is there some underlying story about inductive reasoning lurking in the unacknowledged background of such a description. His response *should* be – and that is both a descriptive and proscriptive should – immediate and unequivocal. Such decisive immediacy is not a common characteristic of deliberative reasoning, quite the opposite in fact – but it *is* an intrinsic feature of *recognition*.

Recognition, as experienced ordinarily, is immediate and (in the first moment at least) decisive. The experience of perceptual recognition is different to, for instance, the experience of using a list of known features to ascertain whether a photo is of a particular person. We do not, when we recognize someone normally, tick off a list of criteria to determine (inductively) who they are; it is only when our ability to recognize someone cannot operate that we take this highly artificial step, and it is clearly a very different phenomenon to that of 'normal' recognition. Wittgenstein makes the point about recognition that it is not, as we might prereflectively think, a process of comparing what we are looking at with some sort of mental representation, as if reading off similarities between a template and an exemplar. Recognition is not experienced as a phenomenon of comparison that points to some external criterion; instead, we see the object *as* what it is, without thereby referring to anything else outside the object:

> 605. And it is not so much as if I were comparing the object with a picture set beside it, but as if the object *coincided* with the picture. So I see only one thing, not two.[11]

The well-worn concept of the 'leap' (*spring*) described in *Postscript* provides a useful template for conceptualizing what happens in recognition. The moment of recognition is, to borrow a Climacan phrase, a 'qualitative transition' from seeing *something* to seeing something *as* what we recognize it to be.[12] There is no moment of pause to consider reflectively what we are looking at within the phenomenon of recognition itself – if this happens, it happens prior to recognition rather than within it. As with our discussions of *interesse* in consciousness and the experience of self-referentiality in imagination, we once again seem to be dealing with a phenomenon central to human agency which appears to be embedded in vision and perception itself, rather than being a function of reflective cognition. That's not to say it is nonrational – presumably great scientific and technical advances often involve the immediate recognition of highly complex states of affairs, and we sometimes 'see' medical diagnoses or the answers to mathematical problems – but the non-reflective immediacy of perception is essential here.

Secondly, the peasant fails to *see himself*. In failing to recognize the legs as his own, the peasant fails to see himself as imperiled, and as such, he fails to see the situation as pertaining – essentially, immediately, and concretely – to *him*. Certainly, he knows, legs are going to be crushed; but his failure to look beyond purely external determinants means he does not see that the danger is danger to *him*, something he should care about very much. The comic appeal of this scene rests mainly upon the disjunction between the peasant's object of consideration and his attitude towards it. If the peasant failed to recognize someone *else's* legs the joke simply wouldn't work. The peasant is crucially involved in the situation in which he finds himself because he is *co-identical* with what he contemplates. To draw an attractive if admittedly tenuous natural language point, if we said 'The peasant was run over by a carriage,' no one would correct us by saying 'No, the peasant was not run over, his legs were' – that *itself* would sound like a (rather insensitive!) joke. His attitude of unconcern therefore is completely inappropriate; this is not a situation he can reasonably be indifferent to. He does not perceive (and it is precisely a perceptual relationship, as we saw above) *himself* in the situation, and so his vision is every bit as disconnected from reality as the ungrounded imagination of infinitized selfhood. The peasant sees legs, but in not *experiencing* this perception as a perception *of himself* in the sense picked out by the term *interesse*, his perception and thereby his response to the situation goes awry.

Finally, the peasant is *responsible* for this failure, and is therefore a legitimate object of fun. There is nothing sympathetic in the portrayal of the peasant, and nothing to suggest that his blunder is mitigated by any extraneous circumstances. Even the peasant's drunkenness, which he is clearly responsible for, does not seem to be entirely to blame for the mistake, for his highly unusual mode of flawed perception is clearly not a typical effect of alcohol. Nor is a contingent fact such as a sub-par intellect or lack of talent to blame for this failure of vision. Kierkegaard is not above delighting in folktales which deal in derogatory 'rustic' stereotypes (such as stories of the hapless *Molboer*, the inhabitants of Mols lampooned as hopelessly dim-witted in Danish folklore). But Kierkegaard's use of this stereotype goes beyond straightforward snobbish disdain.

The peasant's inability to see the legs in front of him as *his* legs neatly parallels references to the absentminded bookseller Soldin, who 'When he wanted get up in the morning, he was not aware that he was dead' (CUP, 1:167/SKS 7, 155). Like the peasant, Soldin displays a lack of self-consciousness that seems to be the result of an inhuman inattention rather than any lack of mental acuity: when a customer impersonates Soldin's voice while his back was turned, Soldin has to ask his wife if it was he who was speaking (CA, 51/SKS 4, 356). Just as the peasant does not see his own presence in the situation before him, Soldin fails to see his absence. While this character too can be taken as a simple object of fun, the point Johannes Climacus makes in the *Postscript* is that the most esteemed speculative scholar, in abstracting himself out of the existence which he claims to encompass with complex systems of thought, *is no better*. Intelligence is no guarantee against becoming ridiculous.

The peasant should simply *see* the legs as *his*. Not to do so is not simply to be exceptionally dull, it is to be *less than human* in an important respect. He is not lacking in some human attribute or virtue that may be unequally distributed across individuals; rather, the peasant lacks an aspect of what we take it as necessary to *be* human in the first place. And as this is not due to any mitigating inequitable distribution, the peasant is to blame for this failure.

Reflecting the world: the self as mirror

A similar crisis of self-recognition can be found in the discourse 'To Need God Is A Human Being's Highest Perfection.' Here, however, the crisis takes on a positive aspect, as a means for uncovering the self as a being distinct from its externalities (the 'inner being' of the *Upbuilding Discourses*). A self who has suffered a catastrophic failure of externalities, who has lost 'wealth and power and dominion [...] the flattering attention of the crowd, and all the envied grandeur of his appearance' but avoids the despair described in *Sickness*, also becomes unrecognizable to himself and the world at large (EUD, 298/SKS 5, 292). The world barely recognizes him because of the trivialities of his changed appearance and circumstances ('Is it not wretched that it is clothes that make a person unrecognizable, so that one does not know him when he is unclothed' [EUD, 298/SKS 5, 292–3]), but he himself also struggles to recognize himself:

> Just as the world is unable to recognize him again because of the drastic change, so he can scarcely recognize himself – so changed is he, that he who needed so much, now needs so much less.
>
> (EUD, 298/SKS 5, 292)

The self uncovers a previously unsuspected disjunction between itself and the world, finding itself to be less dependent upon the trappings of its socially constructed identity than it took itself to be.

What is missing from immediate, socially constructed selfhood such that it cannot sustain the perceptual conditions necessary for self-recognition? Partly, the problem is, as noted above, the lack of stable, persistent identity conditions. For Kierkegaard, the self-knowledge of the immediate self is nothing more than 'a relation between a dubious self and a dubious something else,' the dubiousness inhering in the potential for either the self or that to which it compares itself to change (EUD, 313/SKS 5, 305). The inconstancy of the external world is such that the self is made correspondingly inconstant where it defines itself by externalities. External qualifications are always relational, and relational properties can change at any time. Those I compare myself to 'could be changed, so that someone else became the stronger, the more handsome, the richer' (EUD, 313/SKS 5, 305). Where these externalities change, I am still left with myself, a self that no longer knows what it is or, in the case of the self that declares 'either Caesar or nothing' and then fails to become Caesar, becomes intolerable to itself by virtue of its continued, volatilized existence (SUD, 19/SKS 11,134–5). William James says much the same thing when he discusses 'the paradox of a man shamed to death because he is only the second pugilist or the second oarsman in the world' – though he can beat everyone on earth minus one, if he cannot beat that one person, 'He is to his own regard as if he were not, indeed he *is* not.'[13]

But it is not only the volatility of the immediate, world-immersed self that makes self-recognition in ideality impossible (or at least dangerously unreliable). Just as the failure of external predicates makes it impossible for the self to 'see itself' in any radically altered possible future self, so too nothing in the external world offers anything like the *distinctiveness* of a self. Here, like his pseudonym Anti-Climacus, Kierkegaard incorporates a mirror metaphor to explain what is lacking:

But if he nevertheless is unwilling to be like an instrument of war in the service of unexplained drives, indeed, in the service of the world, because the world itself, which he craves, stimulates the drives; if he nevertheless does not want to be like a stringed instrument in the hands of unexplained moods or, rather, in the hands of the world, because the movement of his soul is in accord with the way the world plucks its strings; if he does not want to be like a mirror in which he captures the world, or, rather, the world mirrors itself [...].

(EUD, 308/SKS 5, 301)

The immediately constructed self is a self composed of the 'stuff' of the world. As such it never succeeds in becoming more than the reflection of the world in/out of which it is constituted. The entire content of my selfhood is determined and shaped by the outside world, and takes on the forms and appearances given by this world. Even my immediate desires and inclinations are 'external' in this sense, in that they are distinct from what I reflectively take to be *me* (and thus can be repudiated), and they are shaped and given direction and expression by the outside world. That I manipulate the world and my place in it does not change this fact. If I am just the sum of my social relationships, then my self is constituted passively, even if (on a level shallower than the self-constitutive role choices espoused by Judge William in *Either/Or*) I actively take these roles on. I may choose to become Mayor, but what it is to *be* Mayor – powers, responsibilities, expectations, perks and vestments – will be determined by the social context. There is nothing distinctive to *me* about these externalities. They are merely supplied by the world and as such cannot support or sustain the radical schism between the inner and the outer self uncovered by the awareness of 'distinctness' from the world. For self-recognition to be possible in ideal presentations of oneself, the contents of these representations must carry something *more* than just the forms given by the external/material/social world. I must supply this something more, so as not to become *merely* a reflection of the world, and so that I can see myself as more than what the world gives me to wear.[14]

This 'more' that must be present in self-representations if self-recognition is to occur will here take us beyond the sustainability of visual metaphors. For Anti-Climacus, humans are more than their finitude and externality, but are also potentially spirit (*aand*). Spirit, we recall, is a self-relation where the self 'relates itself to itself or is that in the relation whereby the relation relates itself to itself' (SUD, 13/SKS 11,129). Plainly, we cannot straightforwardly assign any visible content to this definition – in other words, we cannot *see* what it is to be a self. In *Upbuilding Discourses in Various Spirits*, Kierkegaard declares 'To be Spirit is humanity's invisible glory' (UDVS, 193/SKS 8, 290), and that this invisibility, like that of God, is important in terms of successful reflection:

> But God is Spirit, is invisible, and invisibility's image is indeed in turn invisibility: in this way the invisible Creator reproduces himself in the invisibility, which is the qualification of spirit, and God's image is precisely the invisible glory. If God were visible, well, then there would be no one who could resemble him or be his image; for the image of all that is visible *does not exist*, and amongst the visible there is nothing, not even a leaf, that resembles another or is its image. If that were the case, then the image would be the object itself.
>
> (UDVS, 192/SKS 8, 289–90)[15]

This claim that there are no likenesses seems unduly strong, but it really amounts to a truistic assertion that the best image is still *only* an image, not the object of which it is the image. Of course, Kierkegaard is not talking about self-recognition here, but rather about making oneself capable of reflecting the image of God. To be human is to be made in the image of God, but this likeness consists in the ability to emulate God, which, paradoxically, involves becoming as nothing.[16] This is a special quality of the divine, that being infinite, no positive, finite image can present it; it requires, therefore, a negative presentation. This is why, as Louis Mackey puts it (indirectly citing CUP, 1:472/7, 428) the 'negative' seen from a human perspective always stands for the positive seen from the viewpoint of divinity.[17] As George Pattison notes in his discussion of the religious discourses, being made in God's likeness cannot be a simple matter of erect carriage and superior cognitive abilities compared to nonhuman animals: 'if humanity defines itself in terms of its external powers it will necessarily make itself incapable of *being* (rather than merely reflecting) the image of anything else, including, pre-eminently, God.'[18] So Kierkegaard's direct point is to do with becoming *oneself* a surface for reflection, becoming, in effect, the only surface that can reflect the invisible: nothing. Paradoxically, the need to break with immediacy, in which the self only *is* as a passive reflection of externality, will drive the self ultimately to become *nothing but* a reflective surface, but this of a different and very particular kind. But this passage also has important implications for Kierkegaard's model of self-recognition in ethical imagination.

We saw earlier that a crucial feature of ethical imagination is the transcendence of possibilities as being not merely representations of possible actions, but of *my* possibilities, as live, genuine features of my ethical situation. The possibilities I represent to myself *are me* in a vital, but necessarily partial, sense. But here Kierkegaard lays out the limitations inherent in visual language: no image, no matter how lifelike, succeeds in becoming the object it represents. Insofar as the 'image' of myself posited in ethical imagination succeeds in being me, it must achieve this by some 'invisible' factor built into the representation. Hence, visible, material, external cues such as the immediate self makes use of to 'know' itself are incapable of carrying the sense in which my representations of my possible self *are* me in an essential sense. Such representations don't, to put it bluntly, just *look* like me. Indeed, when we try to visualize ourselves in some situation we generally *don't* construct a perfectly lifelike image, and this doesn't seem to create problems for imagination in ordinary life. Equally, when we dream, we don't recognize ourselves primarily because of what we look like, but because the figure in the dream is *meant to be* me.[19] What is important to the meaning of the image is not given by the immediate (visual) content of the image but is something that, as we saw in the previous chapter's discussion of imagination, *supervenes upon the image*.

This is certainly the case in the peasant example – while the peasant's failure is a failure to see something, we cannot describe what he was to see in purely visual terms, as the visual content of the experience would be the *same* in a case of successful vision. The experience of seeing one's legs as one's own in a situation of immediate peril is qualitatively and decisively different to that of, say, recognizing my luggage on an airport carousel, ticking off particular visual clues to recognize my bag when I see it. And the difference here is not simply one of familiarity or repeated experience. The peasant fails to see not his legs as objects, but his involvement in the situation. In effect, he sees legs but not *himself* in the situation, and what one sees when one sees oneself goes beyond the merely visual. The successful way of seeing involves significance nonreflectively supervening upon the visual content of the experience.

Master and cow: Kierkegaard's dialectic of recognition

Kierkegaard develops a complex and subtle interplay of reflection and self-recognition to describe the process whereby the self comes to recognize itself in its ideal representations. Arne Grøn has shown that

Kierkegaard, like Hegel, makes much of a dialectic of recognition, one which is crucial to the project of the 'second ethics' of *Works of Love*.[20] Grøn argues that recognition is tied to our ability to see the Other *as* Other, as another distinctive self exercising moral claims upon us. Apart from the moral dimensions of this dialectic of vision, it has important implications for one's self-understanding. To *see* the other wrongly – to fail to see my essential kinship with the other – is to do 'damage' to my 'soul.' To fail to see the other correctly is therefore to ensnare one's own sense of self-constitution in the merely finite, external dissimilarities between myself and the other to which my vision is misdirected.[21]

Equally, though, Grøn's argument can be extended to the forms of self-recognition where the issue is not seeing the *other* correctly, but myself. In many respects *this* form of recognition is no less crucial for Kierkegaard's ethical project, because it is central to the integrated sense of self he takes as necessary for moral life. It is, admittedly, less fully dialectical in that there is no reciprocity of vision – when I recognize myself, what I recognize cannot be taken to be looking back at me. In this sense the dialectic of self-recognition is 'thinner' than that Grøn takes to be at work in the ethical apprehension of the distinctiveness of the other.[22]

Kierkegaard deals directly with Hegel's dialectic of recognition (the Master/Slave example) in, appropriately enough, *The Sickness Unto Death* – a work sometimes viewed as a parody of the dense dialectical style of *Phenomenology of Spirit* (while also dealing with themes familiar from the *Phenomenology* such as Unhappy Consciousness and Despair). Here, Anti-Climacus discusses the self's constitution 'before God,' and contrasts this with other dialectical means of self-constitution:

> And what infinite reality does the self gain by being conscious of existing before God, by becoming a human self, whose criterion is God! A cattleman who (if this were possible) is a self directly before his cattle is a very low self; likewise a master who is a self directly before his slaves, and is properly not a self – for in both cases a criterion is lacking. The child, who previously had only the criterion of his parents, becomes a self as a man by getting the state as criterion; but what an infinite accent falls on the self by getting God as criterion!
>
> (SUD, 79/SKS 11, 193)

This is a two-part claim. Firstly, Anti-Climacus is asserting that the self derives its discrete identity through a dialectical process of mutual recognition *a la* Hegel. To be a self-before-cattle is to be no self at all; to be a self before slaves is to attain, at least, marginal selfhood. To be a self before one's parents and then the state is to achieve progressively fuller understandings of one's selfhood, but being a self before God, by definition the most extreme 'criterion' (*maalestok*) available, provides the fullest expression of what one is.[23] As Pattison shows, God becomes a regulating concept, and being a self before God becomes the fullest expression of being what one is.[24]

What is present, or missing, in these progressively fuller criteria against which to define oneself? Our interactions with animals are, of course, vastly richer and more significant than a philosopher like Descartes would maintain,[25] but there are distinct limits. The clear alterity between the human self and the herd – which irresistibly evokes other Kierkegaardian images of inhuman, selfless masses and crowds – is such that whatever we can see of ourselves in a cow (and there is arguably much more there than Anti-Climacus would allow), it seems a brute fact that such identification will not provide meaning adequate to the self-conception of a being with language and a capacity for transcendence. As Norman Lillegard has argued, to be a self before cattle is to take on a life-view or project that simply cannot be fully comprehensive for the task of living a human life, any more than a passion for ping-pong could be the unifying principle of one's life; so much of what we find meaningful in life is left out by such a passion that such a self would be left out by such a commitment.[26] In both cases, I do not see *enough* of myself reflected in what I define myself in relation to.

An important aspect to this, then, is what we find in the relations by which we construct self-identity that answers to our self-awareness – in other words, the extent to which we can recognize ourselves in what we compare ourselves to. This brings us back to the idea of a criterion (*maalestok*) against which we compare ourselves – and in measuring ourselves we enter into a relationship of self-recognition, *seeing* our likeness in the process of evaluative comparison. Family, state, and society might provide us with progressively *more* adequate contexts in which to see ourselves, but in Anti-Climacus' theologically qualified ontology, human beings are impelled to become *spirit* – something that goes well beyond the capacities of the *merely* visual, but that we are to recognize in all things, to see ourselves *as eternal*, and *as nothing* before God. As pointed to in the Peasant example, this process of self-recognition will be one of immediate self-referentiality, in which our own involvement in what we see supervenes upon what we see. To explore this process of self-recognition more deeply, we must pass through Kierkegaard's frequent use of mirror-metaphors and what they reveal about the dialectic of self-recognition.

7
Mirrors

The mirror of possibility

Mirror metaphors crop up throughout Kierkegaard's authorship, and this should come as no surprise given his emphasis on self-recognition. The mirror represents *the* paradigmatic experience of self-recognition, where I literally see myself, and so where awareness of 'what I look like' is generated and altered in an immediate way. Obviously, the experience *is* mediated on a physical level (through carefully arranged glass surfaces), but on the subjective level, the experience is immediate. We do not, under normal circumstances, stop to consider whether the mirror is accurate, or whether imperfections in its construction distort the image in it. We typically do not even notice that the image in the mirror is precisely that, a 'mirror image,' inverted along its vertical axis. We might think that's simply a product of familiarity with the experience of seeing ourselves in the mirror, where we only *ever* see our image in its inverted form. However, that we rarely notice the difference between how we look in the mirror and how we look in photographs (where we're not inverted) suggests that the specifics of the image *qua* image are not what we attend to when looking at images of ourselves. In the usual, unreflective run of things, we simply *see ourselves*, rather than an *image* of ourselves. This fact, with its curious volatilization of the subject/object schema, makes the mirror a powerful metaphorical and exploratory tool in Kierkegaard's phenomenology of moral perception.[1]

In a previous chapter, we considered Anti-Climacus' analogy of the 'mirror of possibility,' a device which bears repeating here:

> to [see] one*self* in a mirror it is necessary to recognize oneself, for if one does not, then one does not see one*self* but only a human being.
>
> (SUD, 37/SKS 11, 152)

As we have seen, Anti-Climacus presents us here with two different ways in which we can see ourselves in this mirror. Either we see the mirror as making demands upon *us*, or we see it simply as positing possibilities without any real existential connection to the self looking into the mirror. In this later case, we are looking not at us essentially, but merely at *a* person. A connection is missing. And the missing connection is not to be found in any kind of *reflection* upon the image. I've argued at length that in the process of interested ethical imagination we see ourselves immediately in our positing of possibilities – there is no moment of stepping back from the image to determine reflectively what relation it bears to me as a present-situated ethical agent.

Yet the choice of the mirror as a metaphoric device is not, in some respects, an entirely felicitous one. Anti-Climacus qualifies his use of the image of the 'mirror of possibility' with the caveat that 'in the highest sense, it is valid to say that this mirror is untrue' (SUD, 37/SKS 11, 152). In other words, by presenting us with an image of an 'us' we are *not* yet (but which is nonetheless 'us' in the sense of shared identity), this metaphoric mirror goes well beyond what a mirror is normally taken to do. Outside of fairy tales, mirrors show us what *is*, not what will be. Moreover, in real life we almost never seem to have the experience of *not* recognizing ourselves in the mirror. Kierkegaard himself acknowledges this in his discussion of the 'Mirror of the Word' (discussed below):

> *The first requirement is that you must not look at the mirror, contemplate the mirror, but must see yourself* [*see Dig selv*] *in the mirror.*
> This seems so obvious that one might think it would scarcely need to be said.
>
> (FSE, 25/SV2 XII, 315)

The idea of looking into a mirror without recognizing ourselves is so contrary to normal experience as to be immediately suspect. Why, then, use the mirror as an analogy at all?

Part of the answer may be that the Mirror is used metaphorically in the tradition of *lectio divina* which Kierkegaard echoes in his discussion of the mirror in *For Self-Examination*, and religious writers such as Meister Eckhart are also drawn to the mirror as a metaphor for union with God.[2] For Kierkegaard, though, the main reason for his use of the Mirror seems to be that the *immediate* self-recognition involved in seeing oneself in a mirror captures something crucial to the experience of self-recognition in moral thought. We have already seen how this immediacy operates in creating the link between moral perception and decision in the context of deliberation. The immediacy of self-recognition in considering possibilities serves to ground deliberation in the context of my present, concrete self, and prevents imagination from becoming detached from the moral context in which it takes place. In the context of moral self-examination, however, Kierkegaard places a slightly different (yet fundamentally connected) emphasis upon this immediacy. The experience of looking into a mirror is not just one of immediate self-recognition. Most of the time, it is also an immediately *evaluative* experience.

This evaluative aspect of the experience of looking into a mirror is essential to the power Kierkegaard finds in the mirror metaphor.[3] This is already prefigured in his choice of epigram for *Stages on Life's Way*, the quote from G.C. Lichtenberg: 'Such works are mirrors: when an ape looks in, no apostle can look out' (SLW, 8/SLW 6, 16).[4] The reaction to such a work shows the reader to himself in an evaluative light; the ape sees itself as an ape through reading it. In the *Postscript*, the mirror metaphor is again used to specify the specifically *ethical* character of the evaluation in question:

> Let world history be a mirror, let the observer sit and look at himself in the mirror, but let us not forget the dog that also looked at itself in the mirror – and lost what it had. The ethical is also a mirror, and the person who sees himself therein certainly loses something, and the more he sees himself in it, the more he loses – namely, all the uncertain, in order to win the certain.
>
> (CUP 1:153–54/SKS 7, 143)

The reference to the Aesopian dog, who drops his bone when he catches sight of his reflection, shows us that the self-reflection inherent in the ethical which Climacus expresses through this metaphor is one which does not leave the observer unchanged. Whereas the pursuit of understanding of world history may remain simply an idle 'pastime' (CUP, 1:154/SKS 7, 143) with no real impact upon the contemplator, ethical contemplation shows the self to itself in a way that is both evaluative and effects actual change upon the self. *This* reflection offers an evaluation that confronts us and forces us to change the qualifications under which we live (losing 'all the uncertain in order to gain the certain' – that is, trading the approximation-knowledge of the objective for the certainty of resolution and decision). The metaphorical mirror, then, does not simply reflect the self but presents the self back to itself transfigured by the judgments appropriate to it (in this case, ethical). Evaluation is *embedded* in the reflection.

We are familiar with the embeddedness of evaluation in looking into a mirror (in a rather banal sense) from our everyday, non-moral use of mirrors. The experience of looking into a mirror and declaring 'I look terrible' is familiar and unremarkable. But in this experience too we see that the act of self-recognition is in no sense prior to the evaluative act. If asked to describe our thought processes after having this experience, there would surely be something artificial and untrue in responding: 'I saw an image in the mirror, I then recognized the image to be that of myself, and then concluded, by reference to some standard or other, that I look terrible.' Rather, the looking, the recognition and the evaluation are experienced as a unitary moment.

We've seen that recognition is not (on the phenomenal level at least) a *comparative* phenomenon, where we note similarities between what we perceive and some pre-existing template, eventually crossing a threshold of confidence that permits definite identification. I also quoted, approvingly, Wittgenstein's assertion that in the moment of recognition, 'we see one thing, not two.'[5] If we are to concede this to Wittgenstein, and further insist that evaluation is embedded *in* the experience of recognition rather than following it in sequence, then Kierkegaard's notion of a criterion (*maalestok*) against which we are to compare ourselves takes on a different aspect. We cannot examine the criterion and *then* look to see if we meet its requirements; rather, examination of the criterion and how we stand (in evaluative terms) towards it will be bound together in a single perceptual experience. I will, as it were, *see* myself *in the light of* the criterion – and the use of the word 'see' here retains the immediacy inherent in the mirror metaphor. To illustrate the immediacy of vision in the context of self-examination against a set of moral or religious imperatives, Kierkegaard (relatively late in his career) gives us his most sustained and fruitful deployment of the mirror metaphor: the discussion of the 'Mirror of the Word' in *For Self-Examination*.

The mirror of the word: observing the mirror

The first chapter of *For Self-Examination*[6] is a discourse on the injunction in James' Epistle to be a 'doer' and not merely a 'hearer' of the word of God:

> If anyone is a hearer of the Word and not a doer of it, he is like a man who observes his bodily face in a mirror, for he would observe himself and go away and at once forget what he was like.
>
> (James 1:23)

Kierkegaard picks up upon this mirror simile and uses it as the basis of an extended discussion on the correct approach to Scripture, driven by the question 'What Is Required In Order To Look at Oneself with True Blessing in the Mirror of the Word?' In this discourse, Scripture *itself* becomes the mirror:

> God's word is the mirror – I shall, in reading or hearing it, see myself in the mirror.
>
> (FSE, 25/SV2 XII, 315)

Equating the act of reading Scripture with looking into a mirror conflates both the self-representation (the image in the mirror) and the 'criterion' we are to compare it to. Thus Scripture both simultaneously provides a moral standard *and* evaluates us against that standard. We are to look into the mirror and see ourselves as *judged* by the Word; that is, in reading the moral imperatives of Scripture we are to experience this reading as disclosing to us – *showing* us – how we stand. Again, the experience is thoroughly evaluative in a self-referential way, not as a postscript to reading Scripture, but as an inextricable element of that reading. Kierkegaard goes on to lay out a schematic account of the conditions necessary for seeing oneself in the mirror of the Word, dividing the discourse into three sections, each detailing another 'requirement' for 'seeing oneself in the mirror of the Word.' In so doing, he reveals much about what is at issue in moral reflection and the psychological state picked out by his earlier use of the term *interesse*.

The first requirement for appropriate engagement with Scripture 'is that you must not look at the mirror, contemplate the mirror, but see yourself in the mirror,' which 'seems so obvious that one might think it would scarcely need to be said' (FSE, 25 SV2 XII, 315). Already, then, Kierkegaard has run up against a seeming infelicity in the mirror-metaphor. Yet he persists with it.[7] The injunction not to 'observe the mirror' becomes, in the context of Scripture, a reiteration that the essential meaning of Scripture is that it is *to be acted upon*, and not made into fodder for endless interpretation.

Kierkegaard gives the arresting extended metaphor of a man who receives a letter from his beloved, written in a language foreign to him (FSE, 26–8/SV2 XII, 316–17). He takes a dictionary and toils away at attempting to interpret the letter. He angrily dismisses an acquaintance who remarks 'Well, so you are sitting and reading a letter you've received from your beloved' by making a distinction between translating and reading:

> 'Have you taken leave of your senses, you think this is reading a letter from one's beloved? No, my friend, I am sitting here in toil and drudgery in order to get it translated with the help of a dictionary; at times I am ready to burst with impatience, the blood rushes to my head, and I could just about hurl the dictionary onto the floor – and you call that reading, you must be having me on! No, soon, thank God, I will be finished with the translation and then, yes then, then I shall read the letter from the one I love; that is something quite different.'
>
> (FSE, 27/SV2 XII, 316)

The Lover thus 'distinguishes between reading and reading' (FSE, 27/SV2 XII, 317), or two different forms of reading, the first taken as preparatory to the second (for the sake of clarity I'll refer to the translative form as 'reading' and the second mode as 'Reading'). In the second sense, 'he understood [R]eading to mean that if the letter contained a wish, one should begin fulfilling it at once; there was not a second to waste' (FSE, 28/SV2 XII, 318). The act of reading in preparation for Reading concerns the attempt to discern exactly what Scripture says – the literal meaning of Scripture – while Reading (taken as the whole purpose for biblical scholarship) concerns a more immediate, agent-directed engagement with the text. Precisely the same distinction is captured in the case of the diligent needlewoman in 'An Occasional Discourse' who hopes no one will 'look wrongly [*saae feil*, lit. 'see mistakenly'] and see her artistry instead of the meaning of the cloth or [...] look wrongly and see a defect instead of seeing the meaning of the cloth' (UDVS, 5/SKS 8, 121). In both cases, attention is misdirected towards the mechanics of the production rather than its meaning. The distinction between these two modes of attention neatly parallels the Objective Truth and Subjective Truth distinction in the *Postscript*; only in the second, subjectively qualified form of engagement does the individual's personal relation to the truth under consideration become the decisive factor. Both 'reading' Scripture and paying attention to the needlewoman's cloth rather than its meaning are species of 'observing the mirror' rather than what it discloses.

Within a religious context like Kierkegaard's, rigorous Biblical exegesis at least notionally understands itself as the attempt to determine precisely *what* is required of us, so that, once this is determined, scriptural injunction can serve to tell us *how* we are to live, or how we stand. But of course, the task of biblical scholarship never does reach this state of perfect perspicuity whereby all moral demands are known and all moral questions settled. Like asking questions about the nature of the afterlife, scholarship, it seems, is actually a strategy for *evading* responsibility (FSE, 32/SV2 XII, 321). The act of interpreting Scripture becomes a device for deferring the moment of having to Read the Scriptures, to 'be alone with' the Word of God and so have to experience it as judging and claiming oneself. Kierkegaard uses 'being alone' with the Word here to express a certain kind of comportment *to* the Word where the Word is received as speaking *specifically* to the hearer. Scripture is here understood as irreducibly moral – that is, it immediately confers responsibility and obligation – and consequently, inescapably agent-directed:

> To be alone with Holy Scripture! [. . .] it traps me at once; it asks me (yes, it is as if it were God himself who asked me): have you done what you read there?
>
> (FSE, 31/SV2 XII, 320)

In this picture, spending the finite time apportioned to us attempting to determine *exactly* what is required is a *moral* failure, as it actually seeks to excuse us from acting upon those requirements we *can* readily understand. Kierkegaard takes it that there is much in Scripture which is, as a point of empirical fact, easy to understand – and the only thing that could distort that clarity would be interpretative scholarship (FSE, 34-5/SV XII, 323). In terms of non-Christian ethics, the translatability of Kierkegaard's thought is somewhat hampered here by his apparent blindness to the possibility of genuine moral dilemma.[8] In several places Kierkegaard appears to dismiss the possibility that there can be any real question over what is normatively required of us; for instance, in *Christian Discourses* he takes it as a sign of the corruption of the age that the content of duty has been 'changed into a problem for thought [...] There must not to be a question about duty, but there must only be the question about whether I am doing my duty' (CD, 205/SKS 10, 214). If such an approach to normative ethics is problematic (or at least unhelpful) in Kierkegaard's ostensibly Christian, culturally homogenous context, it is all the more so today. As Julia Watkin has argued that Kierkegaard's position on revealed morality in *For Self-Examination* suddenly looks considerably weaker in a modern pluralist context, where many religions, and atheism, exist as live alternatives.[9] Equally, there are a great many metaethical options open to the contemporary ethicist, each of which will tend to throw up radically different answers to ethical problems. Such conflicts are endemic between Consequentialist to Deontologist positions. In such a context, surely we can be excused for a little perplexity in ethical matters? Or is Kierkegaard committed to some form of ethical Intuitionism, whereby we simply *see* the right thing to do in moral situations on the basis of some sort of mental intuition, in the same way that we *see* the correctness of a mathematical axiom?[10]

I don't think Kierkegaard *is* committed to anything like Intuitionism; indeed, his entire emphasis on revealed morality would speak against the notion that we have some innate ability to determine moral truth for ourselves. The entire point of the 'second ethics' of *Works of Love* is to replace an immanent, calculative human ethics with a transcendent, divine command towards infinite self-emptying love – and this *essentially* requires revelation, according to Kierkegaard. For us, however, the choice needn't be between Intuitionism and Divine Command theory if we want to recover something of value from Kierkegaard's moral psychology, for the teleological model of moral vision Kierkegaard recommends would cohere equally well with a number of other metaethical positions as well. A claim that we should immediately apprehend the ethical import of a situation placed before us would also be a legitimate outcome of Aristotelian moral education (thus the largely perceptual character of *phronesis*), or perhaps a claim that we are to absorb certain principles until their application in the world becomes a matter of 'second nature.' Common to all these cases is an understanding that 'how the observer himself *is* indeed become decisive' (EUD, 59/SKS 5, 69). What I'm claiming for Kierkegaard here is a form of ethical *perceptualism*, which is fundamentally a matter of moral psychology; it needn't necessarily equate to Rossian Intuitionism or Murdochian neo-Platonism.[11]

Moreover, there is a defensible – if daunting – point that can be recovered from Kierkegaard's apparent refusal to sanction the possibility of genuine moral uncertainty. It may be that reason can't help us out of our contemporary moral situation, which is characterized by increasingly divergent claims as to what considerations (if any) can have normative force, but this no more excuses us from the realm of the ethical than, according to Kierkegaard, uncertainties in biblical scholarship excuse Christians from following Scripture. The murkiness of morality does not excuse us from being legitimately claimed by it; the unclarity and uncertainty of practical reason are in nowise exculpatory. Perhaps that is an unattractively austere, even tragic picture of moral life, but it has a certain terrible plausibility: why should the categorical pull of the ethical make allowances for human ignorance?

Mirrors and normative vision

The (moral) imperative to see oneself rather than the mirror – that is, attending to how one appears seen through the prism of God's Word, rather than trying to discern the objective meaning of Scripture – therefore calls us to a particular engagement with Scripture, one where the Word speaks directly to me about *my* condition. The Word is a mirror in that it immediately presents back to us how *we are*. The act of Reading such texts therefore shows us *ourselves* in a way that is lost to detached, objective scholarship. We *see ourselves* in the Word, and this in an evaluative light.

This immediacy of vision is reinforced by the second condition to be met:

> The second requirement is that when you read God's Word, in order to see yourself in the mirror you must (so that you actually can come to see yourself in the mirror) remember to say to yourself continuously: it is me that is being spoken to, it is me that is being spoken about.
>
> (FSE, 35/SV2 XII, 324)

This is simply a restatement of the need for a personal, direct relationship to the Word instead of an objective, disinterested one (FSE, 36/SV2 XII, 324–5). Kierkegaard urges us to bear in mind when reading that the subject of Scripture is ourselves and our own moral condition. The simplest interpretation of this passage would be that one need simply keep reminding oneself of this periodically, as if pausing every so often to suffix passages of Scripture with 'thou art the man' (FSE, 38/SV2 XII, 327). Indeed, Kierkegaard provides fuel for such a straightforward reading when he alludes to the Persian king Darius, who had a servant remind him each day to remember to take vengeance upon the Athenians (FSE, 37/SV2 XII, 325).

Yet as we have seen, the mirror metaphor entails a form of immediacy in vision, and we've seen many times now that in Kierkegaardian ethical imagination, there is no moment of reflective 'stepping back,' but instead the immediate experience of self-involvement here labeled *interesse*. Such immediacy, which we have shown to be intrinsic to the mirror-metaphor, is plainly at odds with the account of Reading sketched in the previous paragraph. Inescapably, though, Kierkegaard does speak throughout this discourse as if the reading of Scripture should be punctuated by moments of overt self-relation that are temporally separable from comprehension of the text itself. Kierkegaard's description of correct Reading is characterized by phrases such as 'Here you shall say ... ' and 'Then you shall say ....' Is there, then, any evidence of the sort of immediate self-relation built into vision that our discussion has identified as the phenomenon of *interesse* in Kierkegaard's thought?

To begin with, there is evidence both within the text and elsewhere in Kierkegaard that needing the device of 'reminding' oneself is actually a concession to the failure of moral vision. In the *Postscript*, Climacus claims explicitly that the 'subjective thinker,' a self whose orientation is such as to allow for genuine moral engagement with the world rather than selfless, disinterested contemplation, does not need of such reminders. His self-presence in his thought is such that his thought becomes *action* itself rather than a prelude *to* action, such that:

> ... he, acting, works through himself in his thinking about his own existence, that he therefore actually thinks the thought by actualizing it, that he therefore does not think for a single moment: now you must keep watch every moment, but he keeps watch at every moment.

(CUP, 1:169/SKS 7, 156–7)

This has parallels with the psychology sketched in *The Sickness Unto Death* already described. Just as our relation to what we imagine is not given in a temporally separable moment of reflection, here thought does not declare 'this is what I must do,' but orients itself such that in the moment of thought *it is already doing it*. Instead of the precursor to action, thought becomes action itself; thinking takes on the character of resolution, rather than standing outside agency's theater of activity as the deliberative precondition for decision and deed. Such a reading is only possible insofar as Climacus considers decision itself to be a form of action, even if not action in the 'external' sense. (CUP, 1:339–40/SKS 7, 310–11).[12] According to this unforgiving, normatively qualified psychology, thinking about an imperative to act, to the extent that this is not *doing* it, is a dereliction of that imperative. When it operates correctly, thought instantiates the imperatives it apprehends without needing to bring those imperatives to conscious attention. The good night watchman does not need to tell himself to pay attention: his thought *is attentive* without needing to remind himself to be so.

This description of perfected moral agency may appear psychologically unfamiliar to us, precisely because we are accustomed to a mechanistic folk-psychology (given philosophical respectability by Hume, among others) in which belief, desire, and deliberation play discrete and distinguishable roles in the overall process of volitional action. It seems natural to tell ourselves a story in which our beliefs by turn inform, actuate, and restrain our desires, competing desires are mediated by deliberation, our desires determine our decisions acting through the conduit of our beliefs, and so forth. And in working our way through such descriptions, we can apparently distinguish between knowing and desiring, believing and deciding, and can tell a temporal story about how all these elements operate in a definite sequence like some sort of psychic Rube Goldberg machine.

Kierkegaard too offers us exquisitely nuanced images of such psychological pneumatics – but he does so not as instances of how thought *should* be, but how, in its fallen, sinful state, human volition *does* operate. Anti-Climacus holds that modern speculation, like the Socratic, cannot account for *akrasia* (knowing what is right and yet doing what is wrong) because it confines its understanding to 'pure ideality' in which 'there is no talk of the individual, actual person' and hence the transition from knowing to enacting the good happens with the instantaneousness of pure logical necessity (SUD, 93/SKS 11, 206). According to Anti-Climacus, however, *akrasia* occurs because our defiant will corrupts the process *from the beginning*, and this finds expression in a fragmented psychic environment in which the will plays knowledge and desire off against each other in a ballet of dissimulation. 'In the life of the spirit there is no standing still,' and accordingly 'if a person does not do what is right at the very second he knows it – then, first of all, knowing goes off the boil' (SUD, 94/SKS 11, 206). This is then followed – a *temporal* sequence – by an appraisal of this object of knowledge by the will, which then defers decision ('We shall look at it tomorrow') in order to allow still more time to elapse. In the course of this additional time, 'knowing becomes more and more obscure' until eventually *what* the self knows has been transformed into something more amenable to the will (SUD, 94/SKS 206–07). Thus the self has re-shaped its beliefs in light of its desires, a process of gradually 'eclipsing [one's] ethical and ethical-religious comprehension' to avoid being '[lead] out into decisions and conclusions that [our] lower nature does not much care for' (SUD, 94/SKS 11, 207).

This, according to Anti-Climacus, is how 'perhaps the great majority of men live' rather than a description of an abnormal psychology (SUD,

94/SKS 11, 207). Yet however common it may be, it is still nonetheless defective, for this power of 'stretching things out' operates in the service of our 'lower nature,' whereas 'the good must be done at once, as soon as it is known' (SUD, 94/SKS 11, 207). The temporal sequentialization of cognition already points to its always-already sinfulness, to its primordial corruption ahead of each and every act of apprehension. In perfected agency, by contrast (whether this ever actually occurs or not), knowing and willing simply collapse into a single moment, in which there is no temporal or psychological schematization but only unity of consciousness and purpose. The machine metaphor will break down at this point: while a machine's malfunction will tend to call our attention to the distinct parts and local mechanisms that it is composed of, we *can* regard the separate parts of a fully functional machine in this way if we choose to. By contrast, in perfected moral cognition it is not simply that the transitions from knowledge to desire-formation to decision occur too fast to be empirically discernible: on the phenomenal level at least, there *are* no such discrete moments, only the experience of a unitary, volitional consciousness. The mechanistic description of cognition can only be given of a process *that has already failed.*

'Thou art the man'

Returning to the Mirror of the Word discussion in *For Self-Examination,* we find the same thought: that the need for 'reminders' points to a failure of moral cognition. In hearing the story told by the Prophet Nathan, King David fails to see that the story is about himself. He requires the interpretative postscript 'thou art the man' to make 'the transition to the subjective' (FSE, 38/SV2 XII, 327). This statement is needed to tear David out of the objectivity with which he had approached the story in order to keep awareness of his own moral culpability at arm's length. Had David been more concerned for his own moral condition, the implication seems to be, he would have seen himself in the story *without* needing to be told that it was a story about himself (even though the story itself concerned the slaughtering of sheep). In the same way, Kierkegaard re-tells the Good Samaritan parable and claims we are to understand that the Priest who passes the injured man by *is us* (FSE, 40–1/SV2 XII, 328–9). We are to *see* our co-identity with the person presented in the story – and as has previously been argued, seeing our co-identity with the content of imaginatively projected possibilities is precisely what is meant by *interesse.*

The story of David and Nathan seems to have been of enduring interest for Kierkegaard, who cites it as early as William's opening epistolary address in *Either/Or* (EO, 2:5/SKS 3, 15). Kierkegaard again mentions it briefly in *Works of Love* in a passage stressing that Scripture speaks directly and exclusively to the reader. When read *properly*, 'What the prophet Nathan added to his parable, "You are the man," the Gospel does not need to add, since it is already contained in the form of the statement and in its being a word of the Gospel' (WL, 14/SKS 9, 22). Sacred text contains an in-built message to the reader, such that 'beside every word in the holy books a disturbing notice in invisible writing confronts [the reader] that says: go and do likewise' (WL, 46/SKS 9, 53). This message removes the need for 'thou are the man' reminders by making reader-referentiality determinative of the meaning of Scripture itself – for those with eyes to see the invisible ink. Accordingly, the correct interpretation of the phrase 'The tree is to be known by its fruits' is that 'you [the reader] are the tree,' not 'You or we are to know the tree by its fruits' (WL, 14/SKS 9, 22), which only becomes manifest when we read the text in the appropriately self-reflexive way. Thus how we approach the content of Scripture will be decisive for the meaning we ascribe to the language, in a way that is both dependent upon the language and yet not determinable by it.

Importantly, the Nathan example seems to push the notion of *self-recognition* to breaking point here. We claimed earlier that Kierkegaardian self-recognition is essentially a matter of seeing our involvement in what we contemplate, rather than noting a merely visual similarity with ourselves. Just as our ability to recognize ourselves in a visual representation such as a dream is not dependent upon visual similarity,[13] so here Nathan shows David to himself in his sinfulness in a story about sheep. David is to *see himself in* the story even though there is nothing in the objective conceptual content of the narrative that resembles or alludes to him: unlike the straightforwardly literal play *The Murder of Gonzago* that Hamlet uses to prick Claudius' conscience, it takes a not inconsiderable stretch of imagination to read Nathan's parable of a rich man slaughtering a poor man's lamb as an analogy for adultery and murder. Once again, the *meaning* conferred by the image is nowhere to be found in its direct content, but in the 'viewer's' engagement therewith. This is not, however, to say that David simply imports a meaning into the story that 'properly' doesn't belong there; rather, he uncovers a meaning that is only accessible if he engages with the story in the self-referential attitude of *interesse*.

That the meaning of morally exemplary narratives can only be apprehended through a mode of direct identification, and therefore crucially depend upon the listener to make this meaning manifest, is explicitly claimed in *An Occasional Discourse*. Here Kierkegaard claims that '[t]he discourse does not address itself to you as a specific person, it does not even know who you are,' as exemplified by David's ostensible absence from Nathan's parable. Yet this apparent indifference on the part of the narrative itself can be overcome through a specific mode of contemplation, one that is entirely dependent upon the listener:

> The discourse does not address itself to you as a specific person, it does not even know who you are; but if you think about the occasion very vividly [*ret levende*], then it will seem to you, whoever you are, as if it were speaking directly to you – this is not the merit of the discourse, it is your self-activity's doing, that you for your own sake assist the discourse and of your own accord will to be the one to whom it says: you.
>
> (UDVS, 123/SKS 8, 223–4)

Again, Kierkegaard is *not* suggesting that we project meaning onto discourses such that we 'find' meanings in these discourses that are actually in ourselves. Rather, it is only through a specifically self-reflexive mode of receptivity that the moral meaning of the discourse can become evident. The capacity of a discourse to prove morally upbuilding depends upon the 'self-activity' of the reader, without which the moral communicator is helpless to communicate her message. In the same work, the pious needlewoman faces the same problem in that she cannot communicate her message in the *conceptual* content of her embroidery but must rely upon its viewer to see it in such a way that its meaning becomes manifest to them:

> She could not work the sacred meaning into the cloth; she could not and did not sew it onto the cloth as one more ornament. This meaning lies precisely in the beholder and in the beholder's understanding, when he, at separation's infinite distance, faced with himself and his own self, has infinitely forgotten the needlewoman and her part.
>
> (UDVS, 5/SKS 8, 121)

The embroidery's capacity to impart moral meaning is entirely dependent upon the observer's relation to it; the communicator is impotent without this correct comportment on his listener's part. The same is true of a further Anti-Climacan mirror-metaphor: that of contradiction-as-mirror developed in *Practice in Christianity*. Here, contemplation of

the 'contradiction' of the utterly paradoxical figure of the God-Man
discloses the self to itself:

> And only the sign of contradiction can do this: it draws attention to
> itself and then it presents a contradiction. There is a something that
> makes it impossible not to look – and look, as one is looking one sees
> as in a mirror, one comes to see oneself, or he who is the sign of the
> contradiction looks straight into one's heart while one is staring into
> the contradiction.
>
> (PC, 126–7/SKS 12, 131)

Once again the self is being asked to 'see itself' in something that
objectively does not resemble it. At least this 'mirror' is another human
being; the God-Man is a concrete human being, 'not a fantastic unity
that has never existed except *sub specie aeterni*' who 'discloses the
thoughts of hearts' (PC, 126/SKS 12, 131). However, in another sense,
insofar as the God-Man is God, and as God-Man is also an irremedia-
ble contradiction, He is radically other to the contemplator and so not
something a detached observer should be able to see herself in. Yet
this contemplation discloses the self to itself, transfigured as though
viewed through the God-Man's evaluative gaze which 'looks straight
into one's heart' (PC, 127/SKS 12, 131). Thus one 'comes to see oneself' (PC, 126/SKS 12, 131) but in such a way that the disclosure is not
merely reflective but is itself performative:

> A contradiction placed squarely in front of a person – if one can get
> him to look at it – is a mirror; as he is judging, what dwells within
> him must be disclosed. It is a riddle, but as he is guessing the rid-
> dle, what dwells within him is disclosed by the way he guesses. The
> contradiction confronts him with a choice, and as he is choosing,
> together with what he chooses, he himself is disclosed.
>
> (PC, 127/SKS 12, 131).

Again, the evaluative meaning of the experience of staring into this
mirror is not prefigured in the content of the 'image' one sees there. Narratives about the exploits of Jesus of Nazareth, or claims for his divinity,
do not *prima facie* include the contemplator in them, yet the contemplator is revealed to herself in the contemplation through her subjective
engagement with it.[14] And this engagement takes the form of action,
namely, a choice (PC, 127/SKS 12, 131), rather than in the making of
objective judgments regarding the content of the 'image.'

Non-theticality and immediacy in mirror-vision

Scripture, wherein we are to see our own moral condition in stories and injunctions that do not contain *us* in their conceptual content seems to be a prime example of the supervenience of self-referentiality on conceptual content. Kierkegaard elsewhere makes similar points with respect to, for instance, the 'earnest thought of death.' For Kierkegaard, the moral value of the thought of death is lost if mortality does not become part of the content of *all* my thought: 'To think this uncertainty [of death] once and for all, or once a year at matins on New Year's morning, is of course nonsense and is not to think it at all' (CUP, 1:166/SKS 7, 154). Climacus thus enjoins us 'to think it [death] into every moment of my life,' or 'to think it every moment.' As Westphal observes, this obviously makes little sense if it is read as an injunction that one must constantly be thinking of the fact of their impending death, even if they also happen to be thinking about other things at the same time: 'Under this impossible, morbid, and no doubt immoral scenario, whenever offered a penny for my thoughts, I could answer, "I am thinking about my death and immortality." '[15]

Westphal argues that what Climacus is urging here is that death not be treated as a topic for objective reflection at all. Instead, 'thinking death into every moment' would be more akin to Sartre's non-thetic consciousness (of) consciousness, discussed in Chapter 3. Just as, for Sartre, a pre-reflective consciousness of consciousness is built into every moment of intentional consciousness, as a nonreflective awareness, so for Climacus, the thought of death attends every thought without every thought thereby being about death.[16] Awareness of death will be built into intentionality itself without every thought thereby intending death *per se*. Note, too, that if Westphal is right, this will be necessary for any discussion or contemplation of death to be legitimate in Climacan terms, in that it is only this pre-reflective awareness of mortality which preserves a link between the 'object' (the thought of death) and the 'subject' (whose death it is).

Death is not the content of the thoughts, actions, and intentions which the subject forms in the course of their daily round, yet the thought of it is *present* in all these other thoughts and actions. This is reasonably easy to envisage if we imagine the thought of death as a certain mood or attitude inherent in everything we think or do; think of a person whose every action seems to proceed from or be somehow colored by anger, or fear, or insecurity. But the thought of death – the thought of *my* death – is more conceptually fully fleshed than this. Kierkegaard's idea seems to be that this specific, fairly concrete thought – that it is certain that I will die and that I cannot know when this will occur – must somehow be built into my deliberation over which tie to put on, who to marry, and where to vacation next year. In the same way, in *For Self-Examination* Kierkegaard claims that the correct engagement with Scripture will involve seeing my own moral involvement in the text even though the actual content of Scripture does not contain me personally. Meister Eckhart seems to accord a similar status to the thought of God in theist consciousness:

> Whoever possesses God in their being [...] for them, all things taste of God and in all things it is God's image that they see. [...] It is the same as when someone has a great thirst and, although they may be doing something other than drinking and their minds may be turned to other things, the thought of a drink will not leave them for as long as they thirst, whatever they do, whoever they are with, whatever they strive for, whatever their works or thoughts; and the greater their thirst, the greater, the more intense, immediate and persistent the thought of a drink becomes.[17]

Note that Eckhart here presents thirst not merely as a state of feeling (which the physiological aspect of it clearly is), which we could easily envisage as *accompanying* any thought or action. We can, for instance, imagine Eckhart writing the above-quoted passage in a state of pain, hunger, exhaustion, elation or anxiety, without its actual content being perceptibly different. But Eckhart claims something stronger: the 'thought of a drink' will accompany every thought, action and utterance of the thirsty person. Thirst here is not merely a feeling, it is the desire for something *conceptually* specific. Nor is it simply that a thirsty person 'wants' a drink in the sense that a drink would contingently alleviate the feeling of thirst (essentially the same sense in which a dying plant 'wants' water). The person desires this specific thing to slake their thirst, even when they are thinking and talking of other things (and so their intentional consciousness is directed at these other things). Eckhart goes on to claim that when a person is in love, 'the object of their love will never be extinguished in them, but they will find its image in all things, and the greater their love becomes, the more present to them it will be.'[18] There is a parallel with our imaginative youth from *Practice in Christianity*: obsessed with the image of a moral exemplar, his 'eyes see nothing of what lies closest around him' until the 'world of actuality in which he is standing and the relation of his surrounding world to himself' reasserts itself (PC, 189/SKS 12, 188). Seeing the image every-where and at the same time seeing the concrete reality in which he finds himself causes the image to overlay the world as a moral imperative.

Eckhart sees attaining this condition as necessary if the individual's every action is to be 'made radiant' by the ever-present thought of God. For Eckhart, this process seems to be one of habituation, like learning an instrument: while it requires hard work and concentration initially, it ultimately becomes easy to do through practice, until concentration is no longer required.[19] Kierkegaard certainly does *not* want to claim that practice at Reading the bible will make attaining the appropriate interpenetration of subjectivity (which will prevent us from ever being distracted by 'the mirror itself') easy, or that habitual rumination on death will *automatically* integrate death non-thetically into our other thought. Only earnestness (*alvor*), described by Vigilius Haufniensis in *The Concept of Anxiety* as 'the acquired originality of disposition' (CA, 149/SKS 4, 448) marks the difference between dispositions of character and thoughtless habit. Kierkegaardian earnestness is not something that can be acquired by habituation. Nonetheless, he does seem to imply that when moral vision is operating *correctly*, these things – our fini-tude, our moral implicatedness in what we contemplate – are contained immediately in thought. The need for reminders such as David's 'thou art the man' or Darius' 'remember the Athenians' indicates a *failure of vision*.[20] Just as the drunken peasant in the parable in *Sickness Unto Death* should not need someone to remind him that the legs facing destruction were his own, so too we would not need these reminders or proddings if our vision were correctly oriented towards our moral emplacement. But the moral capacities of humans are highly prone to failure, and indeed failure, according to Kierkegaard, is their usual condition. This characteristic failure of vision can actually work *for* the person who, like Nathan, seeks to communicate some moral claim via an ostensibly unrelated discourse, as Kierkegaard claims in *Christian Discourses*:

> One tells him a story. This now puts him quite at ease, because he understands well enough that since it is a story it is not him that is spoken about. A word is introduced into this story that perhaps does not immediately have its effect, but sometime later suddenly transforms itself into a question of conscience.
>
> (CD, 235/SKS 10, 242)

The moral communicator can thus use the indirectness of the para-ble form to get under their listener's guard; the effect is more insidious than a direct, didacticizing address which the listener might reflexively or defensively reject.[21] This does not remove the moral communicator from their dependence upon the 'self-activity' of the listener, but it makes it easier for the conditions necessary for that self-activity to arise. This awareness of the characteristic fallibility of moral vision also forms the basis of Kierkegaard's third condition which must be met to look into the Mirror of the Word: not immediately forgetting what one has seen. Kierkegaard takes it that we almost certainly *will* forget, but that sufficiently humble effort (such as trying to remember for an hour rather than grandiosely assuming we can remember forever) increases our chance of partial success (FSE, 44–6/SV2 XII, 331–3).

Jamie Lorentzen's reading of Kierkegaard's metaphors merits discussion at this point. Lorentzen notes the methodological significance of metaphoric constructions in which the reader's involvement in the construction is only indirectly given, thereby preserving the necessary maieutic distance between communicator and receiver; thus in discussing this mode of reception Kierkegaard intimates to his reader that the subject of his text *is the reader*.[22] Lorentzen therefore notes many of the examples of Kierkegaardian 'mirrors' of self-recognition we have discussed above, and also references a parable in *Stages on Life's Way* about a repentant gambler witnessing the corpse of a suicide, a fellow gambler, being drawn out of the Seine:

> My gambler is a man who has understood the old saying *de te narratur fabula* [the tale is told of you]; he is no modern fool who believes that everyone should court the enormous objective task of being able to rattle off something that applies to the whole of humanity, just not to himself.
>
> (SLW, 478/SKS 6, 440)

Lorentzen reads this as Frater Taciturnus' way of alerting the reader that the tale is told of *them*: they too are a repentant or unrepentant 'gambler' in some sense (whatever sins might stand for 'gambling' here). He also takes it that Judge William's reference to Nathan (EO, 2:5/SKS 3, 15) is an attempt to alert the reader to the fact that *Either/Or* is a text about *the reader* rather than simply about the thoughts of A and Judge William. The reader is brought to see themselves in the parable or metaphor, establishing 'relation or similarity between themselves and a character or situation in the story either because of or despite the distancing effect of metaphor,' that allows the metaphor to 'become very close, personal, and thereby potentially transformative for the reader.'[23]

For Lorentzen, the 'activity' of reminding ourselves that 'the tale is told of us' constitutes 'authentic earnestness for Kierkegaard.'[24] Yet this language of 'reminders' seems incompatible with the normatively charged immediacy of apprehension that we've been discussing. Lorentzen is right that what characterizes the 'conscientious' reader will be a particular way of seeing rather than a particular form of reflection upon metaphor, but he describes this vision in terms of 'comparison.'[25] But comparison is largely a reflective and diachronic process, whereas the moment of self-recognition is a synchronic experience of *seeing-as-myself* in which the parable shows me myself in my culpability. So the end-point of true 'earnestness' will not be simply an 'activity,' but a way of seeing in which David, for example, sees himself in what is presented to him without needing incessant reminders. Thus Lorentzen's account, though fundamentally correct and laudable as a description of Kierkegaardian methodology, misses part of the psychology that is intimated in these discussions of self-recognition in metaphoric material.

Willing to see

For Kierkegaard, doctrine – understood as the Word of God regarded *impersonally* – cannot act as a mirror, for acting as a mirror involves not merely being reflected, but looking at oneself in the mirror:

> it is just as impossible to mirror oneself [*at speil sig*] in an objective doctrine as to mirror oneself in a wall. And if you want to relate yourself impersonally (objectively) to God's Word, there can be no question of contemplating yourself in the mirror, because to mirror oneself certainly requires a personality, an *I*; a wall can be seen in a mirror, but a wall cannot mirror itself or observe itself in the mirror.
>
> (FSE, 43–44/SV2 XII, 331)

The reflective function of a mirror therefore requires a volitive act – the act of looking at oneself, as here captured in the reflexive verb *at speil sig*. This seems self-evident, but in a sketch for *For Self-Examination*, Kierkegaard elaborates on this by outlining (in somewhat skeletal detail) further requirements necessary 'to Look at Oneself with True Blessing in the Mirror of the Word.'

Firstly, 'One must to a certain extent know [*kjender*] oneself beforehand. For one who does not know himself cannot recognize [*gjenkjender*, lit. "re-know"] himself, either' and this self-knowledge must ultimately equate to God-knowledge or standing before God (FSE, 234/SKS 24,

425). This reiterates what was said in the previous chapter about the conditions for self-recognition: one must have a sense of oneself that goes beyond immediate or external categories, and ultimately measures the self before the limiting-concept of God.

Kierkegaard further claims here that when we 'accidentally' see ourselves in a mirror, without expecting too, we do not recognize ourselves. This seems to be plainly wrong, although we can certainly imagine circumstances in which it might happen. The point of this empirical claim seems to be to emphasize that self-recognition involves a certain degree of openness to the experience, an attitude of receptivity, and that adopting such an attitude appears to be in part a willed act, implicitly or otherwise. This is the thrust of Kierkegaard's second condition presented in the sketch:

> (2) You must not be afraid to see yourself [. . .] it takes great courage to dare to look at oneself, which can indeed only occur in the mirror of the Word, for otherwise it so easily become a fraud.
>
> (FSE, 234/SKS 24, 425)

This emphasis on the volitional aspects of seeing oneself in a comparative, evaluative light is interesting. By positing a volitional aspect to the process of vision, while at the same time arguing that we must be prepared to accept what the mirror shows us (having *what* we see determined by something external), Kierkegaard opens up a tension within vision itself. The act of *seeing* contains within itself an uneasy and irreducible interplay between voluntary and involuntary elements. Rick Anthony Furtak expresses this volitional ambiguity in vision in his discussion of seeing lovingly:

> Love is not a product of the will, and the mode of receptivity in which value is perceived is not one in which the self projects value outward; but passionate impressions are not so coercive that we are entirely passive in yielding to them, either.[26]

Ferreira has used the example of *Gestalt* shift to illustrate this tension between volitional and non-volitional elements in vision. In the familiar example of seeing Jastrow's figure as a duck *or* a rabbit, there is an ambiguous relation between active and passive elements of the experience:

> In a situation where a *Gestalt* shift occurs, we initially see only one possibility; at some point, after concentrated attention or perhaps

coaching, a different figure comes into focus for us. Seeing the latter figure is not the direct or immediate result of any decision or volition, nor is it a choice in any standard sense [...] We can decide to *look for* the figure we are told is there and cannot yet see, but we cannot decide to see (recognize) it. Recognizing the new and qualitatively different figure is not the direct result of willing or the necessary result of the effort to look for it.[27]

We can make a deliberate effort to try to see something in a specific way – in the context of Kierkegaard's use of mirror-metaphors, to see *ourselves* in the full existential import of that term. But the actual moment of vision itself has the quality of being imposed upon us rather than chosen. The relation between the volitional and the non-volitional in vision therefore remains essentially opaque. *Contra* Ferreira, James Giles has contended that Gestalt shifts and indeed Kierkegaardian leaps in general do, in fact, resolve straightforwardly into clear choices.[28] This objection points to the need to locate the exact moment of ambiguity in a Gestalt shift: what is at issue is neither the moment of involuntary seeing nor subsequent voluntary shifting from seeing one thing to the other, but rather the specific moment of looking for what we know is there but cannot yet discern. This is plainly something we can *try* to do, yet no specific action corresponds to that trying (except perhaps a sort of disengagement from the image we can see – trying *not* to see the rabbit in the hope that the duck will appear to us). Moreover, in that the leap is construed by Kierkegaard as something that occurs in all non-tautological thought, the category of the leap does, as Ferreira contends and Giles implicitly denies, pervade cognitions that do not answer to the name of 'choice' or 'decision' at all. So there is indeed an implicit and unresolved tension in the Kierkegaardian category of the leap.

Kierkegaard seeks to emphasize, in passages like the sketch for *For Self-Examination*, the volitional aspects of self-recognition. This is to be expected in a work concerned with moral self-examination; morality is, truistically, principally concerned with the will. However, in developing a *moral* phenomenology of vision, the partly involuntary character of seeing would seem to present a challenge. The drunken peasant does not *choose* not to recognize his legs – and if this is the case, how can his failure of vision be regarded as a *moral* failure? David's failure to see himself in Nathan's parable could likewise hardly be called deliberate, yet it seems clear he is *responsible* for that failure, his failure to see compounding his earlier guilt rather than merely and neutrally keeping it hidden from him a little longer. In *Either/Or*, Judge William claims that David 'wanted to understand the parable the prophet told him but was unwilling to understand that it applied to him' (EO, 2:5/SKS 3, 15) – yet to understand, to 'get' something, is, like seeing or realizing something, a largely passive experience of apprehension characterized by a non-volitive transition into comprehension. How can such apparently unintentional features of the mental landscape attract moral approbation or opprobrium?

Of course we frequently *do* attach moral culpability to failures of vision or attention, on the basis that vision occurs in the context of projects and responsibilities. The peasant does not choose to fail to see his legs, but insofar as he is responsible for himself his failure is blameworthy. David does not (consciously) choose not to see himself in the parable told to him, but insofar as he is a moral agent, and thus ought to be concerned for his ethical status, his failure is a moral failure. We can, therefore, regard the failure to see ourselves in these various mirrors – possibility, ethical exemplars, Scripture – in a way characterized by the sense of self-involvement picked out by *interesse* as one for which we are culpable. Seeing ourselves in representations of ourselves becomes an inherently moral act, even though, in the process of seeing, there is much that is beyond our control.[29]

8
Seeing the Other

The other as mirror

Kierkegaard seems to make a viable case that Scripture and ethically edifying narratives can operate as 'mirrors,' in which moral agents see their own condition reflected to them in conceptual content which ostensibly does not include them. But what of *persons*, other ethical agents, and moral patients, as mirrors? Relating ourselves to moral exemplars is, as John Lippitt notes, 'a vital part of ethical and religious development and self-understanding' for Kierkegaard.[1] But the *way* in which we relate ourselves to exemplars is potentially problematic for other aspects of our moral vision.

While the discussion of the 'mirror of the Word' in *For Self-Examination*, and the God-Man as a mirror of contradiction in *Practice in Christianity* both speak of identification with other persons, such as Jesus and figures in the Good Samaritan narrative, the self so identified with is immediately transfigured into an imperative for action. The figures considered cease to be actual persons (if indeed they ever were that) and become simply ethical claims. This also seems to be implied more starkly by the Anti-Climacan claim that in imitation, as opposed to mere admiration, 'I straight away begin to think about myself, simply and solely to think about myself [. . .] I quite forget [the admired one] in favor of myself' [*jeg glemmer ganske ham over mig selv*] (PC, 242/SKS 12, 235). As we saw in Chapter 5, the admired/imitated one remains imaginatively present in the simultaneity of ideal and actual that characterizes Anti-Climacan imagination, but transfigured as 'a requirement upon my life, like a sting in my soul that propels me forward' (PC, 242/SKS 12, 236).

This would seem to imply that these selves, once they are seen as the site of a disclosure of an ethical demand, are not preserved in their distinct individuality, but are instead absorbed as imperatives into an ethical outlook. If this is the case, it would seem Kierkegaard is susceptible to the critique leveled by post-structuralist ethics of norm-based ethical systems: namely, that they fail to attend to the other's unique particularity or 'respect the absolute singularity of the other, and/or the irreducibility of otherness.'[2] This particularity is a 'residue' which cannot be captured by moral norms which, insofar as they aspire to universality, necessarily generalize across persons.

Perhaps few individual works of moral philosophy have been as roundly condemned from this critical perspective as Kierkegaard's *Works of Love*. Virtually from the outset of Kierkegaard's twentieth-century reception this work has drawn repeated accusations of acosmism, abstract indifference to persons in their concrete specificity, and an apparently callous indifference to worldly inequality and suffering. In a typically Kierkegaardian irony, a string of influential critics such as Theodore Adorno[3] and K.E. Løgstrup[4] have found this book, built around the biblical injunction to love the neighbor (Matthew 22:39), to display Kierkegaard at his most otherworldly, inhuman, patronizing, austere, and isolationist.

Part of what critics like Adorno and Løgstrup respond to is the sense that the ethics of *Works of Love*, which directs vision to the curiously vacant concept of 'the neighbor' (*den næste*) reduces the actual selves we encounter to contentless 'vehicles' or occasions for the apprehension and enactment of normative demands. In response to the scriptural question 'Who, then, is one's neighbor?' Kierkegaard offers an account that seems to hollow out the neighbor completely:

> The concept 'neighbor' is actually the redoubling of your own self; the 'neighbor' is what thinkers would call the Other, that by which the selfishness of self-love is to be tested. As far as thought is concerned, the neighbor does not even need to exist. If a person living on a desert island had developed his mind in accordance with this commandment, so he could, by renouncing self-love, be said to love the neighbor.
>
> (WL, 21/SKS 9, 29)

This claim that the ethics of the 'Royal Law' can be satisfied without achieving any relation at all to an actual other person has seemed troubling to some commentators. Peter George provides an instructive example of such an objection to Kierkegaard's 'second ethics,' holding that the ethics of *Works of Love* are actually profoundly anti-social.[5] George claims that in reducing all human relationships to the God-relationship (God becomes the object of love, and the neighbor and beloved are accordingly loved only *through* the loving of God), in decrying reciprocity and thus reducing relationships to one-sided affairs, and in describing the love of neighbor in a way that effaces the actuality of the other, Kierkegaard articulates an entirely inward-looking ethics on which genuine social relations cannot be built. As Løgstrup puts it, 'Never before has ethics so shut itself in and so shut out the world as it has in Kierkegaard's thought.'[6]

Moreover, *Works of Love*, perhaps more overtly than any other Kierkegaardian text, is concerned with the place of *vision* in our moral engagement with others. It decries certain ways of seeing[7] and insists on the normative value of other ways of seeing: 'one sees the neighbor only with closed eyes or by looking *away from* the dissimilarities. The sensate eyes always see the dissimilarities and look *at* the dissimilarities' (WL, 68/SKS 9, 75). This emphasis on vision means we can add to the charge that the category of 'neighbor' effaces the other-as-other another possible objection: that in moral vision the other-as-actual-person is reduced by the self-concerned moral seer to a mere surface of emergence for a moral imperative. Hence, if Kierkegaard's entire moral psychology is to be shown to be adequate to the experience of concern for others *as others*, rather than as bare loci of duty, we need to show that the psychology we have outlined, and the account in *Works of Love*, attends sufficiently to concrete persons.

In *Works of Love*, Kierkegaard attempts to supply a corrective to forms of love which, in aiming at an object of preference or inclination, essentially loves an 'other-I,' and is therefore effectively self-love (WL, 53–4/SKS 9, 60–1). All forms of preferential love, including *Elskov* (somewhat unhelpfully translated 'erotic love' in the *Kierkegaard's Writings* series) turn out upon examination to be fundamentally selfish. Thus far at least, Kierkegaard seems to be pointing to the discriminatory aspect of these preference-driven forms of love, arguing instead for an ethic built, as Ferreira notes, on a type of blindness – a willing blindness to the concrete differences and distinctiveness of individuals.[8] All persons are subsumed under the rubric of *den næste*, which is a category of pure duty (the duty to love). Kierkegaard does allow that we can *have* a beloved or a friend, but such a relation must be secondary to the duty-directed neighbor love: 'Your wife must first and foremost be to you the neighbor; that she is your wife is then a more precise specification of your particular relationship to each other' (WL, 141/SKS 9, 143). Yet the lack of personal content essential to the concept of *den næste*, which 'is like the category "human being"' (WL, 141/SKS 9, 143), seems to foreclose whatever could be considered essential to 'preferential' love.

Some of the more extreme claims in *Works of Love* that critics like George alight on can be dismissed relatively easily. One alone on a desert island can conform to the Royal Law 'as far as thought is concerned' (WL, 21/SKS 9, 29) – yet this threshold case is so far removed from everyday moral experience as to have no real bearing on the experience of actual humans.[9] Pia Søltoft notes that many readings of this passage that accuse Kierkegaard of 'acosmism' miss the fact that the object of the passage is the *concept* of the neighbor, not actual persons, and that 'to love one's neighbor in fact requires that there be at least *one* other person present to the self.'[10] The passage is concerned with what *thought* requires in order to conform to the Royal Law, not what is required to *actually* practice it.[11] Kierkegaard claims one of the purest works of love[12] is that of remembering one who is dead (WL, 345–58/SKS 9, 339–52). This work is the 'most unselfish' (WL, 349/SKS 9, 343) because 'one who is dead makes no repayment' (WL, 350/SKS 9, 344) and so there can be no possibility of reciprocity between lover and object of love. Here, the duty to love is apparently discharged not towards a concrete other but a nonbeing. Yet the notion of a moral duty to the dead does seem to be intuitively accepted in everyday moral life independently of any belief in posthumous survival, and our concern for the dead – respecting their corpses, honoring their memory, keeping promises made to them while alive – does treat the *person* who has died as the object of this moral concern, despite their no longer existing.[13]

In other respects, however, it is difficult to exonerate Kierkegaard completely of the charge of blindness to the other in their concrete particularity. Ferreira notes that even those commentators who hold that the abstraction implicit in the category of 'neighbor' coexists in *Works of Love* with emphases on distinctiveness and difference fail to account for how these might be compatible.[14] Ferreira attempts to show that the compatibility consists in these rival emphases belonging to two different contexts: a context of 'law,' characterized by a purely formal analysis (a statement of the law) and 'love,' to which is proper a material analysis (a description of love).[15] The 'blindness' to morally irrelevant distinctions actually emerges as a clearing away of those factors that, by distracting us, themselves make us blind to the other in their concrete, morally compelling actuality.[16] Grøn makes a similar case with his emphasis on *Works of Love*'s insistence on 'ways of seeing' that variously disclose or obscure the distinctiveness of the other;[17] nor are we to substitute the actual other for '*an imaginary idea of how we think or could wish that this person should be*' (WL, 164/SKS 9, 164 original emphases). We are to become blind to those differentiating factors that obscure our essential kinship with the other – 'Law' serves to direct our loving attention to all through the catch-all category of the Neighbor, but our duty remains specifically to love the people *we see* (WL, 154–74/SKS 9, 155–74). As Ferreira puts it, 'Even if the call on us by all is equal in principle, our duty is to respond to need as manifested in our actuality.'[18]

Ferreira makes a sound textual and exegetical case and her divisions into two contexts can comfortably be accepted. However, on the level of moral psychology this division into contexts does not tell us how the empty formalism of the normative category of *den næste* and attention to the other in their concrete particularity are to be held together. If *vision* is central to the moral psychology of *Works of Love* (as the text makes clear and as both Ferreira and Grøn emphasize), how are we to unify these disparate elements in the immediate unity that I've repeatedly claimed is an essential feature of vision? How are we to see *both* the other in their concrete distinctiveness *and* the apparently abstract formal requirement to love the neighbor *qua* neighbor (purged of distracting specificities) without losing sight of one or the other or alternating between the two? To be an earnest Kierkegaardian moral agent is, according to John Davenport, to always have *oneself* as a proper object of earnestness, but this does not mean that the earnest agent cares primarily *about* herself, but rather that 'earnest caring about anything or anyone else will also involve a reflexive effort to control and organize our own character in accordance with our concern, if it is truly earnest.'[19] But how is this dual concern, with its self-effacing reflexivity, possible? This question can also be rephrased in light of our discussion of mirror metaphors: how can we see our own moral condition in the mirror of the other *and yet still see the other?* If we are to look at ourselves, not the mirror (FSE, 25/SV2 XII, 315), how are we to see moral imperatives as proceeding from the persons before us and yet still attend to their concrete actuality?

Ideality and the concrete other

To answer these questions we need to return to the account of imagination given in *The Sickness Unto Death*. In his discussion of the despair of infinitization, Anti-Climacus describes the despair of infinitization (recall here that this is a loss of oneself in the infinite at the expense of one's finite grounding) as expressing itself in the self's 'feeling, knowing and willing' (SUD, 31–2/SKS 11, 147–8) with forms appropriate to each. Infinitized feeling is particularly relevant in the present context. Anti-Climacus chooses to explicate this form of despair by describing it in terms of a person whose emotional identification with others amounts to no more than 'abstract sentimentality.' The self whose feeling has become fantastic feels a form of pity which is essentially meaningless, in that it has no real object:

> When feeling becomes fantastic in this way, the self becomes only more and more volatilized, until it becomes a kind of abstract sentimentality that inhumanly belongs to no human, but inhumanly, so to speak, sentimentally participates in the fate of one or another abstraction, for example, humanity *in abstracto.*
>
> (SUD, 31/SKS 11, 147)

This is a self whose object of sympathy or emotional identification essentially does not exist. Someone who is emotionally concerned by the plight of people who exist for the sympathizer as part of some overarching, amorphous abstraction – for instance, 'the poor,' 'the proletariat,' 'the oppressed' – does not, on Anti-Climacus' view, actually pity anyone. Their pity is not directed at *persons*, we might say, but only at the *idea* of persons. This looks worryingly close to *den næste*, which Kierkegaard explicitly equates with the category of the 'human being':

> The other human being, that is the neighbor who is the other human being in the sense that the other human being is every other human being. Understood in this way, the discourse was therefore right when it stated at the beginning that if a person loves the neighbor in one single other human being, then he loves all human beings.
>
> (WL, 58/SKS 9, 64)

(Note the similarity with Derrida's formula 'Every other (one) is every (bit) other' [*Tout autre est tout autre*]; the individual other, in their otherness, stands simultaneously for otherness as such and all individual others who participate in alterity.)[20] Anti-Climacan 'abstract sentimentality' belongs to no human because it is not in fact a relation between humans, and therefore stands in only a false relation to the lived experience of the sympathizer. It is not, despite appearances, a self's relation to the moral situation it finds itself in at all. *Works of Love* seems to make the same point when it decries the 'wasting' of love on the unseen (WL, 163/SKS 9, 164). Ferreira, among others, notes the congruency here with

Richard Rorty's rejection of the notion of a sympathetic identification with 'humanity in general.'[21] If we are to experience genuine empathy it must be with beings who, whether actually present or merely envisaged, exist on the level of concrete particularity. We cannot truly identify with abstract groups, only with actual individuals. When we are swept up with this sort of 'universal pity' we are in fact feeling sorry for no one, at least no one actual.[22]

Consider too the case of emotion felt for fictional characters without any sort of reintegration into lived experience of the moral meanings such sympathy discloses. When we experience fiction correctly, as Furtak puts it, 'our "aesthetic" emotions are not founded on belief, but on the entertaining of propositions unasserted.'[23] Fiction has enormous power to illuminate the world of moral value by eliciting emotional responses from us; the 'grief' we feel when a fictional character dies reveals to us something of the singular preciousness of nonfictional human beings. But sometimes we react to fiction in a way that seems to covertly 'assert the propositions,' as it were: experiencing the appropriate emotional response to a presented fictional situation but failing to acknowledge the ontological 'suspension' of the facts in question. Thus we get the overwrought reader who weeps for days at the plight of a Brontë heroine, or the obsessive viewer who writes angry, grief-inflected internet rants about the killing off of their favorite TV character: passionate people, certainly, perhaps even admirable on some level. Nevertheless, on the Anti-Climacan account, they would have to be regarded as demonically lost in a state of radical disconnection from their concrete reality. And here again we see that interest is not simply a synonym for passion: as a call back towards the existing self, *interesse* actually acts as a *corrective* to the functioning of *lidenskab* in these instances.

Genuine sympathy, then, must be found in a concern for actual persons, not merely the idea of persons. Yet if the ideal needs the concrete for authentic moral concern to be possible, the concrete too needs the ideal. A true comprehension of certain evils requires me to understand the full scope of that evil across all its sufferers, not merely individual instances of it. This is why the evil of genocide is more than the mereological sum of however large a number of individual racially, ethnically or sectarianly motivated murders. As is all too familiar, we often lapse into a dehumanizing mode of speaking about genocide in which the concrete suffering of actual humans is abstracted into large numbers that seem meaningless to us. The suffering of individuals demands our attention if we are genuinely to *understand* what is done when such crimes are committed. But equally, the scope of the crime is also part of its qualitative evil, because the attempted destruction of an entire race is an evil over and above mass-murder; yet this is not to say that the perpetrator commits the separable crimes of mass murder *and* genocide.[24] Moreover, the *individual* is essentially a victim of genocide; it is not the case that they are merely murdered while the *sum* of such victims instantiates the further crime of genocide. Hence in some instances at least, morally salient facts are only revealed by a consideration that simultaneously keeps sight of both the suffering of the individual I see before me and the broader scale of the problem.

This is, at least in part, why the use of the term 'genocide' has been so fraught in discussions of events as long ago as the 1915–17 Armenian massacres or as recent as the conflicts in Rwanda or Darfur. Even where the number of dead or the racist nature of the crimes is not in dispute, the attribution of genocidal intent transfigures a sum of hate crimes into a qualitatively new evil that supervenes upon the existing moral facts. This point can be seen more clearly when a natural evil is compounded by a moral one: if I look at, say, a person dying of AIDS in sub-Saharan Africa, can I coherently accuse the developed world of callous indifference to *one* such sufferer in the way I can accuse it of indifference to *millions* of like sufferers? Scale here seems to be part of the moral evil itself, not a fact over and above the sum of individual suffering, though the evil still inheres precisely in what is being done to individuals, not masses of individuals.

We are therefore drawn back to the *Sickness Unto Death*'s account of moral vision as a holding in tension of the concrete and the ideal, the actual and the imagined. In our apprehension of the other, the actual person before us is unified in our vision with the ideal claims they make upon us, neither element dissolving or collapsing into the other. Reiterating the Wittgensteinian point about recognition, we see not a person *and* a moral demand, but a person who constitutes, *in their concrete specificity*, a moral demand in themselves. The other presents itself to me immediately as making claims upon me, not in such a way that the other is obscured by these claims, but appears in its moral fullness. This holds even where the other is an ethical exemplar rather than (or in addition to being) a moral patient. The life of Gandhi can become a prototype for me without me thereby losing sight of Gandhi himself in his human particularity and individual preciousness.

The account of ethical imagination enunciated across Kierkegaard's writings requires the built-in, non-thetic self-referentiality of *interesse* in order to constitute the self's relating itself to itself *in* its relating the ideal and actual. Without this, the sense of my own involvement in that which I contemplate would have to be supplied by a secondary cognition, which would run counter to Anti-Climacus' structure of selfhood and the phenomenology of vision at work in the mirror-metaphors. The absence of *interesse* from the *Sickness* structure would open up a temporal priority in which I would have to turn away from the unity of ideal and concrete before me to contemplate my own relation thereto. Such a temporal priority is foreign to the Kierkegaardian normative moral vision, and in the case of *Works of Love*, such a temporal priority would be accordingly alien to the phenomenon of loving attention. We would need to look away from the other (seen as making moral demands) to contemplate our own involvement therein (these demands are made of *me*).

Non-theticality has a role to play here too. That interest attends thought without itself being the *object* of thought is crucial in the present context, for if I am to avoid the 'effacement' of the other, the moral evaluation of myself I apprehend in seeing the other must not constitute the objective content *of* my seeing the other. My involvement in the moral demand contained in the figure of the other – and its attendant judgment upon me – must remain part of the non-thetic background of my vision. Accordingly, where vision is *perfected* (where, for instance, David no longer needs 'thou art the man' reminders), I will not move *diachronically* from a contemplation of the self/text/exemplar before me to an awareness of what *I* must do; otherwise 'repentance must acquire itself as an object, inasmuch as the moment of repentance becomes a deficit of action' (CA, 118/SKS 4, 419). This perfection never in fact comes about – the temporal structure of moral existence itself exponentially compounds guilt, causing the self to 'flee to faith in grace' (JP, 692/SKS 21, 13) – but the *telos* is no less real for being finally unattainable. Kierkegaard's model of moral psychology contains a demanding teleology that does not excuse us from its instantiation even though temporally it can never be fully achieved.

In the case of sympathy, the self-referentiality picked out by *interesse* is crucial to an understanding of what is morally at issue in such apprehensions. In *The Concept of Anxiety* Haufniensis claims explicitly that sympathy (which, as Ferreira notes in relation to Humean moral psychology, is closely related to imagination)[25] must contain within it a form of self-referentiality if it is to operate in a fully ethical way:

Only when the sympathetic person in his compassion relates himself to the sufferer in such a way that he in the strictest sense understands that it is his own case that is here in question, only when he knows how to identify with the sufferer in such a way that he, as he fights for an explanation, fights for himself, forsaking all thoughtlessness, softness and cowardice, only then does the sympathy acquire significance, and only then does it perhaps find meaning.

(CA, 120/SKS 4, 421)

The 'meaning' and 'significance' here are explicitly ethical ones: the fullness of compassion requires a self-reflexivity for it to attain moral significance. Without this self-concern, sympathy becomes 'a means of protecting one's own egotism' (CA, 120/SKS 4, 421), a stratagem for keeping the Other's suffering (which is only contingently not *my* suffering) at bay. A full understanding of the other's suffering requires my sympathetic identification with it ('there but for the grace of God go I') but if this is to remain attention to the *other*, and not turn in on itself to become a concern for my own welfare, this self-reflexivity cannot be allowed to become the *object* of cognition. The non-thetic nature of *interesse* allows for the self-reflexivity necessary for sympathy while maintaining sympathy's status as a concern for the other rather than for ourselves.

Such non-theticality may be necessary to avoid a related type of moral egotism. It is one thing to see the plight of another as a reason to act generously towards them; it is quite another to do so out of a desire to be (or to preserve a self-image according to which I already am) a generous person, even if my other motives, and the outcome, are the same in both cases. Admitting 'I am a generous person' into the set of motives one brings into play in deliberation is fundamentally different to possessing the motives *of* a generous person.[26] Yet in seeing another as a moral exemplar in particular, or as disclosing my own moral status to myself, there is a real risk of such egocentric motives being brought into play. If, however, we can somehow see the other as presenting a moral demand and as disclosing our moral status to us without that status being *thematized*, then this danger can perhaps be circumvented. The non-theticality of *interesse* provides an answer as to how we can properly be concerned for our moral status without thereby admitting cognitions *about* it into our deliberation.

Moreover, the account of vision in *Works of Love* contains the same *telos* as that of the account of vision implicit in the use of mirror metaphors. In *Works of Love*, the end-state of perfected moral vision is presented as one in which vision issues immediately and unimpededly in action. This expresses itself in love's inability to reflect upon itself and remain love:

> *As soon as love dwells upon itself, it is out of its element.* What does dwelling upon itself mean? It is to become an object to itself. But an object is always a dangerous matter when one is supposed to move forward [. . .] when love dwells finitely on itself, all is lost. Think of an arrow flying, as is said, with the speed of an arrow; imagine that for one moment it occurs to it to want to dwell upon itself, perhaps in order to see how far it has come, or how high it is soaring above the earth, or how its speed compares with the speed of another arrow that also flies with the speed of an arrow: in that same second the arrow falls to the ground.
>
> (WL, 182/SKS 9, 182)

Love, therefore, cannot become an object to itself (at least not finitely – love can dwell 'infinitely' on itself which simply means a 'redoubling' without the intrusion of a 'third factor' that would make the love itself an object of contemplation) because love expresses itself in forward movement. To contemplate love is to cease loving. The self occupied with Christian love is 'occupied *at the speed of action*' (WL, 188/SKS 9, 188) and has no time to contemplate their love as object. Again, in this idealized picture of perfected agency, to look lovingly on the other is immediately to be impelled to action, just as seeing oneself in the mirror of the Word or a moral exemplar is to turn immediately to action rather than contemplation.

Kierkegaard's account of moral vision therefore is capable of overcoming charges that it effaces the other (either by insisting on the moral primacy of categories like *den næste* which appear to exclude concrete differences, or that in following another as a moral exemplar we ignore them as an actual concrete human being). Interest emerges as a crucial element in securing this proper attention to the other-as-other, by virtue of both the self-referentiality it insinuates into the combination of concrete and ideal in vision, and its non-thetic character. Taken together, these allow us to see the other in their concrete specificity whilst simultaneously attending to the formal, ideal moral requirements they place upon us. In that sense *interesse* both helps rescue the ethics of *Works of Love* from certain accusations that have been made against it, and shows how Kierkegaard illuminates a path that avoids moral egotism and indifference to individual others while still preserving a concern for one's moral status at all times.

Part III

Knowledge and Meaning

9
Concern, Misfortune, and Despair

Interest and concern

We've seen that the property of thinking we have identified as *interesse* plays a sort of regulative role in the exercise of moral imagination, keeping feeling, knowing, and willing from becoming hopelessly infinitized. So far we've considered infinitized willing and feeling, and how *interesse* prevents these states from coming about; in the final part of our investigation, we will consider the relationship between interest and knowledge. But we begin in a place that might, at first, be surprising: the *Upbuilding Discourses*.

The signed religious discourses are an essential part of Kierkegaard's authorship, but at least among the more overtly philosophically inclined commentators they have generally received second-billing. This is perhaps not unexpected, as these discourses are designed for the moral edification of a generalist reading audience and are non-technical in character and style; most philosophers might be excused for thinking they would find little of clear theoretical value in what looks, for all intents and purposes, like a sermon. In *Being and Time*, Heidegger famously declares that there is more of philosophical value in the signed discourses than anywhere else in Kierkegaard's writings apart from *The Concept of Anxiety*,[1] but this declaration perhaps does more to hinder the philosophical reception of the discourses than to promote it: Kierkegaardians, convinced Heidegger harbors a vast and poorly concealed debt to texts like the *Postscript*, might see this assertion as more of a diversion than an endorsement. In any event, Heidegger's distinguishing these texts from Kierkegaard's 'theoretical' works goes unchallenged. Yet there has nonetheless been some important work on the *Upbuilding Discourses*, helping us to appreciate their importance to Kierkegaard's thought and the surprising philosophical depth and complexity of their themes.[2]

In one of the first works to discuss Kierkegaard explicitly as a philosophical psychologist, Kresten Nordentoft draws a connection between the term *interesse* as it occurs in the pseudonymous works, and the use of *bekymring*, 'concern,' in the *Upbuilding Discourses* of 1843:

> 'Concern' is the edifying discourse's translation of the Climacus fragment's 'interesse,' and it is the name of the situation which Anti-Climacus describes when he says that 'the relationship relates itself to itself.'[3]

If this equation of 'concern' and 'interest' holds good, then we can use the understanding of *interesse* we've been developing here as a way into the *Upbuilding Discourses*, showing that the model of moral cognition, imagination, and perception we've recovered from the pseudonymous works is also at work in the veronymous writings. But there are reasons to be cautious here. Nordentoft provides no substantive defense of his identification,[4] and *bekymring* (like *interesse*) is a fairly prosaic, everyday Danish word; its presence in a series of short texts written for generalist readers is hardly startling. We therefore need to consider whether Nordentoft is right, which will amount to asking whether there *is* some philosophically interesting sense of *bekymring* at work within the *Upbuilding Discourses*, and further, whether it plays a role cognate to that of *interesse* in the pseudonymous works we've been considering. In what follows, I'll argue that one discourse in particular not only affords *bekymring* a role equivalent to *interesse*, but also offers us several insights into relation of *interesse*, knowledge, and self-understanding.

The nature of concern

The 1843 discourse 'Strengthening the Inner Being' contains several fascinating psychological and ontological undercurrents. It takes as its starting point Ephesians 3:13-end, where Paul speaks of his sufferings as being undertaken for Christ's followers, and prays that God will grant 'strengthening in the inner being' to the believers in Ephesus. The discourse therefore concentrates largely on the relation between suffering and misfortune and strengthening in this 'inner being' (*Indvortes Menneske*). *Bekymring* plays a key role in delivering such 'strengthening,' in a way that is at once epistemic, affective, and ontological: concern, Kierkegaard tells us, is an attitude towards not merely the world, but also towards one's relationship *to* the world, which somehow serves to actualize this 'inner being.' In a crucial passage he tells us:

Through every deeper reflection, which makes him *older* than the moment and lets him grasp the eternal, a person assures himself that he has an actual relation to a world, and that this relation therefore cannot be mere knowledge about this world and about himself as part of it, since such knowledge is no relation, precisely because in this knowledge he himself is indifferent toward this world, and this world is indifferent through his knowledge of it. Not until the moment when there awakens in his soul a concern about what meaning the world has for him and he for the world, about what meaning everything within him by which he himself belongs to the world and he therein for the world – then the inner being first announces itself in this *concern*.

(EUD, 86/SKS 5, 93)

The move described here is a familiar one in Kierkegaard: the move away from a purely immediate self-understanding towards something more self-reflective. As we saw in Chapter 6, this movement underlies the journey from an unconscious life of immediacy to one of self-transparency before God in *The Sickness Unto Death*, a journey in which the self comes to know itself progressively better by differentiating itself over against contexts that supply increasingly more adequate 'criteria' (family, society, state, and God). In the passage above, this 'deeper reflection' pulls the self away from its selfless immersion in the immediate and so makes it 'older than' the moment, something with history, something that, in self-collection, transcends the temporal instant it inhabits. Indeed, it distinguishes itself from the very *fact* of emplacement in temporality and thus 'grasps the eternal.' Concern, therefore, as a desire for meaning, operates as a *principium individuationis* that radically differentiates the self from the world of spatiotemporal things. Yet concern is not mere impersonal Cartesian doubt or Husserlian *epoche*: it differentiates subject and world in such a way that the self's connections *to* the world, 'everything within him by which he himself belongs to the world and he therein for the world' (EUD, 86/SKS 5, 93) are preserved. In contemplating the external in a way that seeks to assign transcendent meaning to itself *in its relation to* the external, the self uncovers its *alterity* to the world, with 'alterity' here preserving the sense contained in its Latin root *alter* – 'one of two.'[5]

The point of departure for the search for meaning is our 'assuring' ourselves of our 'actual relation to the world,' and this starting point conditions everything that follows. Concern is directed towards our *relationship to* existence, not merely to existence *itself*. The desire for meaning is therefore implicitly self-referential, even when directed outward. If we were to find a meaning for the phenomena we see in the external world that *lacked* this self-referentiality, this would not constitute any sort of relation to the world, 'simply because in this knowledge he himself is indifferent toward this world and this world is indifferent through his knowledge of it' (EUD, 86/SKS 5, 93). Only meaning which explains the world *and my place in it* will satisfy the demand for meaning engendered by my becoming 'older than the moment.'

So 'concern' emerges as a self-referential mode of contemplating my relation to the world. 'Indifferent' knowledge simply won't satisfy the demands of concern. Indifferent knowledge contains only specific data, hypotheses, conjectures, and so forth concerning how the world is. Concerned knowledge, by contrast, also contains a *reflexive* element: it apprehends how the world stands and simultaneously how I stand in relation to it. Already, we can begin to discern important congruencies with *interesse* as it has been understood in the foregoing chapters: a sort of self-referentiality built directly into consciousness, perception, and imagination. But we've also seen throughout that this self-referentiality supervenes non-thetically upon thought rather than becoming a thematized object for contemplation. Even if *bekymring* shares the quality of self-referentiality with *interesse*, does it also partake of this non-thetic immediacy?

Part of the answer can be found in the claims Kierkegaard makes with respect to concern's function of generating *and sustaining* the 'inner being.' In *Johannes Climacus, interesse* is identified *with* consciousness; in other words, interestedness is another *name* for the actuality of consciousness. A cognate role, one of ontological grounding, seems to be accorded to *bekymring* in 'Strengthening the Inner Being.' Here, the Pauline 'inner being,' a self that is distinct from (yet nonetheless interrelated with) its surroundings, only 'announces itself' (*forkynder sig*) when concern is operative. This 'inner being,' insofar as it is a function of seeing oneself as individuated over against the world in which one finds oneself, corresponds to the way Anti-Climacus later uses the terms 'self' and 'spirit.' Like consciousness in *Johannes Climacus* and spirit in *Sickness* it depends for its existence upon self-referentiality in thought, such that the inner being is not a given but something *achieved*.

But this achievement must have the character of *ongoing* concern in order to count as an achievement *at all*:

> At no moment does this concern cease; for the knowledge he wins is
> no indifferent knowledge. If, for example, a person were intended to

decide this matter once and for all and then be finished with it, then the inner being in him would only be stillborn and would vanish again.

(EUD, 87/SKS 5, 94)

Normal concerns can present themselves as time-limited in various ways: I can be concerned about how I am going to deal with a difficult semester, about getting a problem with my car fixed (in which case I have a concern which I expect will cease when the problem is addressed), and I can anticipate becoming concerned at a future time when my child will be old enough to go out alone. Yet *bekymring* in the philosophically interesting sense cannot present the object of its concern – the meaning of the world and my relation to it – as temporally circumscribed in this way, as if I could be concerned about such matters at some time and not others, or ever *stop* being concerned about them ('I've finished working out my salvation in fear and trembling, now let's go grab a beer'). The concern that establishes (or perhaps indicates the establishment of) the inner being presents itself as something that must be of concern to the self at all moments of its existence. Yet if such concern were a matter of thinking *about* the meaning of one's relation to the world, this would necessitate an inhuman constant meditation upon this one topic – and again, this doesn't seem to be a picture of moral life that Kierkegaard wants to endorse.

We will now take a few moments to consider the key example Kierkegaard gives in the discourse – the meaning of misfortune – and show how concern, as it is explicated in this example, displays the same features we discerned for *interesse* in the previous chapters: non-thetic, self-referential, and expressive of a sense of finding oneself *in* what one contemplates.

Misfortune and fortune

'Strengthening the Inner Being' is primarily a discourse on the nature of suffering and tribulation, and with the self's desire to discover some transcendent meaning, purpose or justification for these sufferings. This is a familiar theme: the almost instinctive human need to ask *why?* in the face of misfortune. Confronted with some moral or natural evil, we seek an explanation that goes beyond the immediately apparent mechanistic causes (the explanatory resources available to the 'moment' – hence, again, a 'deeper reflection...older than [that is, transcending] the moment' [EUD, 86/SKS 5, 93]) to find some transcendent, final cause or meaning of our suffering. However, this attitude of concern as a craving for meaning is not concerned simply with obtaining *any* answer, but an answer that provides a meaning sufficient, in itself, to structure the agent's projects and determine her actions:

> This concern is not calmed by a more detailed or a more comprehensive knowledge; it craves another type of knowledge, a knowledge that does not remain as knowledge for a single moment, but in the moment of possession transforms itself into an action, for otherwise it is not possessed.
>
> (EUD, 86/SKS 5, 93)

Consider a man who survives an earthquake that kills his entire family. He asks why such a thing has happened, and is approached by two people, each offering different answers: a seismologist and a priest. Both offer (apparently causal) explanations of what has occurred, explanations the sufferer may accept or reject. The fundamental difference between the two accounts is that while the seismologist offers an explanation that the sufferer can understand and yet be indifferent to, any explanation the priest could give in terms of 'the will of God' will direct itself essentially to the sufferer as a moral being. The priest's explanation speaks directly to the sufferer and implicitly *about* the sufferer; the agency of a reportedly loving personal God addresses itself to the inquirer in their moral concretion in a way that the shifting of tectonic plates does not.[6] If the sufferer accepts the priest's explanation without 'finding himself' in the explanation in this sense, a term like 'the will of God' would become simply another link in a chain of causes which will be entirely outside the sufferer and to which he can remain indifferent.[7]

What *bekymring* seeks, therefore, is a form of explanation in which the self is essentially involved, and which therefore provides knowledge the self *cannot be indifferent to*. The knowledge it yearns for is not merely factual, but is rather knowledge that – like Scripture in *For Self-Examination* – speaks to and concerns the agent directly and personally, without mediation or further reflection. The self seeks an understanding of the order of things that will include *itself* in a fully determinative way. This type of meaning belongs to that rather peculiar order of knowledge that can only be known in a certain subjective orientation if it can be said to be known at all: if such knowledge does *not* connect with the subjectivity of the agent, such that it transforms the agent's volitions in and of itself, then this knowledge has not, in fact, been acquired. Moral and religious knowledge are generally acknowledged to be of this type. With respect to moral beliefs at least, Jonathan Dancy notes that these are 'somehow officially in the motivating business' in a way that other types of belief are not, even if the latter types of belief *can* often be motivationary.[8]

Consider these conjunctive statements: 'I'm in love with Mary, but this fact doesn't really matter to me;' 'I think what I'm doing here is profoundly ethically wrong, but it doesn't really bother me;' 'I believe God has a plan for me, but I don't really care.' These statements seem to be expressions of flawed *understanding* in a way that, say, 'I believe that osmium is the heaviest known metal, but I don't really care' is not. To use an example given by Christopher Cordner, a knowledge-able geographer could lose interest in geography without losing their geographical understanding, but 'someone who came to think that all or even most of what they had taken seriously in ethics was simply use-less facts would *thereby* show themselves to have suffered a genuine lose of moral understanding.'[9] Equally, someone who claims to hold reli-gious beliefs that do *not* meet the need for satisfying meaning would also not seem to hold genuinely *religious* beliefs. 'No one,' as Raimond Gaita puts it, 'can seriously say, "It is cheap, sentimental, banal and does the dirt on life, but it is my religion and true nonetheless." '[10] It seems that in the curiously unintelligible locutions about moral and religious topics that I gave a moment ago, what Hare would call the phrastic (the part of the sentence which tells us what the proposition is about) and neustic (the part that expresses my attitude towards the proposi-tion) in each statement simply cannot go together *if* we understand the phrastic element correctly.[11] In belief-reports of this type, an incorrect neustic actually invalidates the truth-value of the phrastic. At the very least, moral and religious statements require no further statements to explain why they are taken to be normatively significant, whereas if I *was* profoundly affected by the atomic weight of osmium, I would have to explain the circumstances that made this the case.[12]

Yet the domain of the questions asked by *bekymring* is, according to 'Strengthening the Inner Being,' wider than simply that of 'why did this bad thing happen?' or 'what is the moral meaning of this mis-fortune?' Rather, concern interrogates *good* fortune equally, demanding transcendent purpose or justification even for the goods we already enjoy:

> But the person in whose soul the Inner Being announces itself in that concern does not become happy when good fortune indulges him in everything. He is seized by a secret horror of the power that is bent

on capriciously squandering everything in such a way; he becomes anxious about being involved with it.

(EUD, 89–90/SKS 5, 96)

Concern therefore is not simply actuated by the experience of misfortune, but also by *good* fortune, or indeed, simply by consideration of the status quo. Moreover, *bekymring* does not simply ask about the origin or cause of the prevailing state of affairs, but instead asks an evaluative question that is simultaneously and essentially about the subject's own status or state. Hence, in considering the 'indulgence' of good fortune, the question that arises is already not merely about origin, but *legitimacy*. Kierkegaard here draws a suggestive analogy with 'civil' or 'human justice,' which, we are told, is 'only a semblance of divine [justice]' and which 'also directs itself to the single individual, and its scrutiny is more rigorous' (EUD, 91/SKS 5, 97). When a person in civil society is found to have astonishing wealth, the authorities demand he explain how he got it; if he cannot, he is suspected of being a thief (EUD, 89/SKS 5, 95–6). Asking the question of the origin of wealth is here *simultaneously* an interrogation of the legitimacy of its possession. Demanding an explanation is, in the same instant, demanding justification. The question of origin is therefore an irreducibly *moral* question, and an inability to answer it makes the person morally suspect. Like human justice, Divine Justice asks this question and demands answer:

> If a person, in reply to its question as to how he comes to have all that he has, has no other answer than that he himself does not know, then it judges him, then it becomes a suspicion against him, that he is not in *legitimate* possession of it. This suspicion is not a servant of justice, but is justice itself, which accuses and judges and passes sentence upon him and guards his soul in prison, so it cannot escape.
>
> (EUD, 89/SKS 5, 96)

The final phrase, equating justice itself with the mere *suspicion* of illegitimacy, broadens the scope of justice from the retributive or redistributive (which can only commence *after* moral judgments have been made) to the interrogative. Rather than a necessary prelude *to* justice, the act of moral interrogation becomes *itself* justice, as justice becomes principally a matter of justification. Accordingly, the moral ambiguity arising from an inability to explain the source of one's wealth (broadly construed) becomes itself a violation of justice. Our involvement in a 'squandering' distribution of goods for which we have neither explanation nor justification makes us culpable even in our ignorance. So the demand that one be able to 'make an accounting' of oneself is properly a moral demand, regardless of what condition such an accounting might subsequently disclose. There are definite echoes here of a Kantian 'pathology' that Bernard Williams denounces as a 'leveling of the sentiments' that regards 'admiration or liking or even enjoyment of the happy manifestations of luck' as 'treachery to moral worth.'[13] Kierkegaard could perhaps respond that however uncomfortable this 'pathology' may make us, it nonetheless follows from our need for transcendent meaning, which is not prepared to accept a response that provides justifications for some regions of the distribution in which we find ourselves while quarantining others from the need for justification altogether. This particularly strong version of justice won't content itself with explanations that go as far as, say, 'I've worked hard for everything I have' while excusing itself from considering the fact I was lucky enough to be born at this time, in this country, to this family, with these talents, and so forth.

If the self is to meet the demands of Divine Justice, it must examine its place in the order in which it finds itself in a way that is morally self-evaluating. It does not seek a meaning for the goods or ills it undergoes simply from a standpoint of morally neutral intellectual curiosity; such evaluation must take place as part of an interrogation that is essentially moral from its inception. Indeed, seen from the viewpoint of Divine Justice (once the subject accepts the precepts of such a viewpoint), a morally neutral inquiry would already be *morally* in the wrong, insofar as it is actuated by something other than justice. The question about meaning is an immediately, essentially morally self-evaluative one. And this immediately self-evaluating aspect is something that, as we have seen, is central to Kierkegaard's entire moral psychology: our ability to see the world (whether in the form of Scripture or of other people or circumstances before us) in a way that is simultaneously a non-thetic evaluation of how *we* stand in relation to what we contemplate.

Helplessness and fate

The usefulness of misfortune,[14] then, is that it discloses to the subject its involvement in a distributive order that calls the subject's own moral legitimacy into question. It does so in a frighteningly thorough way: nothing is excluded from the purview of justice, and the entire order in which the subject finds itself embedded is brought into question. Moreover, Kierkegaard thinks that the vicissitudes of both fortune and misfortune reveal to the agent that whatever it tries to do under its own power, it is ultimately helpless: all achievement is owed to Providence, while individual effort amounts to nothing in the face of a seemingly capricious order of things that can inflict Job-like loss at any time. This exposure to a causal realm completely indifferent and ultimately impervious to human aims and ends is something that those in a state of pre-reflective immediacy never contemplate. In the *Concluding Unscientific Postscript*, Johannes Climacus develops a similar account of the meaning of suffering, and contrasts it to a naive faith in good fortune [*lykke*, which also carries the simpler meaning of 'happy'] characteristic of the 'immediate' life view:

> *Immediacy is good fortune*, because in immediacy there is no contradiction; the immediate person, viewed essentially, is fortunate, and *the life-view of immediacy is good fortune*. If one wished to ask him from where he gets this life-view, this essential relation to good fortune, he might answer, with the innocence of a virgin: I do not understand it myself.
>
> (CUP, 1:433/SKS 7, 394)

The phrase 'I do not understand it myself' echoes the discussion of justice described above, and we now understand this language as encapsulating an ignorance that is *already morally culpable*. The immediate self has not sought any explanation deeper than the purely causal, or perhaps thin generalizations such as 'fate.' Having not sought any explanation of the order of things that would incorporate his self, such an immediate person '*perceives* the misfortune, but he does not *comprehend* the suffering' (CUP, 1:433/SKS 7, 394). This lack of comprehension (or inability to 'come to an understanding with misfortune' [CUP, 1:433–4/SKS 7, 394]) is necessary so long as the self understands its suffering as something 'alien,' something external and as such essentially unrelated to the self. 'Aesthetically, suffering relates itself to existence as something accidental' (CUP, 1:445/SKS 7, 404). In religious categories of self-understanding, 'Inwardness (the ethical and ethical-religious individual), however, comprehends suffering as essential' (CUP, 1:434/SKS 7, 395).

This move toward comprehension involves a transcendence of the explanatory resources open to the immediate life-view: 'Fortune, misfortune, fate, immediate enthusiasm, despair' (CUP 1:434/SKS 7, 395). This last element, despair, contains the key to this transcendence. So long as misfortune is perceived as something contingent and external, the immediate self must assume that 'it will stop again, because it is something alien' (CUP, 1:434/SKS 7/394). Hence the claim that the immediate life-view is one of good fortune: if misfortune is marginalized as something extrinsic to the self, the self implicitly has a 'default' position in which misfortune is not to be found, and to which, in periods of misfortune, it assumes it must eventually return. But if this doesn't happen and misfortune persists, the self comes to despair (CUP, 1:434/SKS 7, 394–5).

Hannay has noted that Kierkegaard's use of *fortvivelse* is not univocal and varies across different works,[15] and here it is being used in a sense different to the ontological dysfunction articulated in *The Sickness Unto Death*. The usage here, like that in *Either/Or*, is closer to Hegel's use of the term, which understands despair as 'the conscious insight into the untruth of phenomenal knowledge.'[16] For Hegel, consciousness comes to find it is not what it assumed itself to be, and so despair becomes the occasion for a reassessment of its life-view. In much the same way, for Climacus (and more pointedly Judge William in the second volume of *Either/Or*), despair issues in a skepticism about the self's current life-view and so acts as a 'solvent-cum-propellant necessary for keeping the journey [to greater self-understanding] going.'[17] Despair is here understood as the exhaustion of a *livsanskuelse* ('life-view') that precipitates the seeking of a new understanding of the self and its existence – precisely the search for meaning described in 'Strengthening the Inner Being.'

But if misfortune can lead to despair in this way, the Kierkegaard of 'Strengthening the Inner Being' maintains that *good* fortune, just as much as bad, can become the occasion for the titular 'strengthening' (*bekræftelsen*) if it is approached in the self-referential mode of concern. However, whereas bad fortune can disclose the contingency of human happiness and the ultimate inefficacy of human effort, good fortune can, if not appropriated with the understanding conferred by concerned thought, lead to precisely the opposite conclusion, even in the person whose earlier experiences have made him 'intimate with adversity':

He had learned that there is distress in life; in heavy misfortunes, he had confessed to himself just how weak and powerless a person is in his own strength. Yet he did not give up courage, he did not become despondent, he kept on working [...] See! Then the sun of prosperity rose once again, illuminated everything, explained everything, assured him that he had come a long, long way, that he had won what he had been working for. Then he cried out in his joy, 'It just had to happen this way, for a person's exertions are not fruitless and meaningless toil.' With that he had spoiled everything and received no strengthening in the inner being.

(EUD, 92/SKS 5, 98)

By forgetting the 'lesson' of misfortune – the ultimate total impotence of finite beings – the self actually defers the imperative of explaining misfortune. Good fortune becomes a function of personal effort, while misfortune becomes essentially extrinsic, something imposed from without. Under these determinants, no deeper comprehension of misfortune, one that will incorporate the self *into* the explanation in the way required by concern, will be possible. An opportunity to strengthen the inner being – that is, to collect oneself in an order of meaning disclosed by the fact of misfortune – has been squandered. Later in the authorship, Kierkegaard speaks of hardship as 'awakening' the spirit from its 'dream-life;' hardship breaks the self out of its immediacy and gives it a deeper conception of itself (CD, 108–9/SKS 10, 119–20).[18] This later account, however, gives hardship an explicit teleology, one directed towards an understanding of the self's transcendent condition:

> …hope, eternity's hope, is like a gentle breeze, like a whisper in a person's innermost being, only all too easy to ignore. But what, then, does hardship want? It wants to have this whisper brought forth in the innermost being […] It is eternity's voice within that wants to be heard, and in order to secure a hearing it uses the clamor of hardship [to drown out the other voices].

(CD, 109/SKS 10, 120)

Once again, misfortune, hardship, and suffering serve to clear the ground for a deeper understanding of existence that locates the sufferer in something transcendent – an understanding that awakens or presents the 'inner(most) being.' The self in concern is never outside the explanation it seeks, and it is this that differentiates concerned and unconcerned inquiry. Concern seeks to comprehend misfortune in such a way that the concerned self's own relation to the order of things is contained within the explanation, rather than being secondary to or derivative from the explanation. The search for answers is inherently self-directed; concern seeks an explanation that will incorporate the self, in its ethical totality, into the explanation, such that this understanding *immediately* translates into normatively conditioned action.

For this reason, concern, just like interest, has a teleological import, in that it refers thought towards its own involvement in what it contemplates and so gestures towards the moral. Just as *interesse* provides a *telos* for consciousness by referring it back towards itself, so *bekymring* constitutes a *telos* for thought by gesturing towards a transcendent meaning that will have immediate implications for the self in its moral agency.

But this will only be possible if the explanation appears in terms that will be sufficient to the self's transcendence of the causal realm in which it finds itself. As we have seen, in facing catastrophic misfortune, we seek an explanation that goes beyond the purely causal or mechanical – we seek an ultimate justification, a *meaning* that answers to the capacity for transcendence that we find within ourselves. What concern ultimately aims at is a *final justification*, an explanation in which the self is given a personal teleology. In short, concern is ultimately concern for personal *salvation*. This is perhaps hinted at in the quote from *Christian Discourses* above in which the inner being is presented as speaking with 'eternity's voice;' and, as we'll now see, it is made even clearer in the way Johannes Climacus negotiates the relationships between knowledge, interest, and eternal blessedness in the *Concluding Unscientific Postscript*.

10
Interest in the Postscript: The Telos of Knowing

Climacan interest

In the published works, the term *interesse* occurs nowhere as often, nor with such apparent philosophical valence, as in the *Concluding Unscientific Postscript to Philosophical Fragments*. No discussion of the role of interest in Kierkegaard's account of self and vision would therefore be complete without engaging with the way *interesse* is used in this work. Moreover, the primary usages of *interesse* (in its philosophically interesting sense) in Kierkegaard's work are to be found in two of the three works 'written' by Johannes Climacus – *Johannes Climacus or De Omnibus Dubitandum Est*, and the *Postscript*. Though I've argued that the mode of cognition picked out by *interesse* in *Johannes Climacus* plays a central role in other works as well, the *explicit* use of the term is largely confined to the Climacan writings and the journals. To a large extent, then, the identification of *interesse* with the non-thetic self-referentiality built into thought that the present work has attempted to demonstrate will succeed or fail depending on whether this sense attaches to the use of *interesse* in the *Postscript*.

The question that motivates and structures the inquiry of *Philosophical Fragments* is 'Can a historical point of departure be given for an eternal consciousness; how can such [a point of departure] be of interest more than historically; can one build an eternal happiness on historical knowledge?' (PF, 1/SKS 4, 213). The question, then, concerns the relation of certain types of knowledge to their knower: can at least some subset of historical knowledge become the basis for a subjective orientation? This question is explicitly about Christianity, and the existence of the historical Jesus of Nazareth as the basis for hope for personal salvation. In the

Postscript, an ironically titled addendum to the *Philosophical Fragments*, this motivating question is restated thus:[1]

> …the issue is not about the truth of Christianity but about the individual's relation to Christianity, thus not about the indifferent individual's systematic eagerness to arrange the truths of Christianity in paragraphs but rather about the infinitely interested individual's concern regarding his own relation to such a teaching.
>
> (CUP, 1:15/SKS 7, 24–5)

Thus *interesse* reenters the Climacan account in relation to specific ways of knowing, an attitude to knowledge that is not 'indifferent' but subjectively 'concerned' – language that we have heard before in our discussion of 'Strengthening the Inner Being.'

However, the object of this knowledge is something very specific. The thought of salvation from sin through the paradox of the incarnation is a conceptually concrete *revealed teaching*, a transcendently given body of knowledge rather than something immanently derived from human thought. It is towards this divinely revealed body of knowledge that Christianity 'presupposes the infinite interest' (CUP, 1:16/SKS 7, 25) in that the *telos* of Christian doctrine is one's personal salvation:

> I have at least understood this much, that it [Christianity] wants to make the single individual eternally happy, and that precisely within this individual it presupposes this infinite interest in its happiness as a *conditio sine qua non*.
>
> (CUP, 1:16/SKS 7, 25)

The interest presupposed by Christianity is therefore one directed towards a specific object: one's eternal *salighed*, variously translated as 'happiness' or 'blessedness.' Such an interest is subject to qualifiers such as 'passionate,' 'personal,' and 'infinite,' and it stands in contrast to other types of interest which are not adequate to the *telos* of eternal happiness. It is therefore, in these respects, qualitatively different to all other interests – yet it remains *an* interest, albeit the preeminent one.

The claimed *infinity* of interest in an eternal happiness is linked to the inadequacy of finite things to answer to the need for meaning (especially, as we've just seen, in the face of misfortune or crushing loss) for beings whose nature contains something 'eternal.' In our capacity to go beyond the given and the temporal in thought, we express a transcendent nature that requires a correspondingly transcendent *telos* for its demand for meaning to be satisfied. We need whatever structures our approach to what Climacus considers the 'task' (*opgave*) of living an entire life of human selfhood to be grounded in some purpose or meaning that transcends our finite, exhaustible and fallible human chains of justification for our lives.[2] Our 'sense for' our eternal happiness requires absolute ends, and therefore such a sense 'can surely be nothing other than an *infinite* concern' (CUP, 1:16/SKS 7, 25).

Our 'interests' are clearly among those things by which we order or structure our lives meaningfully, and certain interests have a greater capacity for providing this meaningful coherence (what Norman Lillegard has called 'dimensional wholeness')[3] than others. This thought is in large part behind Judge William's insistence that the young aesthete of *Either/Or* lacks a self, because he has no integrating ethical passions or commitments to give coherence to his psychological makeup and history. Yet Kierkegaard ultimately rejects the adequacy of the merely ethical life-view and, in the journals of 1854–55, he vociferously rejects marriage, Judge William's paradigm example of a self-conferring, freely chosen ethical commitment.[4] Though ethical commitments such as marriage do confer a higher degree of 'dimensional wholeness' to a life than, in Lillegard's example, a passion for Ping Pong, such commitments cannot relieve the self of the infinite guilt (infinite separation from God) that it uncovers as it develops a fuller understanding of itself.

Accordingly, infinite interest constitutes the possibility of faith (CUP, 1:27/SKS 7, 34), as it is only from the perspective of an *infinite* concern for one's eternal *salighed* that the content of Christianity can be appropriated in its full import. If Christianity is viewed merely as an historical rather than a transcendently religious matter, such a merely historical subject will be inadequate to grounding the self's infinite interest in eternal blessedness; a self so infinitely interested 'would here despair at once' (CUP, 1:23/SKS 7, 30) through such a view. An historical approach to truth can only furnish us with 'approximation' objects of knowledge due to its inductive character. This is no problem for a self that approaches the question objectively; that is, a self who is 'merely historically interested' (CUP, 1:23/SKS 7, 30). A self motivated by such an interest may enquire into Christianity but necessarily misses the essential point of Christian doctrine: *personal* salvation.[5] The objective self *is* interested, but 'not infinitely, personally, in passion, in the direction of his eternal happiness, interested in his relation to this truth' (CUP, 1:21/SKS 7, 29).

So what separates the merely historical interest from the interest in one's eternal blessedness is apparently captured in these qualifiers 'infinite,' 'personal,' and 'impassioned,' which are, in turn, appropriate or inappropriate to their object. Interest becomes inappropriate when the relationship between the nature of the object and the mode of the interest do not correspond. Not surprisingly, most of the discussion of *Postscript* is dedicated to the incorrect mode Climacus sees as adopted by modernity's relation towards Christianity. A dispassionate, detached, and objective approach to Christian doctrine is wholly inappropriate to the central meaning of Christianity; if a person were ostensibly to enquire into their personal salvation in a dispassionate mode we would be entitled to wonder if such a person *really* understood the object.[6] Conversely, though of less interest to the *Postscript*, a passionate engagement with an inappropriate object has its own perils. 'Infinite interest' in the wrong sort of object yields comic self-contradiction; adding passion to such a misdirected interest yields 'zealotism.' The zealot at least has the merit that she has passion (CUP, 1:36/SKS 7, 42) but is nonetheless 'comical' because her infinite interest is directed towards a mere approximation-object (CUP, 1:31/SKS 7, 38). Zealotism is therefore a cognate of the 'lunacy' of relating absolutely to such relative ends, which issues in phenomena such as jealousy and vanity (CUP, 1:422/SKS 7, 384). For the same reason, a self who intends to base his eternal happiness on the historical fact of the continuity of the church is equally comical; though his passion is commendable, he becomes comic because the objectivity of historical fact is 'incongruous' with his interest (CUP, 1:43/SKS 7, 48-9). Passion, too, may go awry here, as where the pastors Climacus decries cause purely aesthetic emotion to arise in their listeners by dressing up their religious discourses through a 'dabbling' with the poetic (CUP, 1:446/SKS 7, 406).

So the terms 'infinite,' 'personal,' and 'passionate' do qualify the interest in an eternal *salighed* in ways that set it radically apart from all other interests – for instance, the claimed infinity of this interest confers a sort of urgency on the interest that makes 'every iota' of infinite worth (CUP, 1:31/SKS 7, 38).[7] Yet Climacus does not thereby appear to be using *interesse* in a sense different from that captured by the everyday English use of 'interests.' In this sense, having an interest in, or being interested in, one's eternal happiness, stands at the far end of a spectrum that includes having an interest in or being interested in a sport, pastime, or relationship. The difference is vast, but at base it would seem to be one of degree and scope, not fundamental type. We saw in Chapter 3 that the way *interesse* is used in the *Johannes Climacus* fragment rules out such an interpretation. If consciousness *is* interestedness, then interest cannot simply be a dispositional or characteristic attitude towards a specific object, or even the *totality of* such attitudes in a self. Yet in the *Postscript*, interest in an eternal happiness appears to be simply one interest among others, albeit one that attracts rather strident adjectives like 'passionate,' 'infinite,' and 'personal.'

Is salvation an object?

There is, therefore, good reason to suspect that the use of *interesse* in the *Postscript* does not conform to the sense we've seemingly recovered from elsewhere in the Climacan writings and which I've claimed pervades Kierkegaard's wider phenomenology of moral perception. It is *this* context that allows Merold Westphal, as we saw in Chapter 3, to interpret the interest of faith as being *an* interest, albeit one with a privileged status in relation to other interests by virtue of its object: "an interest superior to, and unconditioned by, all other interests."[8] Such a reading seems to be backed up by Climacus' insistence from the outset of the work that, from the perspective of the interest of faith, all other interests become not merely subordinate, but potential *temptations*: 'faith is precisely the infinite interest in Christianity and any other interest easily becomes a temptation' (CUP, 1:21/SKS 7, 29). The object of Christian interest, therefore, is 'superior' in Westphal's terms because other interests will tend to distract or divert the self from the all-pervasive task of creaturely selfhood. Though the object of Christian interest is shown throughout the *Postscript* to be something unique, distinct, and irremediably paradoxical (namely, the eternal appearing in time through the historical event of the Incarnation), we are still firmly located in the language of object-directed *preoccupation*. It is certainly not clear that Climacus is talking about a non-thetic self-referentiality built into thought such as we have defined *interesse* to mean in specific contexts.

Moreover, insofar as the question relates to appropriate *modes* of interest, the popular reading that conflates passion (*lidenskab*) with interest will be able to get a foothold here. This reading is supported in the context of *Postscript* by considerations of contiguity, for as we've already seen, *lidenskab* and *interesse* occur together with demonstrable frequency in the *Postscript*.[9] Given that Kierkegaard uses passion (an accessible, everyday household word) frequently, whereas the sense of *interesse* I'm arguing for here is specialized and must be recovered exegetically, assigning a distinct, specialized sense to the use of *interesse* in the *Postscript* seems, at first blush, superfluous. Unless the *Postscript* yields internal evidence that *interesse* has a sense importantly distinct from that of *lidenskab*, parsimony will compel us to take the two terms as co-referent.

Otherwise we'd needlessly complicate Climacus' philosophical psychology to no explanatory benefit, and obscure the possibility that the sense of *interesse* used in the *Postscript* is importantly different to that used elsewhere.

Beyond simple contiguity, Climacus sometimes comes close to directly identifying passion with interest: 'subjectivity is, in its essence, passion, at its maximum infinite, personally interested passion for one's eternal happiness' (CUP, 1:33/SKS 7, 39). Here, interest seems to serve merely as a qualifier for *lidenskab*, while in other places this relationship is reversed: 'the expression for subjectivity's utmost exertion is the infinitely passionate interest in its eternal happiness' (CUP, 1:53/SKS 7, 57). Either Climacus the humorist is playing with us – always a possibility – or these terms are more or less interchangeable. 'Interested Passion' and 'Passionate Interest' are equally valid names for full subjectivity; does this mean that each of these two names contains a tautology? Climacus implies that they do not:

> As soon as one takes subjectivity away, and passion from subjectivity, and *infinite interest from passion*, there is in general no decision at all, whether on this or any other problem.
>
> (CUP, 1:33/SKS 7, 39; emphasis added)

So Climacus *does* regard passion and interest as separable, and therefore distinct. And it is here that the flaw in the argument from contiguity becomes apparent: if passion and interest are the same thing, why does Climacus use these terms – passion, interest and infinite – in such regular and somewhat awkward concatenations? If the terms are genuinely interchangeable, the only purpose such clustering could have is rhetorical intensification. Though this remains a possibility, the separability of interest and passion cited above suggests something more substantive.

This conceptual separability of *interesse*, however, does not dispose of the object-centered, dispositional sense of the term evident in Westphal's reading. Yet the *Postscript*'s discussion of subjectivity does contain important uses of *interesse* that would seem to go beyond this prosaic sense of interest and require the elements of non-thetic self-referentiality and immediacy crucial to the specialized use of *interesse* I've argued for. The object-directed sense is already volatilized in this passage:

> In the infinite, passionate interest in his eternal happiness, the subjectivity is, in his utmost exertion, at the utmost point, not where

there is no object (the imperfect and undialectical distinction) but where God is negatively present in the subjectivity, which in this interest is the form of the eternal happiness.

(CUP, 1:53/SKS 7, 57)

Climacus here seems to fold the concept of the object of such an interest (an 'imperfect and undialectial distinction') into the fabric of subjectivity itself. At the extreme point of subjectivity, this interest expresses itself in the 'negative presence' of God, the infinite gulf between the self and God as uncovered by immanence ('Religiousness A' as the *Postscript* describes this stage) which can only be bridged via a transcendent, paradoxical intervention on the part of the infinite (the Incarnation, which structures 'Religiousness B'). The self focused on its eternal salvation expresses the need for God, but in a way that would lead us to think its salvation is not an *object* of thought. The need for salvation expresses itself in all moments of subjectivity, not, it would seem, in specific cognitions about eternal *salighed*.

Immediate self-referentiality

Eternal blessedness represents 'the expression for subjectivity's utmost exertion' (CUP, 1:53/SKS 7, 57), and as such, an interest in *salighed* is a determinative characteristic for what Climacus calls 'the subjective thinker.' Importantly, Climacus tells us that such a subjective thinker's interest is *self*-directed, not just in the sense of being focused on the goal of personal salvation, but in a sense that it pervades all thought:

the subjective thinker as existing is essentially interested in his own thinking, is existing in it. Therefore, his thinking has another kind of reflection, namely that of inwardness, of possession, whereby it belongs to the subject and no-one else.

(CUP, 1:73/SKS 7, 73)

This passage (and equally CUP, 1:325/SKS 7, 296, which claims that 'actuality is interiority infinitely interested in existing, which the ethical individual is for himself') brings into focus what is wrong with the interpretation of *interesse* as a description of specific dispositions and gestures towards a different sense of what *interesse* might mean here. If the existing subjective thinker were 'interested in his own thinking' in the same sense that one is interested in football, then he would be continually reflecting on his own thinking, a sort of self-absorption that is clearly at odds with the active, projective sense of 'exist' (*eksistere*) that Climacus employs to describe the existence of the self. Such a self will be too bound up in reflection to interact meaningfully with the world, yet Climacus explicitly links interest and action: 'Ethically, the highest pathos is that of interestedness (which is expressed in that I, acting, transform the whole of my existence in relation to the object of interest)' (CUP, 1:390/SKS 7, 356). Christianity may want the subject to infinitely concern himself about himself (CUP, 1:130/SKS 7, 122), but not at the expense of agency.

Moreover, if I am interested in the *content* of my thought, then I am thinking about that content; this thought would then *itself* become an object of this interest, and so on *ad infinitum*. As we've seen, it is precisely in these circumstances that the concept of non-thetic states of thought, such as Sartrean pre-reflective self-consciousness, becomes invaluable, and a parallel consideration generated by Climacus' identi-fication of consciousness (*bevisthed*) with interestedness (*interesserethed*) compels us to place *interesse* in this non-thetic category. Here too, the phrase 'essentially interested in his own thinking' (CUP, 1:73/SKS 7, 73) only seems to be intelligible if *interesse* is taken to refer to a non-reflective aspect of thought, rather than designating the content of reflection. It would seem then, that *interesse* as Climacus uses the term (at least in this passage) partakes of the non-thetic character necessarily bound up with *interesse* in *Johannes Climacus*.

Self-referentiality is also implied by the passage just cited. The charac-ter of subjectivity is a state in which the self 'possesses' his thought, such that 'it belongs to the subject and no-one else' (CUP, 1:73/SKS 7, 73). We have shown that in other places, *interesse* and *bekymring* refer to a sense of presence with, involvement in, or ownership of, that which one per-ceives or contemplates. Here too, a sense of self-reflexive involvement is crucial to subjective thought; moreover, it is a key element missing in Climacus' descriptions of objective thinkers as 'absent-minded.' To think subjectively is not to think *about* oneself (that is, to make one's subjectivity an object for itself), but to think about *other* objects of thought such that one's relation to them comes into view. Even as early as *Either/Or*, this thought seems to be in play, in Judge William's picture of the ethically actualized self:

> But when one chooses oneself abstractly, then one does not choose oneself ethically. Not until a person has taken himself upon himself in the choice, has put on himself, has *so totally interpenetrated him-self that his every movement is accompanied by the consciousness of a responsibility for himself* – not until then has a person chosen himself ethically.
>
> (EO, 2:248/SKS 3, 237, my emphasis)

This could superficially be read as a counsel of self-absorption, but our new understanding of *interesse* suggests instead that this 'consciousness of responsibility' will be a *way* of thinking rather than a *content* of thought.

For instance, the self apprehends ethical injunctions as being *about* them, even though they take the form of generalizations that hold good for all persons: 'that it [the ethical] pertains to all human beings is in a sense not at all relevant to him, except as a shadow that accompanies the ethical clarity in which he lives' (CUP, 1:143/SKS 7, 133). Despite its general character, when viewed from the interested standpoint of the subjective thinker, the ethical addresses itself to them *individually*; it does not speak to persons in general 'any more than the police arrest human kind in general' (CUP, 1:320/SKS 7, 291). This is clearly the same account of the appropriation of ethical imperatives as we saw in *For Self-Examination*, where moral exemplars and imperatives of Scripture provide a call to action in the form of an evaluative judgment specifically directed at the individual reader. Though the reader is not contained in the objective content of Scripture, the reader *sees himself* therein, in an immediate, non-reflective apprehension of involvement. This essential meaning of the ethical is only apprehended through a mode of engagement where the self immediately relates itself to that which it contemplates, not as a posterior act of reflection but *in* its reflection.

Kierkegaard often speaks of subjective thought as 'double reflection,' 'redoubled' by virtue of the subjective thinker's relating the content of his thought back to himself. In the course of his excellent discussion of Kierkegaard in relation to Harry Frankfurt, Edward Mooney cashes out the phrase 'double reflection' at one point as 'reflection on reflection' and 'Concerned reflection *on* our reflections.'[10] I think it can be seen here why I think such descriptions are misleading if taken at face value. This may be a useful way of thinking about the formation of second-order volitions in Frankfurt, but for Kierkegaard, subjective thought does not consist principally in overt second-order reflective cognitions about our first-order cognitions (reflective or otherwise). Nor is a 'double reflection' a diachronic pairing of a first- and second-order thought. The 'doubleness' of double-reflection consists in the *conceptual* separability of the content of the thought and its relation to me as thinker, not their temporal or phenomenal separability.

To reiterate: the question that motivates *Philosophical Fragments* and *Postscript* is about the self's relation to *knowledge* (specifically, ethico-religious knowledge). Authentic subjectivity requires us to appropriate this knowledge in certain ways if we are to be said to be 'in truth;' for there is also a mode of knowing 'in which the knower knows nothing at all;' 'his knowing amounts to a delusion' (CUP, 1:52/SKS 7, 57), even if the objective, conceptual content of that knowledge is the same in both cases. We must enter a specific *state* if we are to properly comprehend the subject matter that pertains to subjectivity, a specific mode of appropriative relation. However, the immediacy pointed to in the previous paragraph suggests that our appropriation of this knowledge will not be something that occurs *after* we have learned the objective content of that knowledge, but will be somehow built into our cognitions about that knowledge *itself*. To examine what this might mean, and to complete our discussion of Anti-Climacus' troika of infinitized willing, feeling, and knowing, we must now turn to Kierkegaard's account of 'interested knowledge.'

Interested knowledge

Kierkegaard uses formulations such as 'interested knowledge' and 'concerned knowledge' in several places. The distinction between concerned knowledge and indifferent knowledge is central to the account of the self's search for transcendent meaning as described in 'Strengthening the Inner Being.' I claimed in the previous chapter that concerned knowledge is knowledge that the self finds itself *unable* to be indifferent to knowledge in which the self finds itself essentially involved in a way that structures its projects and actions. The term occurs again much later in *The Sickness Unto Death*, the preface of which declares that all 'Christian knowing' [*Erkjenden*] 'ought to be concerned,' as 'The concern is the relation to life, to the actuality of the personality' (SUD, 5/SKS 11, 117). This is contrasted with the 'indifferent' knowledge of scholarship. It already seems clear from these uses that 'concerned knowledge,' or, if we prefer, 'interested knowledge,' is not merely shorthand for knowledge that the subject finds diverting or engaging. Rather, 'interested knowledge' is knowledge in which we are deeply, indeed soteriologically, enmeshed: knowledge in which the subject essentially finds their relationship to the knowledge precisely in being a transcendent knowing spirit.

However, what *sort* of knowledge will the self be able to find itself so bound up in? The obvious answer is knowledge about oneself. Kierkegaard often endorses Socrates' injunction 'know thyself,' and in places, Anti-Climacus seems to develop a sort of morally normative epistemology that sounds superficially like an amplification of that injunction:

> The law for the development of the self with respect to knowing, insofar as it is the case that the self becomes itself, is that the increase degree of knowledge corresponds to the increase degree of self-knowledge, such that the more the self knows, the more it knows itself. If this does not happen, the more knowledge increases, the more it becomes a kind of inhuman knowledge, in the obtaining of which the human being's self is squandered.
>
> (SUD, 31/SKS 11, 147)

Seen under the ethical aspect of the moral requirement for conscious selfhood, an increase in knowledge that is not correspondingly an increase in *self*-knowledge would seem to constitute a waste of the capacity for knowledge. Superficially at least, Anti-Climacus appears to be suggesting that viewed from the perspective of the moral requirement to become oneself, any acquisition of knowledge that is not *about* oneself (or is not automatically accompanied by or can reasonably be expected to lead to such knowledge about oneself) is a morally illegitimate use of our epistemic capacities. Thus, as a result of the all-pervasive categorical reach of the ethical, the only permissible object of knowledge or inquiry appears to be myself.

The implications are enormous: if this *is* what Anti-Climacus is saying, then almost all fields of human inquiry are morally pernicious wastes of time. Philosophy, psychology, and sociology will only be legitimate insofar as they tell me about myself in a way that speaks to my moral condition. Astronomy, mathematics, and physics, which more or less by definition cannot contain me at all, will probably be illegitimate under *any* circumstances. Similar normative conclusions might be said to result from many metaethical positions (such as some versions of utilitarianism) though for very different reasons. It is also arguably implicit in much Hellenistic philosophy, in which even questions of atomic physics may only be legitimately asked insofar as they serve the ethical ends of promoting human happiness.[11] Disturbingly, such an attitude is indeed suggested at several points in the *Postscript*, and more clearly asserted in a note in which Kierkegaard explicitly connects the 'concept' of *interesse* (and the breakdown of *interesse* into *inter esse*, 'between being') with a 'ranking' of the sciences according to their capacity to serve the ends of existing:

On the Concepts *Esse* and *Inter-Esse*

A methodological experiment.

the various sciences should be ordered according to the different ways in which they accentuate being; and how their relation to being gives reciprocal advantage.

Ontology }
Mathematics }

This certainty is the absolute – here thought and being are one, but in return these are scientific hypotheses.

Existential-Knowledge (JP, 197/*Pap.* IV C 100, *n.d.* 1842–43)

In this sketch, Kierkegaard proposes an 'ordering' of the fields of human enquiry (*videnskaber*) according to their relation to being. Sciences such as ontology and mathematics can only yield hypothetical results; even though (particularly in the case of mathematics) they claim to be the perfect, inviolable unity of being and thought. Accordingly, they offer scant 'reciprocal advantage' to the interested thinker, whose 'interest' expresses precisely that she relates knowledge back to existence and *knows* in order to *be*. Certain sciences will, it seems, 'give back' more to the existentially concerned subject than others.

Yet in *Sickness Unto Death* and elsewhere, the claim appears to be not that certain *objects* of knowledge are morally illegitimate, but that certain *modes of knowing* are so. In a *Papirer* entry near the one cited above, Kierkegaard provides an interesting but never-developed sketch:

The Interested Knowing
and its Forms
Which knowledge is disinterested [*Erkjenden er interesseløs*]
    it has its interest in a third (for example, beauty, truth, etc.)
    which is not myself
    therefore has no continuity.

The interested knowledge enters with Christianity.

    The question of authority
    of historical continuity.
    of doubt.
    of faith.

Is knowledge higher than faith? Not at all. (JP, 2283/*Pap.* IV C 99 *n.d.* 1842–43)

There is a lot going on in this skeletal sketch. Kierkegaard here claims that *dis*interested knowing lacks 'continuity' (*Continuitet*, a key term in the dispositional psychology of both *Either/Or* II and *Sickness Unto Death*). Such knowledge attends to various objects (and here the objects in question are the objects of traditional sciences such as metaphysics and aesthetics), and as such, the reflections which make up this knowledge are scattered across the more or less self-standing domain(s) of human enquiry. There is no common thread running between them. The implication in this sketch is that only knowledge of *my self* can yield essential continuity between forms of knowledge.

Yet Kierkegaard does not speak of the 'object' of knowledge, that is, what knowledge is knowledge *of*, but rather the 'interest' of such knowledge. The interest is in a 'third' (*et Tredie*), rather than the object (which presumably constitutes a 'second' to myself as 'first'). What is in question here is apparently not the actual object of knowing itself, but that which motivates the process of knowing or the end towards which it is directed. For instance, suppose I study Bronzino's *Venus and Cupid* as an art critic, employing the techniques of aesthetics. The actual knowledge I acquire may consist of thoughts about the resonances of the painting – the subtleties of expression and style, the erotically charged undercurrents of the painting with their unsettling oedipal resonances, and so forth. But the 'interest' of the inquiry will be, ultimately, beauty; a psychologist might pick up on *precisely* the same aspects of the painting as I do, but the interest of her inquiry will be the mind of Bronzino, not the beauty of Bronzino. Of course, our different 'interests' will direct our inquiries in distinct ways and limit the sorts of questions each of us can ask and the aspects of the painting and its context we attend to. Ultimately, though, when asked what we have been studying, we can both reply with perfect correctness 'Bronzino's *Venus and Cupid*.'

In having its interest in 'a third…which is not myself' (*et Tredie… hvilket ikke er mig selv*) disinterested knowing constitutes the substance of inquiries for which the ultimate *telos* is something external to my own existence. Continuity can only be secured by having *myself* as the 'third,' as the interest of my knowledge. For some reason, it seems, self-hood is capable of providing continuity to knowledge in a way that other interests of knowledge cannot. Why should this be the case? Kierkegaard cites 'truth' as one of the interests that cannot provide such continuity – yet truth can be said to be the interest of enquiries such as chemistry or mathematics. Such enquiries, moreover, have histories; their contents consist of discoveries that only have their validity by virtue of their place in a developing narrative. What sort of continuity, then, does Kierkegaard take it that knowledge which has its interest in oneself has that is lacking in knowledge that is directed to some other 'third'?

This language of the *Tredie* is of course familiar from the structures of consciousness and selfhood articulated in *Johannes Climacus* and *The Sickness Unto Death*, respectively. In these instances, this 'third' is relational rather than a discrete, separate entity. In the case of consciousness, the third is the self-reflexive relationship between ideality and reality that constitutes the conscious self. In *Sickness'* structure of selfhood, the third is the self-reflexive relationship between a human being's constituent internal oppositions that qualifies the whole as a self. In each case, the self is not to be found in the *relata*, but in the way they are related by a self-relating relation.

Mark C. Taylor has argued that Kierkegaard's model of selfhood is non-substantivist, but that there is still a kind of *de facto* substance provided by the self's presence at all moments of selfhood.[12] Thus whatever the self happens to be doing or contemplating, the self as site-of-contemplation constitutes[13] something continuous in all the discrete moments of contemplation or action. It is in this sense that the self attains the predicate 'eternal' ('and next to God there is nothing as eternal as a self' – SUD, 53/ SKS 11, 168), not eternal in the sense of beyond temporality but in the same sense that Louis Althusser, drawing on Freud, speaks of the eternality of ideology.[14] It would seem, then, that it is *this* sense of continuity that is provided by the self as the interest of knowledge. Only through being unified, in the context of a self that self-reflexively holds them together, do the various thoughts and apprehensions that constitute knowledge of an object attain genuine unity. They cannot attain such unity through their internal thematic coherence or interrelation alone. Just as *Johannes Climacus* claims that reflection does not happen 'on paper' but only attains its actuality through individual, concrete consciousnesses, so here it seems the unity of knowledge is only secured through its being knowledge *for* a knowing subject. It is by virtue of *existing* that the subject is able to give continuity to knowledge, while disregarding existence will only yield 'the eternity of abstraction' (CUP, 1:312-13/SKS 7, 284-5). Yet the self's existence alone does not guarantee continuity (as, for instance, the bare, formal unity of apperception allows the Kantian subject to hold different perceptions together as the apprehension of a unified object persisting in time). Existence is a constant process of becoming, and as such, the existing subject is in a constant state of flux; to give continuity to thought therefore requires that thought be *suffused* by a sense of the existing self:

> ... the difficulty for the existing person is to give existence the continuity without which everything just disappears. An abstract continuity is no continuity, and that the existing person exists essentially hinders continuity, whereas passion is the momentary continuity that at once constrains and is the impetus of motion.
>
> (CUP, 1:312/SKS 7, 284)

The existing self can lose its continuity by virtue of its temporally structured nature as becoming in time rather than being a fixed essence. To avoid such loss requires that its thought, knowledge and apprehension be directed, whatever their objective content, to the self's status as existing. The danger here is one of abstraction, which removes the self from existence, and can only be overcome through *interesse*:

> Abstraction is disinterested, but to exist is for an existing person his highest interest. The existing person thus continually has a τελοσ and it is this τελοσ that Aristotle speaks of when he says (*De anima*, III, 10, 2) that at νουςθεωρετιχος [theoretical thought] is different from νουσ πραχτιχοσ τω τελει [practical thought in its *telos*].
>
> (CUP, 1:313/SKS 7, 285)

Aristotelian theoretical thought here would correspond to what Climacus also calls 'pure thought,' which, being governed in its development by its own internal laws, has its *telos* immanently. 'Practical thought,' by contrast, has an external *telos*; it is undertaken in service of some end outside itself. Interested knowing, then, is apparently directed at the self, though not in the sense of having the self as the *object* of knowledge (though it *may* have that object), but as the *interest* that attends the knowledge, not as its content, but as its *telos*. This teleology is related to the fact of my existence, once I see this existence as ethically qualified, for the ethical makes existence infinitely interested (CUP, 1:315/SKS 7, 287).

Gregor Malantschuk draws upon this structural echo of both *Johannes Climacus* and *Sickness Unto Death* when he treats 'interested knowing' as 'a knowing which is especially concerned with personality, for only in personality can there arise incommensurability between actuality and thought or between two opposing positions... the objective position of "the system" is penetrated by a personal interest in an actuality which lies outside the boundaries of immanental thinking.'[15] Note that Malantschuk here does not claim that 'interested knowing' *excludes* systematic knowledge, but that it 'penetrates' it with a 'personal interest' that refers beyond abstract thought to the concrete actuality that can never be captured in abstraction. Abstraction by its nature is 'disinterested,' and 'disinterestedness' is the expression of *indifference* towards actuality (CUP, 1:318/SKS 7, 290), a state utterly incompatible with an apprehension of one's existence in ethical terms. Abstraction is disinterested, but 'the existing person is infinitely interested in existing' (CUP, 1:302/SKS 7, 275). Malantschuk interprets Kierkegaard's claim that 'Interested knowing enters with Christianity' as 'to be understood in the sense that only Christianity provides an example of an absolute unity of the eternal and the personal.'[16] Kierkegaard's claim that 'Religiousness B,' the religious position centered around passionate appropriation of the paradox of the God-in-time (Christ as 'God-Man'), represents the highest point of the development of the self, comes into play here. It is only in the apprehension of the God-Man as bridging the absolute gap between the eternal and finite human selfhood that the particular and the eternal can ultimately be brought into true relation.

So interested knowledge is knowledge of the self, but the self is not necessarily its direct 'object' of knowledge. Rather, knowledge of facts/objects/states of affairs will be suffused with 'personal interest,' interest which relates directly back to the self in its particularity (its personality). All questions of inquiry (even speculative inquiry) will be attended by a nonconceptualized 'question' of equal importance: 'how does all this relate to *me*?' In the Bronzino example, let us say that I study aesthetics in order to clarify my own existence or find meaning. In that case, the interest of the inquiry will not be beauty *simpliciter*, but beauty as this (somehow) relates to me and my existence. Perhaps in coming to understand the beauty of the image I build upon my understanding of my relation to a world of beautiful things which consolidates meaning for me. Perhaps, in contemplating Bronzino's depiction of the human form, I experience a wonder which opens up to me the ethical import of the Other's ability to so transfix me.[17] Perhaps, in a rather Levinasian way, I experience the look upon Venus' face as *overflowing* with inexpressible meaning that reveals to me the depths and preciousness of human beings. I am nowhere in Bronzino, just as a naturalist is (usually) nowhere in the nature he studies, yet both of us must discover that the meaning of what we study lies in ourselves (CUP, 1:247/SKS 7, 224). And that which attends my studies is not the objective content of that thought; rather it attends them superveniently and changes the *quality* of those studies, investing them with a personal teleology not contained within them objectively. So it turns out we can be ethical *and* be astronomers after all. Or, for that matter, philosophers.

Interest and curiosity

This change in quality is perhaps best thrown into negative relief by Kierkegaard and Climacus in their descriptions of the condition of thinkers whose thought lacks this subjective interpenetration of *interesse*. Climacus describes the objective thinker as 'abstract,' 'absent-minded,' 'inhuman,' and 'insane.' Anti-Climacus goes so far as to call this thought 'fantastical.' Fantastic knowing (SUD, 31/SKS 11, 147) is also the name Anti-Climacus gives to that species of knowing that (like fantastical willing and fantastical feeling) loses itself in infinitization by losing its relation to the concrete actuality of the existing subject. Such selves are so absorbed in abstract thought or imagination as to be utterly disconnected from their reality as existing human beings. The 'squandering' of the capacity for knowledge that Anti-Climacus speaks of consists in the failure of this capacity to serve the teleology given to it by the structure of the knowing subject.

Nonetheless, while interest may well attach to fields of inquiry that do not 'contain' us at all, some fields will not only *demand* such interest, but that interest will direct the *conceptual content* of inquiry as well. In other words, while a disinterested astronomer may be perfectly competent *qua* astronomer, other fields of inquiry *need* interest if their conceptual content is to be grasped at all. This is made clearest negatively, in those cases where matters that should concern the self are treated entirely objectively. We have already seen an example of this in the discussion of disinterested biblical scholarship in *For Self-Examination*. The same failure, caused by a lack of supervenient self-reflexivity, is discussed in *The Concept of Anxiety*. Without *interesse*, the 'interest' of inquiry is reduced to what, in that work, is referred to as 'curiosity' (*nysgjerrighed*). Vigilius Haufniensis declares it to be a form of demonic flight from oneself to be engaged in 'curiosity that never becomes more than curiosity,' which he places in the rather non-illustrious company of indolence, dishonest self-deception, weakness, negligence, and 'stupid' busyness (CA, 138/SKS 4, 438-9). If this flies in the face of our assumption that intellectual curiosity is usually laudable, it needs to be understood that Haufniensis is talking about a very specific domain of inquiry.

In the context of *Concept of Anxiety* curiosity is brought into the discussion of the appropriate 'mood' (*stemning*) in which to discuss sin. One cannot, according to Haufniensis, adequately discuss sin from the standpoint of 'the experimenting inquisitiveness that wants to treat sin as a curiosity' (CA, 57/SKS 4, 361). Any discussion of soteriology must relate itself back to the sinful status of the one discussing it, even though in its generality the discussion does not contain any specific sinner conceptually. Sin addresses itself to the individual, and so any impersonal, non-reflexive discussion of it misses the *essential meaning* of sin. For this reason, Haufniensis argues that none of the various sciences through which sin can be discussed – aesthetics, metaphysics, even ethics – will be appropriate to the study of Sin (CA, 14-20/SKS 4, 321-8). Consider the person who discusses morality in terms of social etiquette, or political expediency. This person has, in a very real sense, not understood what morality *means*. But has the person who spends time (years, perhaps) discussing the finer points of moral theory without stopping to consider how the actuality of their life stands in light of that theory – whether *they* are in the right or wrong – understood morality either? Such an incoherence points to something deeper than straightforward hypocrisy. Sin, of course, for Kierkegaard, goes beyond ethical categories and is a religious term, and as such addresses itself absolutely to the individual (the disinterested moral philosopher might consider himself entitled to inquire as to the morality of *others* while the religious individuality, according to Kierkegaard, cannot distract itself in this way). Therefore, to speak about sin in a way which does not relate it essentially to the speaker is to treat it purely as a curiosity, as a topic for disengaged intellectual contemplation rather a living concern for the individual *qua* individual.

The above considerations, taken in sum, reveal that at least one crucial sense of *interesse* at work in the *Postscript* does partake of the elements we discerned in Climacus' earlier use of the term in *Johannes Climacus*. While superficially the Climacus of the *Postscript* uses 'interest' in a way that does not seem to go beyond the prosaic interest-in-a-particular-object sense, closer examination reveals that the key elements of *interesse* as we've understood it throughout this book are also at work here. The character of *interesse* as a non-reflective, supervenient self-referentiality that attends thought, and *immediately* directs all thought back to the self without making the self the *object* of thought, is also a key feature of the *Postscript*'s account of subjectivity. Without it, Climacus would endorse a kind of inhuman, anti-intellectual self-obsession; with it, he can articulate a manner of thinking that is shot through with subjectivity while allowing the self to act as a genuine moral agent.

Of course this doesn't mean that this account of subjectivity (or indeed perfected moral agency) is any easier to achieve. A self that is constantly uncovering more and more the extent of its sinfulness still requires a salvation that transcends the immanent and bridges the infinite gulf between the self and redemption. The demands of an interested engagement with the world will be more and more strenuous the more the self sees itself as guilty by virtue of ethical requirements it cannot shrug off but equally cannot satisfy. Thus the *Postscript* amplifies the earlier Climacan point that *interesse* confers a teleology on thought, by giving flesh to the *telos* that informs interested selfhood – namely, an eternal *salighed*, a transcendent meaning, justification, absolution, and satisfaction that the self in its immanence cannot provide itself.

Conclusion

The foregoing has thrown light on an under-examined term in Kierkegaard's descriptive armory and developed an instructive reading in which it plays a central role. *Interesse*, a term generally ignored or rolled into other, more prominent terms in Kierkegaard's lexicon of mind, has been shown both to have a distinct, independent meaning, and to play a crucial role in Kierkegaard's phenomenology of moral experience. An important and distinct sense of *interesse* has been recovered from the schematic accounts of consciousness and the ontology of selfhood and shown to ramify through these structures and the phenomena that attend them.

Moreover, a discussion of *interesse* has been shown to be a valuable path to take through the Kierkegaardian corpus in that it opens up aspects of Kierkegaardian moral psychology that otherwise remain obscured. The immediate, non-thetic self-reflexivity built into thought and perception themselves that we have shown to be picked out by the term 'interest' emerge as key features of Kierkegaard's account of thought and perception. Attention to these elements has allowed us to deepen our understanding of key Kierkegaardian tropes, such as self-recognition, mirror metaphors, and the moral blindness of love.

The self-directedness that attends interested thought has also shown a teleology to be embedded in cognition itself. Kierkegaard's account of selfhood is avowedly teleological in that the ultimate goal of selfhood is variously expressed as eternal blessedness/happiness or 'rest[ing] transparently in the power that established it' (SUD, 14/SKS 11, 130). But the reading of *interesse* we have developed here shows this teleology to be derivable from factors built into the very structure of consciousness itself, even if that teleology requires revelation both to move to an understanding of the self's sinfulness and to achieve the salvation it craves.

Accordingly, in an important sense, the true value of the preceding exegesis of *interesse* is not so much in what it uncovers but what it gestures towards. What we have developed, in a sense, is a prolegomena to a Kierkegaardian theory of moral perceptualism, for what *interesse* points towards is a highly specific model of moral cognition. Under such a model, 'vision' rather than 'deliberation' or 'reflection' stands for what is central to successful moral cognition; the normative locus of moral psychology shifts from practical reason and deliberative intention to distinctive modes of apprehension.

Our reading of *interesse* has begun to scope out a Kierkegaardian model of moral cognition which has as its *telos* the immediate coextensiveness of vision, volition, and action. The perfected moral agent – such as never is and possibly never *can* be found – sees, judges and acts in one unitary moment. It is in the moments that characteristically *do* intervene between perception and action, the moments of indecision, hesitation, and (as developed in this book) failure to perceive our own implicatedness in that which we see, that the morally 'fallen' character of human agency is to be located. It is in this space, within a framework laid out by Kierkegaard the philosopher in the service of Kierkegaard the theologian, that Kierkegaard the psychologist diagnoses the evasions and self-deceptions endemic to human beings.

Let's return to the thought-experiment we began with. You'll recall that you and I, two remarkably similar people in all relevant respects, are watching television in our respective homes. Confronted with harrowing scenes of human suffering caused by some distant natural disaster, we experience identical affective responses (pity, sadness and a sense that something must be done). Yet you, *without thinking*, leap to your feet and reach for the phone, dialing the Red Cross to see how you can help. I, by contrast, remain in my seat, my emotional response translating neither into immediate action (as in your case) nor even the thought that *I* should do something. Neither of us has acted reflectively or deliberatively, yet only my response would be described as *thoughtless*. I could be morally blamed, while you, despite the seemingly automatic way in which you've acted, would be morally praiseworthy.

I think that far more of our moral lives are like this than is generally supposed, and if we find this example puzzling, this is partly because so much of moral philosophy is couched in terms of deliberation. Discussions in ethics notoriously tend to make use of pulse-quickening examples involving speeding trolleys, ticking bombs, drowning wives,[1] and burning houses containing famous French theologians and good-for-nothing servants who just happen to be our parents.[2] Yet dilemma cases, even mundane ones, are relatively rare occurrences. Most of our moral 'decisions' seem to be almost reflexive in character ('oh, let me help you with that') rather than deliberative; and when we do in fact deliberate it tends to take the form of weighing moral considerations against nonmoral ones ('I should stop to give that hitchhiker a lift, but I'm worried about my safety and I am also running late') rather than weighing up competing moral facts.

Habit and culture certainly play a role in these reflexive responses, yet we seem to have a real sense that at least *some* of them run far deeper than that. In at least some cases these reflexive responses are somehow deeply expressive of a person's subjectivity, for we can be fully *present in* these immediate actions in a way that we aren't present in our 'absent-minded' habits. Perhaps they even express our moral character *better* than actions that are the outcome of moral deliberation (which can be, though doesn't have to be, 'impersonal' in character). It's sometimes claimed that actions that don't proceed from any sort of at least theoretically articulatable principle are inherently nonethical, however otherwise admirable they may be. Thus Norman Lillegard can claim that Oskar Schindler's passion for saving the lives of his Jewish workers was not essentially ethical because it lacked 'a rational motivational self-concept.'[3] What I want to suggest here, though, is that an immediate response such as Schindler's could still be ethical, even if his moral vision failed him on other occasions; his saving of lives might indeed represent a seeing of the other as neighbor, even while his marital infidelities suggest he failed to see his wife in those terms.

Does the Kierkegaardian model of moral cognition leave us any better equipped to understand what's happened in our thought experiment? I think it does, and not just in the ways I've been able to discuss here. John J. Davenport has shown, in a way that deserves serious attention, that Haufniensis' account of 'earnestness' as 'the acquired originality of disposition' that prevents repetition from devolving into habit (CA, 149/SKS 4, 484) has an important role to play in reconciling our divergent intuitions about moral agency. For if Haufniensis is right, earnestness conjoins the free volitional character of existentialist will (answering to our intuitions about the deliberateness of actions properly subject to moral dis/approbation) with the stable dispositional states required by aretaic conceptions of moral agency (answering to our intuitions about moral character).[4] In our imagined scenario, you have certainly acted with earnestness, which is why what you do isn't merely absentminded habit. It may well be a product of your settled dispositions formed, perhaps, by years of Aristotelian training in the moral virtues, but it is somehow permeated by your subjectivity nonetheless – you are fully *in* what you do here.

Our discussion of self-reflexivity in moral vision has also given us a powerful new grammar of moral motivation, one that allows us to redescribe your actions in ways that better conform to our intuitions about your action's moral worth. You have *seen yourself* in the situation that presented itself to you. 'You,' of course, were in no way the *object* of your cognitions, which were entirely taken up with the suffering of others you saw onscreen. Yet you nonetheless *recognized* yourself in the situation in that you saw it as *directly implicating you personally*. The suffering you saw *claimed you*, made a *demand of you specifically* and revealed you as standing in a certain moral relationship to it. You saw yourself in an evaluative light: every second spent on the couch was already a deficit of action that made you *guilty*. None of this was in any way thematized in your consciousness during the experience, yet it is essential to our description of what was praiseworthy in your consciousness at that time.

The possibilities that opened up for you in that apprehension appeared to you as *your* possibilities rather than merely possibilities for a generalized 'everyone,' which of course would amount to no one in particular. And you inhabited those possibilities so immediately that your perception, imagination and volition were all immediately combined; effectively, they were co-referent. And our sense is that this is how it *should* be, that this is how we *should* react to moral demands; if in fact temporal gaps open up between these elements in moral cognition, this shows us the human, all too human failings that necessarily beset finite beings considered as moral agents.

As for me, in the situation described in the experiment, I'm exactly like all the failures of moral vision we've encountered in Kierkegaard. Like the drunken peasant, I've failed to see my involvement in the situation before me, that it makes demands of me that I cannot be indifferent to. Like David, I've failed to see myself as morally implicated by what's presented to me, in this case on television rather than through a strange parable. Perhaps I hear the phrase 'You can help by calling this number' on TV, but to make the link between the 'you' in this phrase and the 'me' sitting on the couch would require a personalized reminder such as Nathan has to give David ('That means *you*, Pat!'). If I simply sit there pondering the moral evil of this suffering, I am like the person who sees the mirror but not themselves therein. Perhaps, like the person suffering from the despair of infinitized feeling, I lose myself in a rapture of pity for the suffering millions without thereby *actually* pitying any *actual* person. And like the person who discusses sin in a mood of detached intellectual curiosity, my thoughts about the moral dimension of the situation fail to be truly *moral*. I may have studied moral philosophy for some years now, but if I don't see my own moral status reflected to me in these thoughts, do I really *understand* morality *at all*?[5]

A day later we meet in the street and our talk quickly turns to the disaster. When you mention calling the Red Cross, I can't help but feel admiration. 'What a wonderful person, to just leap up and call the Red Cross like that!' But here again, I've missed the point. You aren't merely a figure to be *admired*. I might legitimately admire you for your outstanding singing voice and skill at tap dancing, as through sheer contingent fact I happen to lack these talents and can do nothing to remedy this. But your exemplary *moral* conduct stands as a task for emulation, in light of which static admiration is exposed as a strategy of evasion.

The task that emerges from this exegetical discussion is to reconstruct Kierkegaard's moral psychology along these lines, to see how far a Kierkegaardian picture of moral experience can take us. Our discussion of *interesse* serves both to clear the ground (by disposing of certain needlessly diachronic or over-ontologized descriptions of Kierkegaard's model of thought) and to trace the outlines of such a reconstruction. Such a model of agency will be unique and raise important challenges to many of our conceptions of volition. The ambiguous character of vision, containing both volitional and non-volitional elements, will direct us to look for subjective agency in new and philosophically interesting places. Already in our discussion of the way *interesse*, by virtue of its non-thetic character, allows intentional thought to be 'shot through' with subjectivity, we have begun to discern ways in which agency might be preserved in such an account, ways very different to those we are familiar with. Attention to the central role of vision in Kierkegaard's moral psychology, and the role of *interesse* therein, may reveal other ways in which Kierkegaard can contribute to our understanding of what it is to be a moral being.

Discerning what is of continuing value in Kierkegaard and deploying it in live philosophical contexts remains a vital and largely under-championed role for Kierkegaardians. However much we may ultimately choose to leave aside of the Kierkegaardian project, his thought remains a living, astonishingly rich repository of philosophical insight. Whatever the achievements of Kierkegaard exegesis in the century-and-a-half since his death, the task of mining Kierkegaard's thought for its vast philosophical potential has only just begun.

Notes

Introduction

1. Using the terms more or less interchangeably, in accordance with their pre-theoretical use in everyday language. I'm certainly not using 'character' in the *derivative* moral sense in which we accuse someone of 'lacking character.' Seigel (2005) p. 317.
2. Aristotle (1975) p. 120.
3. See for instance Urmson (1988) p. 92.
4. Aristotle (1975) p. 120.
5. Aristotle (1975) p. 121.
6. Williams (1981) p. 14.
7. My thanks to Poul Lübcke and Paul Muench for pointing this objection out to me.
8. Korsgaard (1996) pp. 247–8. My defense of what Korsgaard would reject as a form of romanticism depends largely on a belief that the dichotomy between an action's being either passively impelled or actively chosen is not exhaustive, precisely because the distinction is more ambiguous than it may appear.
9. This seems to be what Mooney has in mind in his claim that, for Kierkegaard, asking 'what will my *response* now be?' in reaction to an evaluatively-structured apprehension of a morally obligating situation (such as coming across a roadside accident) can constitute an 'acting in reflecting.' Though the phrase 'acting in reflecting' may sound somewhat un-Kierkegaardian, I think it is entirely compatible with Kierkegaard if we take it that this refers to an Aristotelian deliberation on the appropriate *means* of responding rather than a deliberation on whether I *should* respond. Mooney (1996) p. 67.
10. Aristotle (1975) p. 41: 'Now we deliberate not about ends but about the means to ends. For neither does a doctor deliberate whether he should make people healthy, nor an orator whether he should persuade, nor a statesman whether he should enact good laws and enforce them, nor anyone else about whatever the end may be, but positing an end, each of them considers how and by what means that end can be brought about.' This has seemed puzzling to many. Surely, I can deliberate about whether or not to become a doctor, orator or statesman? Don't people at the start of their careers do this all the time? But the point is surely that once we have *posited* the end, it remains static relative to the means which it presents and which can be assented to or vacated on the basis of deliberation. The prior deliberation on whether to *be* a doctor takes place relative to some other fixed end ('I want a career where I help people,' 'I want to use my talents in a noble profession' and so on).
11. Outside of these continents, his reception has been more sporadic. The history of Kierkegaard reception in Japan is a distinctive one; see

Mortensen (1996). In Australasia, Kierkegaard remains a marginal figure, although I suspect his work is somewhat more popular than his near-total exclusion from university syllabi would suggest. See McDonald (2009).

12. Poole (1998) p. 62.
13. Merold Westphal notes that it is tempting to say that 'if Kierkegaard were writing today he would use the term "phenomenology" where he actually uses "psychology"' but argues that such a substitution creates as many questions as it solves. Nonetheless, we can remain within Kierkegaard's terminology while maintaining that his psychology is developed phenomenologically or is fundamentally phenomenological in character. See Westphal (1987a) p. 40.
14. This is Kinya Masugata's description of Kierkegaard (playing on Kierkegaard's description of Socrates) as quoted in Mortensen (1996) p. 100.
15. Despite its rich descriptive value, Kierkegaard's psychology, as Westphal notes, 'is a clinical psychology. Its starting point is sickness, its goal diagnosis and therapy. It is theory for the sake of therapy.' Westphal (1987a) p. 40.
16. Rudd (2001) p. 140.
17. Russell (1959) p. 305. Russell dismisses Sartre's project by comparing it to what, to him, seems like a gross absurdity: 'It is as though one were to turn Dostoevsky's novels into philosophic text-books.' Most Kierkegaardians and a great many others (including an increasing number of Analytic philosophers) would, I suspect, be entirely comfortable with approaching an author like Dostoevsky in such a way.
18. I'm grateful to a comment of Anthony Rudd on an earlier version of this work for helping me to see this.
19. For one specific use of the insights developed by this approach to make useful interventions into contemporary debates, see Stokes (2006).
20. Hannay (1998).
21. For a discussion on this topic, see Furtak (2008) esp. pp. 59–66.
22. Poole (1998) pp. 58–60.
23. ibid. p. 64.
24. Strawser (1994) pp. 639–40.

1 The Interesting and the Interested: Stages on a Concept's Way

1. Variants on the lexeme occur in the *Samlede Værker* with the following frequency: *interessant*, 59, *interessante*, 45, *interessantere*, 6, *interessantes*, 2, *interessanteste*, 9, *Interesserethed*, 9, *Interesseretheden*, 2, *Interesseløshed*, 3, *Interesseløs*, 8. It is notable that *Interesserethed(en)* ('interestedness') occurs almost exclusively in the Climacan writings.
2. Nordentoft notes that Kierkegaard's use of the word changes over time, although he does not outline how (except to say that 'Concern' [*Bekymring*] occupies the same conceptual space as *interesse* in the Upbuilding Discourses). Nordentoft (1978) pp. 84–5.

3. Although it is not the sense which is examined in the present work, Kierkegaard does use the 'vested interest' sense of the term critically in a journal entry from 1854, where he berates the 'practical world' for lacking 'a concept of or respect for uninterestedness, disinterestedness [*Uinteresserethed, Interesseløshed*] (JP, 549/*Pap.* XI² A 124 *n.d.* 1854).
4. Koch (1992) p. 25.
5. Heiberg (1861) p. 371.
6. Koch (1992) p. 28.
7. ibid. p. 42.
8. ibid. p. 50.
9. ibid. p. 34.
10. ibid. p. 44–8.
11. Kant (1997) p. 63n.
12. Kant (1951) p. 41.
13. Kant (1997) pp. 41, 43.
14. Kant (1951) p. 44.
15. ibid. pp. 45–6.
16. Schopenhauer (1966) pp. 186, 196.
17. Kant (1997) p. 54.
18. ibid. p. 63n.
19. ibid. p. 25n.
20. ibid. pp. 63–4.
21. Wood (1990) p. 143.
22. Hegel (1977) p. 194.
23. ibid. p. 240.
24. Wood (1990) p. 152.
25. *From The Papers of One Still Living* and *The Concept of Irony* are notably absent from Kierkegaard's overviews of his authorship in *The Point of View For My Work As An Author* and 'A Glance at a Contemporary Effort in Danish Literature' in *Concluding Unscientific Postscript*. Whatever historical and philosophical value these works may have (and however much *Irony* in particular prefigures crucial Kierkegaardian themes), Kierkegaard clearly came to regard *Either/Or* as the start of the Kierkegaardian program.
26. Watkin (2001) pp. 231–32.
27. Davenport (2001a) p. 85.
28. Frankfurt (1988) p. 17. Importantly, the aesthete may well have what Frankfurt calls 'second-order desires,' without these actually becoming volitions. The aesthetic curiosity that Judge William ascribes to his friend would be quite consistent with the aesthete forming a *desire to desire* marriage and stability, just to see what this is like, without actually *willing* that such a desire become his effective desire. The work of self-construction is done by the self-identification implicit in volition, rather than the fact of second-orderness itself.
29. Koch (1992) p. 49.
30. A point Mooney makes in similar terms: Mooney (2007) pp. 9–10.
31. Cross (1998) p. 146.
32. ibid. p. 148.
33. In the *Postscript*, Climacus interprets de silentio as 'a reflecting person who, with the *tragic hero* as *terminus a quo*, with *the interesting as Confinium* and

the religious paradigmatic irregularity as *terminus ad quem*, continually, as it were, runs up against the understanding's forehead' (CUP, 1:262/SKS 7, 238). In other words, this particular use of *det interessante* is to be understood as the result of the impossibility of representing the 'existence-collision' which is the object of de silentio's inquiry (CUP, 1:261/SKS 7, 238). De silentio *must*, according to Climacus, be presented as holding to this unusual interpretation of the interesting as he must remain essentially detached. If he did not posess the detachment of the interesting, he would be *merely* an aesthete, whereas were he fully involved in the religious categories he describes, he could say nothing about them.
34. Malantschuk (1993) p. 67.
35. Koch (1992) p. 125.

2 The Structure of Consciousness

1. As C. Stephen Evans notes, the self's relatedness to 'the other' does not necessarily have to be towards God and can be directed towards other individuals, the family, the nation-state, and so forth (for more on this topic, see Chapter 6). However, he stresses that this does not negate the ultimately theological grounding of the ontology of *Sickness*, or the role of God as the foundation of authentic selfhood (the attainment of which is the ethical task that arises from the ontology). Alastair Hannay takes a much stronger position. In rejecting the interpretation of the *Sickness* ontology that a self can only escape despair by conceiving of itself as divinely established, Hannay argues that the established nature of selfhood means that despair is always already a flight *from* the divine. Rather than being an ontological malaise that can only be cured by a turn towards God, despair is an ontological malaise occasioned precisely by a turning *away* from God. See Evans (1997) pp. 8–9; Hannay (1994) p. 11. See also Dreyfus' recent revision of his earlier understanding of the nature of the other to which we relate: Dreyfus (2008) and Hannay's reply: Hannay (2008a).
2. I am grateful to Myron B. Penner for this observation.
3. Dunning (1994) p. 204.
4. Descartes (1986) p. 13.
5. Rudd (1998) p. 73.
6. We here follow the assumption made in most (though not all) of the secondary literature that at least Chapter I of *Pars Secunda* is written in Climacus' voice. This approach (exemplified by the Hongs) is criticized by commentators such as Michael Strawser, but with respect to at least some of *Johannes Climacus* it seems, if not indisputably correct, at least acceptable. While everything prior to *Pars Secunda* is written *about* Johannes Climacus rather than by him, the sudden cessation of the narration that characterizes the rest of the work does imply that, even if the voice is not directly that of Climacus, it is a faithful account of his intellectual development and ideas. Strawser (1994) p. 627.
7. *Bevisthed*, particularly as the term is used in *Sickness Unto Death*, is a continuum of development in self-reflexivity rather than a definite on–off state.

Kierkegaard does not need, therefore, to posit a discrete moment where a child goes from non-conscious to conscious. Equally, the Kierkegaardian account could ascribe at least limited consciousness to some nonhuman primates who display such self-reflexive concepts as fearing their own death.

8. Though it is important to note that Kierkegaard is not using this as an absolute term. As Nordentoft notes, ' "Pure" immediacy in Kierkegaard is more a concept, an intellectual construction which is employed for analytic purposes, than the name of a factual condition in man.' Nordentoft (1978) pp. 81–2.

9. Ferguson (2003) p. 124.

10. McDowell (1994) p. 69: '...spontaneity permeates our perceptual dealings with the world, all the way out to the impressions of sensibility themselves.' Søren Landkildehus' recent discussion of McDowell and Kierkegaard initiates a topic that I think will prove important; see Landkildehus (2007) pp. 184–92. I am grateful to Søren for our illuminating conversations on this subject.

11. Kant (1929) p. 93.

12. Elrod (1975) p. 50.

13. The infelicities of language here create traps for Kierkegaard commentators. Stuart Dalton, for example, claims that once it acquires language, the infant 'no longer experiences the world directly,' yet to speak of 'experiencing the world' seems too mediated a description for direct, non-'conscious' sense-reception. Dalton is very much aware of the problems of speaking about such infant 'consciousness' and acknowledges that the infant's 'consciousness' 'is a mystery to us, and the unmediated character is a purely speculative presupposition.' Yet he also uses phrases such as 'Language brings an element of ideality into consciousness' that are potentially misleading by virtue of the ambiguous use of 'consciousness.' What exists after the acquisition of language is radically different to and discontinuous with what was there before it, yet both are called 'consciousness. Dalton (2003) p. 369.

14. McDowell (1994) p. 64.

15. Indeed, the sense given to the term varies *within* individual works; Robert C. Roberts identifies three senses of the term within *Two Ages* alone, each carrying different values in the context of that work's critique of the present age. Roberts (1984) p. 92.

16. Marino (1988) p. 10.

17. Dunning (1985) p. 17.

18. ibid.

19. For an excellent recent discussion of Kierkegaard and the Hegelian problem of the beginning (one which discusses in greater depth many of the themes considered here), see Watts (2007).

20. Evans (1991) p. 78.

21. Davidson (1980) pp. 21–42.

22. For Hegel, 'Spurious Infinity' (as developed in the 'Lesser Logic' of the *Encyclopedia* is infinity regarded as 'endless iteration' or 'endless progression' as in the movement of time. This is opposed to 'genuine (*wahrhafte*) infinity' which involves self-subsistence and self-determination rather than abstract limitlessness. See Westphal (1987a) pp. 58–9.

23. Roberts (1984) p. 93.
24. The charge of irrationalism was given additional currency by MacIntyre's treatment of *Either/Or* in his *After Virtue*. There have since been many forceful and generally successful defenses of Kierkegaard against this charge. The main moments of this debate are collected in Davenport and Rudd (2001).
25. Evans (1991) p. 79. Evans explicitly refers to *interesse* in this context, arguing that decision-making is only possible because the will is not disinterested: 'to exist is to be interested, because for Kierkegaard all actuality is an *interesse*.' However, Evans does not develop this suggestion in his discussion of Kierkegaard's theory of action.
26. Dunning (1994) p. 217.
27. For one helpful explanation of Kierkegaard's use of *realitet* and *virkelighed*, see the Hong's footnotes to *Johannes Climacus* (JC, 331 n. 17). Interestingly, Schopenhauer discerns important differences in sense between the German analog of these synonyms: 'Thus cause and effect are the whole essence and nature of matter; its being is its acting [...] The substance of everything material is therefore very appropriately called in German *Wirklichkiet*, a word much more expressive than *Realität*.' Schopenhauer (1966) p. 9.
28. On this topic, see Evans (1998a) pp. 154–76.
29. Many commentators have noted that Kierkegaard's use of *modsigelse* usually means something weaker than a logical contradiction and have suggested alternative translations. Lippitt and Hutto make this point as part of their response to Conant's claim that, strictly speaking, the notion of the 'Absolute Paradox' (the Incarnation) is 'nonsense' and that as there can be no such thing as 'meaningful nonsense,' the *Postscript* is simply a Tractarian ladder, an attempt to say something finally unsayable. Lippitt and Hutto claim that a failure to appreciate the Hegelian context in which Kierkegaard writes, and the consequently broad use he makes of the term *modsigelse*, leads to the inappropriately 'austere view of nonsense' that underpins Conant's claims – the paradox is not a *logical* contradiction but simply a form of incongruity. See Lippitt and Hutto (1998) p. 279.
30. McDowell (1994) pp. 56–8.
31. On *inderlighed* see Come (1995) p. 94; Cappelørn (2008) p. 136 and Hannay (2008b) p. 152.
32. For a discussion of this distinction between these different modes of apprehending mortality, see Stokes (2006).
33. Hume (1969) p. 146.
34. ibid.
35. There has been considerable recent discussion of Abraham's silence – see Kosch (2008), Lippitt (2008), Conway (2008).
36. This is also made explicit in a sketch for *Johannes Climacus*: 'Doubt arises through my becoming a *relation* between two; as soon as it ceases, doubt is cancelled [...] the remarkable thing about it is that in the world of spirit as soon as one becomes divided it does not become two but three' (JC, 258/*Pap.* IV B 10:2 *n.d.* 1842–43).
37. Elrod (1975) p. 50.

3   Consciousness as Interest

1. Elrod (1975) p. 51.
2. Furtak notes that Roberts uses 'emotion' to refer to episodic states while 'passion' picks out a stable pattern of ongoing concerns. Furtak rejects this vocabulary, appealing instead to the Hellenistic schema that distinguishes between episodic instances of emotion and the underlying commitments that express themselves in those episodes. Furtak (2005) p. 143 n. 2.
3. Note that Roberts does not claim that this is a peculiarly Kierkegaardian sense of 'interest,' and he is actually seeking to explicate Kierkegaard's usage of the word 'passion' (*lidenskab*) rather than interest. In that sense he makes the same identification of interest and passion as other commentators, but in the reverse order.
4. Roberts (1984) p. 88.
5. Westphal (1996) p. 51.
6. ibid. p. 138.
7. Hughes (1995) p. 197.
8. Evans (1983) p. 56.
9. Khan (1982) p. 110.
10. Marino (1985) p. 205.
11. ibid. p. 206.
12. Ferreira (1991) pp. 125–26.
13. ibid. p. 126.
14. ibid. p. 127.
15. ibid.; see also EO, 2:164/SKS 3, 161: 'The personality is already interested in the choice before one chooses, and when one puts off the choice, the personality or the obscure forces within it unconsciously chooses.'
16. ibid. p. 127.
17. Penner (1999) p. 75.
18. ibid. p. 76.
19. ibid. p. 75, n. 9.
20. Taylor (1975) p. 44.
21. Dalton (2003) p. 369.
22. Zahavi (2005) p. 18.
23. Zahavi (2007) p. 189.
24. Zahavi (2005) p. 11.
25. ibid.
26. ibid. p. 20.
27. ibid. p. 24.
28. Sartre (1958) p. xxix.
29. Westphal (1996) p. 110.
30. Heidegger (1962) p. 227.
31. ibid. p. 237.
32. ibid. p. 238.
33. This is why, in the passage from *Works of Love* cited above, it is 'something else' to be 'so turned in thought' as to be interested (WL, 361/SKS 9, 355). This orientation of thought, though *proper to* thinking, is all too often absent.

34. Though these do exist – see, for example (CA, 12-14/SKS 4, 320-1 and CA, 303/SKS 4, 336–7).
35. Marino (1985) p. 205.
36. Malantschuk (1971) p. 161.
37. Nordentoft (1978) p. 86.

4   The Ontology of the Self

1. Elrod (1975) p. 23.
2. '[Anti-Climacus'] personal guilt, then, is to confuse himself with ideality (this is the daemonic in him), but his portrayal of ideality can be absolutely valid, and I bow to it. I determine myself as higher than Johannes Climacus, lower than Anti-Climacus.' (JP, 6433/*Pap.* X^1 A 517 *n.d.* 1849).
3. As I've argued elsewhere, it can also be seen as contributing to a tradition, beginning with Locke, that sees personal identity as a function of psychological continuity – though with some crucial differences, which are beyond the scope of (but place some important constraints upon) the present discussion. See Stokes (2009).
4. Nietzsche certainly came to the same conclusion quite independently of Kierkegaard: *The Gay Science* proclaims that 'We, however, *want to become those we are*' and '*What does your conscience say?* – "You shall become the person you are."' Nietzsche (1974) pp. 335, 270.
5. This opens Kierkegaard up to the charge that his interpretation of the psychological phenomena – and indeed his descriptions of the phenomena themselves – are so influenced and directed by his ontological thesis as to be unreliable. The extent to which Kierkegaard gives accurate and objective renderings of observable psychological states, and whether his philosophical anthropology provides the best explanation of these states, are important questions. There is not scope within the present work to deal with them, other than noting that Kierkegaard's psychology is at least vulnerable to rival psychologies which might provide more comprehensive explanations.
6. Elrod (1975) p. 30.
7. Taylor (1975) p. 104 *passim.*
8. There are, however, reasons to be wary of the Hongs' translation of *vorden* as 'process,' which can suggest a move towards completion, whereas for Kierkegaard there is in fact no such achievable end-point, but only continual becoming. I am grateful to Alastair Hannay for pointing this out to me. For a discussion of process-driven selfhood in Kierkegaard and others, see Bennett (1999) pp. 135–56.
9. Taylor (1975) p. 105.
10. Elrod notes that Anti-Climacus is careful to stress that spirit is a 'third' precisely so as to avoid the Hegelian position that Spirit (*Geist*) is *itself* the synthesis of opposites. Elrod (1976) p. 357.
11. Elrod (1975) p. 30.
12. Murdoch (2001) p. 47.
13. Westphal (1996) p. 110.
14. Hannay holds that Anti-Climacus' exclusion of the nihilistic response to the need for transcendent legitimation is due to his answering that need with

a religious framework which describes all other possible answers in religious terms, as not being answers but religious failures: 'the reason why the framework is a solution is because it does not contain the conceptual resources for describing the need that gave rise to it. The framework heals the breach by leaving no room for the problem.' Hannay (1987) pp. 23–38.

5   Imagination and Agency

1. There is an irresistible comparison here with Sartrean 'bad faith' (*mauvaise foi*), which is made possible by consciousness' ability to privilege one of its modes of being (in-itself, for-itself, for-others) at the expense of the others. The *mauvaise* is precisely that the self is operating in a mode designed to evade full consciousness of what it actually *is*, by taking refuge in a partial description of itself. Both *mauvaise foi* and *Fortvivelse* are therefore quite correctly characterizable as forms of inauthenticity in which the self acknowledges part of what it is in order to avoid acknowledging what it is in its totality. However, the Sartrean account does not seem to admit of degrees of inauthenticity in quite the same way as the Anti-Climacan account, nor does the resolution of *mauvaise foi* necessarily require the maintenance of internal tension as in *Sickness*. Sartre (1958) pp. 47–70.
2. In the first *Critique* (A120), Kant holds that imagination, as the 'active faculty for the synthesis of this [perceptual] manifold,' is necessary for all perception to occur; without imagination, we cannot synthesize the manifold of appearances into the understanding of an object. While Anti-Climacus does not make the same sort of epistemic claims, he nonetheless claims that imagination is essential to cognitive activity. Kant (1929) pp. 143–4.
3. Gouwens (1989) p. 2.
4. ibid. p. 148.
5. Murdoch (2001) p. 57.
6. Magee (2001) p. 236.
7. Murdoch (2001) pp. 36–7.
8. The first use of the term 'Ethical Imagination' in connection with Kierkegaard appears to be Gouwens (1982).
9. A point also made in Currie (2007) p. 17.
10. Murdoch (2001) p. 17. On this topic, see also Lita (2003).
11. Mackenzie (2008) p. 132.
12. See (WL, 280–99/SKS 9, 278–97; EUD, 55–78/SKS 5, 65–86).
13. Gouwens (1982) p. 206.
14. Sartre (1958) pp. 10–1.
15. Ferreira (1989) p. 28.
16. ibid.
17. ibid.
18. In *Christian Discourses*, Kierkegaard draws an instructive contrast between a 'task' and a 'question' (CD, 205/SKS 10, 214) which turns precisely on whether a given object of thought (in the context of that particular discourse, immortality) is engaged with through moral urgency or simply intellectual curiosity.
19. Elrod (1975) p. 57.

20. Elrod argues that reflection and imagination are 'co-operative aspects of the process of "infinitizing,"' but nonetheless distinct entities with different functions. However, Anti-Climacus presents imagination explicitly as 'infinitizing reflection' and implies that the role of imagination in thought is so pervasive that it is difficult to see how imagination and reflection can be teased apart. Gouwens also takes issue with Elrod on this point, insisting on a much closer identification between imagination and reflection. Elrod (1975) p. 34; Gouwens (1989) p. 181.
21. Gouwens (1989) p. 197.
22. Williams (1973) pp. 26–45.
23. ibid. pp. 35–7.
24. Parfit (1984) p. 221.
25. Williams (1973) p. 39.
26. Mackenzie (2008) p. 127.
27. Taylor (1975) p. 43.
28. Ferreira (1989) p. 31.
29. This understanding would not be fundamentally altered if we concede that sometimes, and probably most of the time, the imagination only produces *one* such picture.
30. Gouwens (1982) p. 206.
31. Our reasons for rejecting this theorized 'meta-person' here run parallel to the reasons why cognitive science's 'homunculus solution' to the problem of how knowledge arises came to be discredited: 'The disqualified homunculus solution consisted of postulating that a part of the brain, "the knower part," possessed the knowledge needed to interpret the images formed in that brain. The images were presented to the knower, and the knower knew what to do with them. In this solution, the knower was a spatially defined container, the so-called homunculus [...] The problem with the homunculus solution was that the all-knowing little person would do the knowing for each of us but would then face the difficulty with which we began in the first place. Who would do *its* knowing?' Damasio (1999) pp. 189–90.
32. Murdoch (2001) p. 34. Davenport in particular has attempted to show that Kierkegaard's conception of will, though preserving a sense of the freedom of volition found in the existentialist account, is not thereby irrational or absurd. Choice, though 'undetermined by the present state of [the] personality,' is neither arbitrary nor, in important respects, reversible, precisely because this freedom inheres in a primordial level of choice which will then ramify throughout the individual's higher volitional structure. See Davenport (2001a) and (2001b).
33. Elrod (1975) p. 48.
34. Note that Anti-Climacus uses *i samme Øieblik* here and not *samtidig* (as might be implied by the Hongs' translation 'simultaneously'). *Samtidighed* is a crucial term in Kierkegaard's psychology that I think names more or less the same phenomenon as *interesse*; space does not permit me to explore this in depth here, but see Stokes (2010, forthcoming).
35. There are isolated occasions where some of Kierkegaard's authors seem to find it relatively easy to hold the infinite and the concrete together. Judge William considers that the married man 'solves the great riddle, to live in

eternity and yet to hear the cabinet clock strike in such a way that its striking does not shorten but instead lengthens his eternity' (EO, 2:138/SKS 3, 137). Yet it is clear that Kierkegaard takes this resolution to be too simple, too devoid of struggle, and too cemented in the (relatively) easy certainties of the ethical sphere.
36. Ferreira (1991) p. 82.
37. ibid. p. 83.
38. Roberts (1998) p. 185.
39. Ferreira (1991) p. 60.
40. In *Practice in Christianity*, Anti-Climacus does describe imagination as the 'first condition for what becomes of a person' and will as the 'second and in the ultimate sense the decisive condition' (PC, 186/SKS 12, 186). However, that will and imagination can be discussed and analyzed separately and ordered according to their importance for describing the self does not mean they are *temporally* separable.
41. Gouwens (1989) p. 255.

6   Self-Recognition

1. This is not, however, a requirement for *all* philosophies of self-actualization. Schopenhauer holds that 'Everything primary, and consequently everything genuine, in man works as the forces of nature do, *unconsciously*,' and therefore to achieve the actualization of the personal, or indeed to achieve anything at all, 'you must *follow the rules without knowing them*.' Schopenhauer (1970) p. 176.
2. Marya Schechtman compares a case of ordinary survival (going to sleep and waking up), non-survival (being smothered in my sleep by a killer who also brainwashes my sleeping neighbor to have the same mental states as I would have had on waking), and posthumous survival (I go to sleep, I am smothered, and then someone wakes up on a cloud with wings and a harp). In the last case the question of whether this counts as survival is *prima facie* more difficult than the first two, though Schechtman does not go into this in detail. Schechtman (1996) p. 23.
3. See also (CUP, 1:171–7/SKS 7, 158–63) on these sorts of questions regarding the afterlife.
4. Locke (1731) p. 291.
5. Williams (1973) esp. pp. 46–63.
6. Wiggins (1967) p. 50.
7. Parfit (1984) p. 254.
8. For more on Kierkegaard and these sorts of questions, see Stokes (2008, 2009).
9. There is a useful parallel here with Frankfurt's conception of 'reasonableness' versus being 'crazy'. Frankfurt holds that Hume's account of a preference as being irrational only insofar as it is based on a false judgment of fact or causal connection ("Tis not contrary to reason to prefer the destruction of the whole world to the scratching of my little finger') is too narrow. It is, Frankfurt avers, 'lunatic' to prefer the destruction of the world to minor discomfort in my little finger, 'whatever Hume says.' Hence the Humean

conception of rationality in relation to preferences is too narrow to encompass our actual judgments about which preferences are reasonable and which are not. Though the peasant's decision not to move is clearly based upon factual error, and is thus irrational even in Hume's limited sense, this doesn't seem to be what strikes us as flawed in the peasant's reaction. Consider a radical skeptic in the drunken peasant's place, arguing that there is no compelling reason to suppose that the legs he thinks he sees are his, or indeed that he has legs at all. If, on this basis, he failed to move, would he escape the censure which Kierkegaard's account leads us to bring down upon the peasant? Would we not say, with Frankfurt, 'he *must be crazy*'? Frankfurt (1988) pp. 184–6.

10. Lorentzen (2001) p. 13.
11. Wittgenstein (1953) p. 157e.
12. Even in the example of artificial 'inductive' recognition, the moment of decision (if it ever comes) will itself constitute a 'leap' – a radical shift between the quantitative process of inductive reasoning and the qualitative conclusion of identity. For Kierkegaard, 'analogy and induction can only be concluded by a *leap*. All other conclusions are essentially tautological [*Identitet*]' (JP, 2341/*Pap.* V A74 *n.d.* 1844). See also (JP, 2349/*Pap.* V C7 *n.d.* 1844), which speaks of 'The leap of inference in induction and analogy.'
13. James (1950) p. 310.
14. This still leaves room for active, conscious participation in roles that constitute self-conscious moral identity – for instance, the sorts of role assumption (judge, husband) that Judge William urges, or the self-conscious participation in 'practices' that MacIntyre recommends. Still, the role-based self-construction Judge William commends carries a distinct risk of ossification: as Furtak notes, the Judge is so immersed in the roles he has taken on he cannot seriously entertain the prospect that life could be different, or that the moral precepts of his society that shapes the roles he inhabits could be moribund, or wicked, or in need of reform. See MacIntyre (1984) pp. 183–98; Furtak (2005) pp. 82–7.
15. Similarly, in the *Postscript*, Climacus claims that to speak of Christ in terms of his direct recognizability, for instance in an attempt to win over audiences with descriptions of his 'gentle countenance' is 'paganism.' 'The direct [*ligefremme*, 'straightforward'] recognizability is paganism; all solemn assurances that this is indeed Christ and that he is the true God are of no help, as soon as it ends with direct recognizability. A mythological figure is directly recognizable' (CUP, 1:600/SKS 7, 545). That by which Jesus is God cannot be seen directly; again, spirit is beyond the immediate and hence beyond the visible.
16. Pattison (2002) pp. 53–6.
17. Mackey (1971) p. 257.
18. Pattison (2002) p. 57.
19. Williams (1973) p. 39.
20. Grøn (1998).
21. ibid. p. 150.
22. ibid. p. 149. It is worth noting that not all examples of seeing the Other given in *Works of Love* will have this reciprocal-seeing structure either – 'The Work of Love in Remembering One Who Has Died' for instance, *explicitly*

rules out any sort of reciprocation, which is precisely what makes it a work of the most 'unselfish' love (WL, 358/SKS 9, 343).

23. Elizabeth A. Morelli notes that this relation to the Other (finally, God) is ontologically constituting. This is true, but we must be careful of our phrasing here. Although such a relation is certainly constitutive of our self-understanding (and thus contributes toward the actualization of selfhood), this ontologically constitutive awareness takes place in the context of a self that is *already* structurally given as a derived, established, creaturely being-before-God. Paradoxically, we become what we *already are* through standing before God. Morelli (1995) p. 26.

24. This is one of the major theses of Pattison (1997, 2002).

25. For an excellent philosophical discussion of the depths of our relationships with nonhuman animals, see Gaita (2002).

26. Lillegard (2001) p. 216 *passim*.

7 Mirrors

1. I am grateful for a comment from Eiko Hanaoka for suggesting the framing of this thought in terms of the subject/object schema.

2. For a discussion of the relationship between the Mirror-metaphor in *For Self-Examination* and the *lectio divina* tradition, see Andic (2002).

3. See also *Works of Love*: 'In honesty [*Oprigtigheden*] the lover presents himself before the beloved, and no mirror is as accurate as honesty in catching the smallest triviality, if it is genuine honesty or if in the lovers there is genuine faithfulness in reflecting themselves in the mirror of honesty that love [*Elskov*] holds between them' (WL, 151/SKS 9, 152). Again, the evaluative aspect is crucial here: the mirror of honesty issues its reflections in the form of judgements.

4. Climacus claims this epigram is directed to readers who will dismiss *Stages on Life's Way* as simply the same as *Either/Or*. See (CUP, 1:285–86/SKS 7, 260).

5. Wittgenstein (1953) p. 157e.

6. *Til Selvprøvelse*. As *prøv* is roughly 'test' or 'try,' *selvprøvelse* arguably already carries in-built evaluative overtones.

7. Kierkegaard claims at this point that he is simply reiterating James here, yet Kierkegaard's mirror-metaphor and James' do not seem to intersect until Kierkegaard has reached his third 'Requirement.' In that sense then, even if Kierkegaard takes it that (in the context of a discourse dedicated to Christian doctrine) he is already committed to following the mirror-metaphor through regardless of any apparent limitations, in fact he is not. The discourse takes the mirror metaphor far beyond anything that can be found in James.

8. On Kierkegaard's apparent lack of awareness of the possibility of genuine moral uncertainty, see Marino (2001) pp. 43–60.

9. Watkin (2002) pp. 311–3.

10. A classic example of this form of intuitionism is W.D. Ross from 1930: the *prima facie* rightness of an act 'is self-evident just as a mathematical axiom, or the validity of a form of inference, is evident. The moral order expressed in these propositions is just as much part of the fundamental nature of the universe (and, we may add, of any possible universe in which there were

moral agents at all) as is the spatial or numerical structure expressed in the axioms of geometry or arithmetic.' Ross (2002) pp. 29–30.

11. I'm grateful to John Davenport for pushing me to clarify whether Kierkegaard is an intuitionist on my reading. For an explicit claim that Kierkegaard is *not* an intuitionist, see Lübcke (1991) p. 95.

12. In this passage, Climacus re-tells the Good Samaritan parable and imagines a twist: suppose the Levite priest, after failing to help the wounded man, experiences a twinge of remorse and heads back to help him, only to find the Samaritan has beaten him to it and the wounded man no longer has need of his assistance. Climacus asks if the Levite could then have been said to have acted, and affirms that he has indeed acted, but not in 'the external world' (CUP, 1:340/SKS 7, 311). C. Stephen Evans argues that this shows Kierkegaard to share the 'standard intuition that underlies libertarianism: persons are only truly responsible for that which is within their power. To the extent that results are not within our power, to that extent we are not responsible.' However, as I've indicated here in the discussion of moral ignorance, Kierkegaard seems to have a much wider conception of what we are responsible for than would fit this libertarian conception. It is not, for instance, within our power to alter the temporally arranged structure of consciousness, yet temporality, according to Kierkegaard, compounds our guilt. (See CUP, 1:526/SKS 7, 478: 'since meanwhile time has been passing, a bad beginning has been made…and from that moment the total guilt, which is decisive, practices usury with new guilt;' also CA, 117–18/SKS 4, 419: 'repentance must acquire itself as an object, inasmuch as the moment of repentance becomes a deficit of action' and SUD, 105/SKS 11, 217: 'But eternity, which keeps his account, must register the state of sin as a new sin. It has only two rubrics, and "Whatever does not proceed from faith is sin"; every unrepented sin is a new sin and every moment that it is unrepented is new sin.') Temporality, it seems, builds guilt into the very fabric of moral agency. Evans (1991) p. 81.

13. Williams (1973) pp. 26–45.

14. See also (UDVS, 248/SKS 8, 347), where wishes are also described as a 'mirror' with a similar evaluative/disclosive function: '…there is no mirror as accurate as the wish, and although in other respects a mirror sometimes flatters the one who looks into it, shows him otherwise than he actually is, we must say that the wish, with the help of possibility, flatteringly beguiles him to show himself quite as he is, beguiles him into exactly resembling himself.'

15. Westphal (1996) p. 109–10.

16. ibid. p. 110.

17. Eckhart (1994) p. 11. See also (EO, 2:43/SKS 3, 50): 'A religiously developed person is certainly want to refer everything to God, to *permeate and saturate* every finite relation with the thought of God and thereby sanctify and ennoble it (this utterance is naturally oblique here)' (emphasis added).

18. Eckhart (1994) p. 11.

19. ibid. p. 12. Oliver Davies notes in his introduction (p. xxxiv) that Eckhart often speaks from an idealized position, presenting how things *would* be if the self had attained the oneness with God that is at present beyond it. Kierkegaard, too, seems to be gesturing towards a model of perfected moral

agency – where vision coincides with decision – that for weak and imperfect beings such as he takes us to be may be finally unattainable.

20. Kierkegaard suggests that it is surprising Darius needed someone to remind him to take his revenge: 'That was indeed something to remember; it seems to me it would have been better to have a slave who reminded him every day to forget' (FSE, 37/SV2 XII, 325).

21. See also Jeffrey S. Turner on the difficulty Judge William faces in striking the right 'admonishing' tone in his reply to the young aesthete: 'One does not want to run the risk of telling stories or parables which are so enjoyable to listen to, so aesthetically pleasing, that one's listener or reader forgets that the moral of the story is ultimately meant to apply to him or her [...] On the other hand, though, one also needs to take care lest one's admonitions sound *too serious*: direct criticism of another naturally brings about hostility; the one criticized will in all likelihood become "defensive," and here, too, one's real point will be lost.' Turner thinks Judge William fails to rise to this challenge. Turner (2001) p. 47.

22. Lorentzen (2001) p. 111.

23. ibid. pp. 113–4.

24. ibid. p. 114.

25. ibid. p. 18.

26. Furtak (2005) p. 120.

27. Ferreira (1998) p. 217.

28. Giles (2000) pp. 73–4.

29. This is an important element in Iris Murdoch's moral psychology as well. Her emphasis on attempting to alter how we *see* others, to look upon them in a more loving light, does not imply that we can choose to see whatever we want. Our ability to alter how we look at things – an ability which is not always successful and requires effort – does not amount to a capacity for arbitrary (and therefore easily reversible) interpretation. Indeed, Murdoch's point is precisely that we do *not* ordinarily choose how we see things, and the effort to change how we regard others amounts to an attempt to change how things *impose themselves* upon my vision. See Murdoch (2001) esp. pp. 16–17.

8   Seeing the Other

1. Lippitt (2005) p. 80.

2. Sharpe (2003) p. 25.

3. Adorno (1939) pp. 418–19.

4. Løgstrup (1968).

5. George (1998) pp. 70–81.

6. Løgstrup (1968) p. 63. The translation is Marilyn Piety's, given in Søltoft (1998) p. 114.

7. The term is used in this context in Grøn (1998) p. 148.

8. Ferreira (1997b) p. 206; Ferreira (2001) p. 55–6.

9. Kierkegaard does not seem to take particularly seriously the prospect that there *could* be a person who has never encountered another person. Kierkegaard does seem to have a blind spot for threshold cases – for instance,

his claim that we ultimately can neither help nor harm another spiritually seems susceptible to certain extreme, but plausible, counterexamples. See Jackson (1998) p. 243.
10. Søltoft (1998) p. 117.
11. ibid. p. 118.
12. George interprets Kierkegaard as citing the recollection of the dead as being more than just an example of a particularly pure love, but rather 'a criterion for how love should be.' George (1998) p. 79.
13. Gaita (2002) p. 92.
14. Ferreira (1997b) p. 206.
15. ibid. p. 212; Ferreira (2001) pp. 100–3. Ferreira takes herself to be making a different contrast to other commentators who divide *Works of Love* into 'Law' and 'Gospel' such as Kirmmse (1990) p. 312. She also sees her distinction as cutting across the division of *Works of Love* into two series, unlike other commentators.
16. Ferreira (2001) pp. 50–2; Ferreira (1997b) pp. 214–15.
17. Grøn (1998) p. 148.
18. Ferreira (1997b) p. 219.
19. Davenport (2001b) p. 279.
20. Derrida (1995) pp. 82–115.
21. Rorty (1989) pp. 189–98.
22. Though both Kierkegaard and Rorty seem to hold that the category of 'human being' is devoid of content and therefore inadequate to genuine moral attention to the other, the Kierkegaard of *Works of Love* would have to reject Rorty's assertion that we need to find imaginative points of similarity between ourselves and others in order to feel concern for them. Rorty claims that human solidarity, of the sort evidenced by, for instance, those who helped Jews flee Nazis persecution, is not grounded upon sympathy for people as 'fellow human beings' *per se*, but in our imaginative ability to identify with people as fellow-sufferers. Rorty asserts that it is far easier to make this identification in the case of a person who we can envisage as belonging to some classification we ascribe to ourselves – this person is a fellow-father, fellow-businessperson, fellow-Belgian. 'Fellow-human,' by contrast, doesn't seem to be strong enough to overcome the category of otherness – 'a Jew, unlike me.' On Rorty's line, someone who held a concern for humanity as such invests their altruism in something so abstract and artificial that real empathy with real people would be impossible. For Kierkegaard, however, the duty to love the neighbor transcends all points of similarity (which would lead to 'preferential' love) or difference (which would blind us to our kinship with the other as a member of our moral community). For Kierkegaard, the abstract is not to be *replaced* by the content of concrete social relations, but rather the abstract is to find expression in our relation to the concrete persons we see. In that sense, the Kierkegaardian ethic is more immediately inclusive than the Rortian (which does seek full inclusivity but as the end-state of an increasingly broad process of imaginary identification) and better able to explain the fact that many of those who *did* help Jews escape the Nazis reported that they did so precisely because the Jews *were* human beings, not because they saw any closer identification. See Cordner (2001) pp. 76–9.

23. Furtak (2005) p. 58.
24. For a useful discussion of the evil of genocide (and the claim that the Holocaust represents a new evil qualitatively greater than even genocide), see Gaita (1999) pp. 131–55.
25. Ferreira (1994a). Ferriera also detects in *Works of Love*'s discussion of preferential love as self-love an echo of Hume's claim that 'sympathetic engagement with another can often be reduced to a modification of self-love precisely because it effects an identity in which genuine otherness is precluded.' Ferreira (2001) p. 51.
26. Williams (1981) p. 45.

9   Concern, Misfortune and Despair

1. Heidegger (1962) p. 494 n.vi.
2. On the importance of the *Discourses* to an understanding of Kierkegaard's thought, see Pattison (2002).
3. Nordentoft (1978) p. 85.
4. Climacus does use *bekymring* at one point in the *Postscript* (CUP, 1:54/SKS 7, 58) as apparently synonymous with *interesse*, but this sole example is obviously not decisive in itself.
5. I am grateful to Christopher Cordner for this observation.
6. There may of course be some sort of secondary moral demand that flows from the seismological explanation – perhaps he is culpable for recklessly building his family home on a major geological fault line – but these will remain subsequent and extraneous to the seismologist's explanation rather than essential to it.
7. This suggests that Arguments from First Causes do not address themselves in this way to religious inquirers but are purely metaphysical (or perhaps even belong to a species of physics). It may be possible to defend these arguments from the charge that (even if they work) we can remain indifferent to them, but this task is beyond us here.
8. Dancy (2004) p. 112.
9. Cordner (2007) p. 76.
10. Gaita (2002) p. 135.
11. Hare (1964) p. 18.
12. Indeed, the example of osmium was suggested by a comedy sketch on a 1980s British TV show (*Who Dares Wins*) that I remember seeing as a child, in which a wife tearfully confesses to her hurt and outraged husband that osmium is the heaviest known metal. It is precisely the failure of this fact (and others) to connect to anything we can normally be expected to *care* about that allows the sketch to have its comic impact (which I hasten to add was much greater than my description conveys).
13. Williams (1981) p. 38.
14. While the notion that suffering has its uses is a common thought in various strands of Christian thought, it is also often claimed that this utility must be put aside and tribulation welcomed for its *own* sake if suffering is not to be taken as downpayment towards an eventual reward. Hence Kierkegaard in the *Upbuilding Discourses* holds that sufferings are to be received as a

'good and perfect gift' received 'from above' (EUD, 31–48, 125–58/SKS 5, 41–56,129–58), while Simone Weil declares 'I should not love my suffering because it is useful. I should love it because it *is*.' Weil (2002) p. 81.
15. Hannay (1998) pp. 329–48.
16. Hegel (1977) p. 49 n. 78.
17. Hannay (1998) p. 334.
18. Just as in 'Strengthening the Inner Being,' where misfortune is (at least contingently) better able to strengthen the inner being than good fortune, in *Christian Discourses* we are told that 'hardship is better able to make itself understood' than 'the terrors of powerful thoughts' (CD, 110/SKS 10, 121). This would seem to correspond to the *Upbuilding Discourses'* distinction between *bekymring* occasioned by suffering and *bekymring* that arises as a result of contemplation of the status quo, or perhaps simply the *possibility* of misfortune.

10   Interest in the Postscript: The Telos of Knowing

1. In the *Postscript* the discussion moves from the somewhat hypothetical discussion of *Philosophical Fragments* (as evinced by Climacus' use of *guden*, 'the god,' instead of the proper noun *Gud*) to a direct consideration of the content of Christian doctrine. As the Hongs put it, 'In dealing with Climacus' question of how one becomes a Christian, *Postscript* clothes the algebraic thought of *Fragments* in historical costume' (TM, xx).
2. Thomas Nagel claims that our sense of the absurdity of life derives from the combination of (a) our apprehension that the universe provides no externally valid, transcendent justifications for our goals and commitments, with (b) our inability to stop acting as if these commitments *were* so justified. Nagel (1979) pp. 11–23.
3. Lillegard (2001) p. 219; also Lillegard (2002) p. 255.
4. For a discussion of Kierkegaard's late, vehement rejection of marriage as inimical to the demands of Christianity, see Watkin (1997).
5. In several places, Kierkegaard seems to hold that a purely historical or scholarly interest in Christianity would be appropriate so long as it acknowledges its character. As discussed in Chapter 7, in *For Self-Examination* Kierkegaard (non-pseudonymously) holds that biblical scholarship *per se* is legitimate, but goes astray when it claims to advance ethico-religious knowledge – that is, where biblical scholars take it that their efforts are ultimately directed toward yielding ethically normative results.
6. This demand for concordance between mode and object in the evaluation of interests holds outside the ethico-religious sphere, although examples there are not always as uncontestable. A person who professes a religious faith, including its attendant eschatology, yet is indifferent to it, seems to be missing the 'point' in a clear sense. An art collector motivated by aesthetic appreciation might say something similar to someone who collects art solely for its monetary value: the latter doesn't really 'get' what art is about in some fundamental sense.
7. See also (CUP, 1:92/SKS 7, 91): 'Seen from the perspective of pathos, a second has infinite worth.'

8. Westphal (1996) p. 51.
9. Khan (1982) p. 110.
10. Mooney (1996) p. 67.
11. Nussbaum (1994) pp. 13–47.
12. Taylor (1974) pp. 88–9.
13. Or more accurately, in the present moment it understands itself *as* constituting a continuity even if *in fact* its continuity is broken. For more on this topic see Stokes (2009).
14. 'If eternal means, not transcendent to all (temporal) history, but omnipresent, trans-historical and therefore immutable in form throughout the extent of history, I shall adopt Freud's expression word for word, and write *ideology is eternal*, exactly like the unconscious.' Althusser (1971) p. 152.
15. Malantschuk (1971) p. 160.
16. ibid. p. 79.
17. Such experiences are a key topic of Cordner (2001).

Conclusion

1. Williams (1981) p. 18.
2. Godwin (1793) pp. 76–7. In the first edition, we are told we should save the theologian Fenelon from the burning house in preference to the lowly chambermaid, even if she is our own mother; in the second edition (1796, pp. 128–9), the chambermaid has become a valet and potentially our father, brother of benefactor. Evidently, the gender-swap made the example more palatable to the reading public.
3. Lillegard (2001) pp. 226.
4. Davenport (2001b) esp. pp. 276–83.
5. And this thought, of course, becomes redoubled: I claim (perhaps foolishly!) to understand Kierkegaard, but if I fail to live up to the demands of subjectivity in Kierkegaard's work which I explicate, do I *really* understand Kierkegaard? And so on, *ad infinitum*.

Bibliography

Adorno, Theodore W. (1939) 'On Kierkegaard's Doctrine of Love.' *Studies in Philosophy and Social Science* VIII pp. 418–19.

Althusser, Louis (1971) *Lenin and Philosophy* (London: New Left Books).

Andic, Martin (1998) 'Is Love of Neighbor the Love of an Individual?' in George Pattison and Stephen Shakespeare (eds) *Kierkegaard: The Self in Society* (London: Macmillan). pp. 112–24.

Andic, Martin (2002) 'The Mirror' in Robert L. Perkins (ed.) *International Kierkegaard Commentary: For Self-Examination and Judge for Yourself!* (Macon, GA: Mercer University Press) pp. 335–62.

Aristotle (1975) *Nichomachean Ethics*, trans. Hippocrates G. Apostle (Dordrecht and Boston: Reidel).

Atkins, Kim (2004) 'Narrative Identity, Practical Identity and Ethical Subjectivity.' *Continental Philosophy Review* 37(3), 341–66.

Bedell, George C. (1969) 'Kierkegaard's Conception of Time.' *Journal of the American Academy of Religion* 73(3), 266–9.

Bennett, James O. (1999) 'Selves and Personal Existence in the Existentialist Tradition.' *Journal of the History of Philosophy* 37(1), 135–56.

Burgess, Andrew J. (1975) *Passion, 'Knowing How' and Understanding: An Essay on the Concept of Faith* (Missoula, MT: Scholars).

Cappelørn, Niels Jørgen (2008) 'Spleen Essentially Cancelled – Yet a Little Spleen Retained' in Edward F. Mooney (ed.) *Ethics, Love, and Faith in Kierkegaard* (Bloomington, IN: Indiana University Press) pp. 129–46.

Caputo, John D. (1987) *Radical Hermeneutics: Repetition, Deconstruction and the Hermeneutic Project* (Bloomington and Indianapolis: Indiana University Press).

Come, Arnold B. (1995) *Kierkegaard as Humanist: Discovering My Self* (Montreal and Buffalo: McGill-Queen's University Press).

Conant, James (1993) 'Kierkegaard, Wittgenstein and Nonsense' in Ted Cohen, Paul Guyer and Hilary Putnam (eds) *Pursuits of Reason* (Lubbock, TX: Texas Tech University Press).

Conant, James (1996) 'Reply: Nietzsche, Kierkegaard and Anscombe on Moral Unintelligibility' in Phillips D.Z. (ed.) *Religion and Morality* (Hampshire and London: Macmillan) pp. 250–98.

Connell, George (1985) *To Be One Thing: Personal Unity in Kierkegaard's Thought* (Macon, GA: Mercer University Press).

Connell, George (2006) 'Four Funerals: The Experience of Time by the Side of the Grave' in Robert L. Perkins (ed.) *International Kierkegaard Commentary: Prefaces/Writing Sampler and Three Discourses on Imagined Occasions* (Macon, GA: Mercer University Press) pp. 419–38.

Conway, Daniel D. (2008) 'Abraham's Final Word' in Edward F. Mooney (ed.) *Ethics, Love and Faith in Kierkegaard* (Bloomington and Indianapolis: Indiana University Press) pp. 175–95.

Cordner, Christopher (2001) *Ethical Encounter: The Depth of Moral Meaning* (Hampshire: Palgrave).

Cordner, Christopher (2007) 'Three Contemporary Perspectives on Moral Philosophy.' *Philosophical Investigations* 30(1), 65–84.

Cross, Andrew (1998) 'Neither Either Nor Or: The Perils of Reflexive Irony' in Alastair Hannay and Gordon D. Marino (eds) *The Cambridge Companion to Kierkegaard* (Cambridge: Cambridge University Press) pp. 125–53.

Currie, Gregory (2007) 'Framing Narratives' in Daniel D. Hutto (ed.) *Narrative and Understanding Persons* (Cambridge: Cambridge University Press) pp. 17–42.

Dalton, Stuart (2003) '*Johannes Climacus* as Kierkegaard's *Discourse on Method*.' *Philosophy Today* 47(4), 360–77.

Damasio, Antonio (1999) *The Feeling of What Happens: Body and Emotion in the Making of Consciousness* (London: Heinemann).

Dancy, Jonathan (2004) *Ethics Without Principles* (Oxford: Oxford University Press).

Davenport, John J. (2000) 'The Ethical and Religious Significance of Taciturnus's Letter in Kierkegaard's Stages on Life's Way' in Robert L. Perkins (ed.) *International Kierkegaard Commentary: Stages on Life's Way* (Macon, GA: Mercer University Press) pp. 213–44.

Davenport, John J. and Rudd, Anthony (eds) (2001) *Kierkegaard After MacIntyre: Essays* on Freedom, Narrative and Virtue (Chicago and La Salle, IL: Open Court).

Davenport, John J. (2001a) 'The Meaning of Kierkegaard's Choice Between the Aesthetic and the Ethical: A Response to MacIntyre' in John J. Davenport and Anthony Rudd (eds) *Kierkegaard After MacIntyre: Essays on Freedom, Narrative, and Virtue* (Chicago and La Salle, IL: Open Court) pp. 75–112.

Davenport, John J. (2001b) 'Towards an Existential Virtue Ethics: Kierkegaard and MacIntyre' in John J. Davenport and Anthony Rudd (eds) *Kierkegaard After MacIntyre: Essays on Freedom, Narrative and Virtue* (Chicago and La Salle, IL: Open Court) pp. 265–323.

Davenport, John J. (2008) 'Faith as Eschatological Trust in *Fear and Trembling*' in Edward F. Mooney (ed.) *Ethics, Love and Faith in Kierkegaard* (Bloomington and Indianapolis: Indiana University Press) pp. 196–233.

Davidson, Donald (1980) *Essays on Actions and Events* (Oxford: Oxford University Press).

Derrida, Jacques (1995) *The Gift of Death*, trans. David Willis (Chicago and London: University of Chicago Press).

Descartes, Rene (1986) *Mediations on First Philosophy*, trans. John Cottingham (Cambridge: Cambridge University Press).

Dreyfus, Herbert (2008) 'Kierkegaard on the Self' in Edward F. Mooney (ed.) *Ethics, Love, and Faith in Kierkegaard* (Bloomington, IN: Indiana University Press) pp. 11–23.

Dunning, Stephen N. (1985) *Kierkegaard's Dialectic of Inwardness: A Structural Analysis of the Theory of Stages* (Princeton, NJ: Princeton University Press).

Dunning, Stephen N. (1994) 'The Illusory Grandeur of Doubt: The Dialectic of Subjectivity in *Johannes Climacus*' in Robert L. Perkins (ed.) *International Kierkegaard Commentary: Philosophical Fragments and Johannes Climacus* (Macon, GA: Mercer University Press) pp. 203–22.

Eckhart, Meister (1994) *Selected Writings*, trans. Oliver Davies (London: Penguin).

Elrod, John W. (1975) *Being and Existence in Kierkegaard's Pseudonymous Works* (Princeton, NJ: Princeton University Press).

Elrod, John W. (1976) 'Feurbach and Kierkegaard on the Self.' *Journal of Religion* 56, 348–65.

Elrod, John W. (1984) 'Passion, Reflection and Particularity' in Robert L. Perkins (ed.) *International Kierkegaard Commentary: Two Ages* (Macon, GA: Mercer University Press) pp. 1–18.

Eriksen, Niels Nymann (2000) *Kierkegaard's Category of Repetition* (Berlin and New York: Walter de Gruyter).

Evans, C. Stephen (1976) 'Kierkegaard on Subjective Truth: Is God an Ethical Fiction?' *International Journal for Philosophy of Religion* VII(1), 288–99.

Evans, C. Stephen (1981) 'Reductionism as Absentmindedness: Existentialism and Phenomenology as Strategies for Defending Personhood.' *Man and World* 14(2), 175–88.

Evans, C. Stephen (1983) *Kierkegaard's Fragments and Postscript: The Religious Philosophy of Johannes Climacus* (Atlantic Highlands, New Jersey: Humanities Press).

Evans, C. Stephen (1989a) 'Does Kierkegaard Think Beliefs Can Be Directly Willed?' *International Journal for Philosophy of Religion* 26(3), 173–84.

Evans, C. Stephen (1989b) 'Kierkegaard's View of the Unconscious' in Birgit Bertung (ed.) *Kierkegaard, Poet of Existence: Kierkegaard Conferences I* (Copenhagen: C.A. Reitzel) pp. 31–48.

Evans, C. Stephen (1991) 'Where There's A Will There's A Way: Kierkegaard's Theory of Action' in Hugh J. Silverman (ed.) *Writing the Politics of Difference* (Albany, New York: State University of New York Press) pp. 73–88.

Evans, C. Stephen (1992) *Passionate Reason: Making Sense of Kierkegaard's Philosophical Fragments* (Bloomington and Indianapolis: Indiana University Press).

Evans, C. Stephen (1997) 'Who Is the Other in *Sickness Unto Death?*' in Niels Jørgen Cappelørn and Herman Deuser (eds) *Kierkegaard Studies Yearbook 1997* (Berlin and New York: Walter de Gruyter) pp. 1–15.

Evans, C. Stephen (1998a) 'Realism and Antirealism in Kierkegaard's *Concluding -Unscientific Postscript*' in Alastair Hannay and Gordon D. Marino (eds) *The Cambridge Companion to Kierkegaard* (Cambridge: Cambridge University Press) pp. 154–76.

Evans, C. Stephen (1998b) 'Authority and Transcendence in *Works of Love*' in Niels Jørgen Cappelørn and Herman Deuser (eds) *Kierkegaard Studies Yearbook 1998* (Berlin and New York: Walter de Gruyter) pp. 23–40.

Ferguson, Harvey (2003) 'Modulation: A Typology of the Present Age' in Paul Cruysberghs, Johan Taels and Karl Verstrynge (eds) *Immediacy and Reflection In Kierkegaard's Thought* (Leuven: Leuven University Press) pp. 121–41.

Ferreira, M. Jamie (1989) 'Repetition, Concreteness, and Imagination.' *International Journal for the Philosophy of Religion* 25, 13–34.

Ferreira, M. Jamie (1990) 'Kierkegaardian Faith: "the Condition" and the Response.' *International Journal for the Philosophy of Religion* 28(2), 63–79.

Ferreira, M. Jamie (1991) *Transforming Vision: Imagination and Will in Kierkegaardian Faith* (Oxford: Clarendon Press).

Ferreira, M. Jamie (1993) 'Kierkegaardian Imagination and the Feminine.' *Kierkegaardiana* 16, 79–93.

Ferreira, M. Jamie (1994a) 'Hume and Imagination: Sympathy and "the Other".' *International Philosophical Quarterly* 34: 133, 39–57.

Ferreira, M. Jamie (1994b) 'The Point Outside the World: Kierkegaard and Wittgenstein on Nonsense, Paradox and Religion.' *Religious Studies* 30(1), 29–44.

Ferreira, M. Jamie (1997a) 'Imagination and the Despair of Sin' in Niels Jørgen Cappelørn, and Jon and Stewart (eds) *Kierkegaard Studies Yearbook 1997* (Berlin and New York: Walter de Gruyter), pp. 16–34.

Ferreira, M. Jamie (1997b) 'Moral Blindness and Moral Vision in Kierkegaard's *Work's of Love*' in Niels Jørgen Cappelørn and Jon Stewart (eds) *Kierkegaard Revisited* Kierkegaard Studies Monograph Series Vol. 1 (Berlin and New York: Walter de Gruyter) pp. 206–22.

Ferreira, M. Jamie (1998) 'Faith and the Kierkegaardian Leap' in Alastair Hannay and Gordon D. Marino (eds) *The Cambridge Companion to Kierkegaard* (Cambridge: Cambridge University Press) pp. 207–34.

Ferreira, M. Jamie (2001) *Love's Grateful Striving: A Commentary on Kierkegaard's Works of Love* (Oxford: Oxford University Press).

Frankfurt, Harry G. (1988) *The Importance of What We Care About* (Cambridge: Cambridge University Press).

Furtak, Rick Anthony (2005) *Wisdom in Love: Kierkegaard and the Ancient Quest for Emotional Integrity* (Notre Dame, IN: University of Notre Dame Press).

Furtak, Rick Anthony (2008) 'Love and the Discipline of Philosophy' in Edward F. Mooney (ed.) *Ethics, Love, and Faith in Kierkegaard* (Bloomington, IN: Indiana University Press) pp. 59–71.

Gaita, Raimond (1999) *A Common Humanity: Thinking About Love & Truth & Justice* (Melbourne: Text Publishing).

Gaita, Raymond (2002) *The Philosopher's Dog* (Melbourne: Text Publishing).

George, Peter (1998) 'Something Anti-Social About *Works of Love*' in George Pattison and Stephen Shakespeare (eds) *Kierkegaard: The Self in Society* (London: Macmillan) pp. 70–81.

Giles, James (2000) 'Kierkegaard's Leap: Anxiety and Freedom' in James Giles (ed.) *Kierkegaard and Freedom* (New York: St Martins Press) pp. 69–92.

Godwin, William (1793) *An Enquiry Concerning Political Justice, and its Influence on General Virtue and Happiness* (Dublin: Luke White).

Golomb, Jacob (1991) 'Kierkegaard's Ironic Ladder to Authentic Faith.' *International Journal for Philosophy of Religion* 32(2), 65–81.

Gouwens, David J. (1982) 'Kierkegaard on the Ethical Imagination' *Journal of Religious Ethics* 10(2), 204–19.

Gouwens, David J. (1989) *Kierkegaard's Dialectic of the Imagination* (New York: Peter Lang).

Grøn, Arne (1998) 'The Dialectic of Recognition in *Works of Love*' in Niels Jørgen Cappelørn and Herman Deuser (eds) *Kierkegaard Studies Yearbook 1998* (Berlin and New York: Walter de Gruyter) pp. 147–57.

Grøn, Arne (2000) 'Temporality in Kierkegaard's Edifying Discourses' in Niels Jørgen Cappelørn and Herman Deuser (eds) *Kierkegaard Studies Yearbook 2000* (Berlin and New York: Walter de Gruyter) pp. 191–204.

Grøn, Arne (2001) 'Spirit and Temporality in *The Concept of Anxiety*,' trans. K. Brian Söderquist, in Niels Jørgen Cappelørn, Herman Deuser and Jon Stewart (eds) *Kierkegaard Studies Yearbook 2001* (Berlin and New York: Walter de Gruyer) pp. 128–40.

Hall, Harrison (1984) 'Love and Death: Kierkegaard and Heidegger on Authentic and Inauthentic Human Existence.' *Inquiry* 27, 179–97.

Hamblet, Wendy C. (2004) 'On Sovereignty and Trespass: The Moral Failure of Levinas' Phenomenological Ethics' *Minerva: An Internet Journal of Philosophy* 8, 20–33.

Hannay, Alastair (1982) *Kierkegaard* (London: Routledge and Keegan Paul).

Hannay, Alastair (1985) 'Hamlet Without the Prince of Denmark Revisited: Pörn on Kierkegaard and the Self.' *Inquiry* 28(1985), 261–71.

Hannay, Alistair (1987) 'Spirit and the Idea of the Self as a Reflexive Relation' in Robert L. Perkins (ed.) *International Kierkegaard Commentary: The Sickness Unto Death* (Macon, GA: Mercer University Press) pp. 23–38.

Hannay, Alastair (1994) 'Basic Despair in *The Sickness Unto Death*.' *Kierkegaardiana* 17, 6–24.

Hannay, Alastair (1998) 'Kierkegaard and the Variety of Despair' in Alastair Hannay and Gordon D. Marino (eds) *The Cambridge Companion to Kierkegaard* (Cambridge: Cambridge University Press) pp. 329–48.

Hannay, Alastair (1999) 'Kierkegaard's Levellings and the *Review*' in Niels Jørgen Cappelørn and Herman Deuser (eds) *Kierkegaard Studies Yearbook 1999* (Berlin and New York: Walter de Gruyter) pp. 71–95.

Hannay, Alastair (2008a) 'Kierkegaard on Commitment, Personality, and Identity' in Edward F. Mooney (ed.) *Ethics, Love, and Faith in Kierkegaard* (Bloomington, IN: Indiana University Press) pp. 48–55.

Hannay, Alastair (2008b) 'Kierkegaard on Melancholy and Despair' in Edward F. Mooney (ed.) *Ethics, Love, and Faith in Kierkegaard* (Bloomington, IN: Indiana University Press) pp. 147–52.

Hare, R.M. (1964) *The Language of Morals* (Oxford: Oxford University Press).

Hegel, G.F.W. (1977) *Phenomenology of Spirit*, trans. A.V. Miller (Oxford: Oxford University Press).

Heiberg, Johan Ludvig (1861) *Prosaiske Skrifte*, Vol. 3 (Copenhagen: C.A. Reitzel).

Heidegger, Martin (1962) *Being and Time*, trans. John Macquarrie and Edward Robinson (Oxford: Blackwell).

Hinman, Lawrence M. (1980) 'Temporality and Self-Affirmation: A Kierkegaardian Critique of Nietzsche's Doctrine of the Eternal Recurrence of the Same.' *Kierkegaardiana* XI, 93–119.

Hughes, Edward J. (1995) 'How subjectivity is truth in the "Concluding Unscientific Postscript".' *Religious Studies* 31(2), 197–208.

Hume, David (1969) *A Treatise of Human Nature*. (ed.) Ernest C. Mossner (London: Penguin).

Jackson, Timothy P. (1998) 'Arminian Edification: Kierkegaard on Grace and Free Will' in Alastair Hannay and Gordon D. Marino. *The Cambridge Companion to Kierkegaard* (Cambridge: Cambridge University Press) pp. 234–56.

Jacoby, Matthew Gerhard (2002) 'Kierkegaard on Truth.' *Religious Studies* 38(1), 22–44.

James, William (1950) *The Principles of Psychology*, Vol. I (New York: Dover).

Kangas, David (2000) 'The Logic of Gift in Kierkegaard's *Four Upbuilding Discourses* (1843)' in Niels Jørgen Cappelørn and Herman Deuser (eds) *Kierkegaard Studies Yearbook 2000* (Berlin and New York: Walter de Gruyter) pp. 100–20.

Kangas, David J. (2007) *Kierkegaard's Instant: On Beginnings* (Bloomington and Indianapolis: University of Indiana Press).

Kant, Immanuel (1929) *Immanuel Kant's Critique of Pure Reason*, trans. Norman Kemp-Smith (London: Macmillan).

Kant, Immanuel (1951) *Critique of Judgment*, trans. J.H. Bernard (New York and London: Hafner Press).

Kant, Immanuel (1997) *Groundwork of the Metaphysics of Morals*, trans. and ed. Mary Gregor (Cambridge: Cambridge University Press).

Khan, A.H. (1982) '*Lidenskab* in *Efterskrift*' in Alastair McKinnon (ed.) *Kierkegaard: Resources and Results* (Montreal: Wilfred Laurier University Press) pp. 105–14.

Kirmmse, Bruce (1990) *Kierkegaard in Golden Age Denmark* (Bloomington, IN: Indiana University Press).

Koch, Carl Henrik (1992) *Kierkegaard og 'Det interessante': En studie I en æstetiske kategori* (Copenhagen: CA Reitzel).

Korsgaard, Christine et al. (1996) *The Sources of Normativity*, (ed.) Onora O'Neill (Cambridge: Cambridge University Press).

Kosch, Michelle (2006) *Freedom and Reason in Kant, Schelling, and Kierkegaard* (Oxford: Oxford University Press).

Kosch, Michelle (2008) 'What Abraham Couldn't Say' *Proceedings of the Aristotelian Society Supplementary Volume* 82(1), 59–78.

Landkildehus, Søren (2007) 'Answering Stoicism: Kierkegaard vs. McDowell' in Roman Kralik et al. (eds) *Acta Kierkegaardiana*, Vol. 2 (Mexico City: Sociedad Iberoamericana de Estudios Kierkegaardianos) pp. 187–95.

Lillegard, Norman (2001) 'Thinking With Kierkegaard and MacIntyre About Virtue, the Aesthetic, and Narrative' in John J. Davenport and Anthony Rudd (eds) *Kierkegaard After MacIntyre: Essays on Freedom, Narrative and Virtue* (Chicago and La Salle, IL: Open Court Publishing) pp. 211–32.

Lillegard, Norman (2002) 'Passion and Reason: Aristotelian Strategies in Kierkegaard's Ethics.' *Journal of Religious Ethics* 30(2), 251–73.

Lippitt, John and Hutto, Daniel (1998) 'Making Sense of Nonsense: Kierkegaard and Wittgenstein.' *Proceedings of the Aristotelian Society* 98, 263–86.

Lippitt, John (2000) *Humour and Irony in Kierkegaard's Thought* (London: Macmillan Press).

Lippitt, John (2005) 'Telling Tales: Johannes Climacus and "Narrative Unity".' in Niels Jørgen Cappelørn and Herman Deuser (eds) *Kierkegaard Studies Yearbook 2005* (Berlin: de Gruyter) pp. 71–89.

Lippitt, John (2007) 'Getting the Story Straight: Kierkegaard, MacIntyre and Some Problems with Narrative' *Inquiry* 50(1), 34–69.

Lippitt, John (2008) 'What Neither Abraham Nor Johannes De Silentio Could Say.' *Proceedings of the Aristotelian Society Supplementary Volume* 82(1), 79–99.

Lita, Ana (2003) ' "Seeing" Human Goodness: Iris Murdoch on Moral Virtue.' *Minerva – An Internet Journal of Philosophy* 7, 143–72.

Locke, John (1731) *An Essay Concerning Human Understanding*, 10th Edition (London: Edmund Parker).

Lorentzen, Jamie (2001) *Kierkegaard's Metaphors* (Macon, GA: Mercer University Press).

Lübcke, Poul (1991) 'An Analytical Interpretation of Kierkegaard as Moral Philosopher.' *Kierkegaardiana* 15, 93–103.

Løgstrup, K.E. (1968) *Opgør med Kierkegaard* (Copenhagen: Gyldendal).

Mackenzie, Catriona (2008) 'Imagination, Identity, and Self-Transformation' in Kim Atkins and Catriona Mackenzie (eds) *Practical Identity and Narrative Agency* (New York and London: Routledge) pp. 121–45.

McDonald, William (2003) 'Love in Kierkegaard's Symposia.' *Minerva: An Internet Journal of Philosophy* 7, 60–93.

McDonald, William (2009) 'An Archaeology of Silence of Kierkegaard's Philosophical Reception' in Jon Stewart (ed.) *International Kierkegaard Reception Volume 8, Tome III* (Aldershot: Ashgate) pp. 175–93.

McDowell, John (1994) *Mind and World* (Cambridge, MA and London: Harvard University Press).

MacIntyre, Alasdair (1984) *After Virtue*, 2nd Edition (Notre Dame, IN: University of Notre Dame Press).

Mackey, Louis (1971) *Kierkegaard: A Kind of Poet* (Philadelphia: University of Pennsylvania Press).

McKinnon, Alastair (1971) *The Kierkegaard Indices Vol. II: Fundamental Polyglot: Konkordans Til Kierekgaards Samlede Værker* (Leiden, Netherlands: E.J. Brill).

Magee, Brian (ed.) (2001) *Talking Philosophy* (Oxford: Oxford University Press).

Malantschuk, Gregor (1971) *Kierkegaard's Thought*, trans. Howard V. Hong and Edna H. Hong (Princeton, NJ: Princeton University Press).

Malantschuk, Gregor (1980) *The Controversial Kierkegaard*, trans. Howard V. Hong and Edna H. Hong (Waterloo, Ontario: Wilfrid Laurier University Press).

Malantschuk, Gregor (1993) *Nøglebegreber i Søren Kierkegaards Tænkning* (Copenhagen: C.A. Reitzel).

Marino, Gordon (1985) 'S. Kierkegaard: The Objective Thinker is a Suicide.' *Philosophy Today* (Fall, 1985), 203–12.

Marino, Gordon (1988) *Kierkegaard's Anthropology* Dissertation (University of Chicago).

Marino, Gordon (1996) 'The Place of Reason in Kierkegaard's Ethics.' *Kierkegaardiana* 18, 49–64.

Marino, Gordon (2001) *Kierkegaard in the Present Age* (Milwaukee: Marquette University Press).

Mooney, Edward F. (1996) *Selves in Discord and Resolve: Kierkegaard's Moral-Religious Psychology from Either/Or to The Sickness Unto Death* (New York and London: Routledge).

Mooney, Edward F. (2007) *On Søren Kierkegaard: Dialogue, Polemics, Lost Intimacy, and Time* (Aldershot: Ashgate).

Morelli, Elizabeth A. (1995) 'The Existence of the Self before God in Kierkegaard's *The Sickness Unto Death*.' *The Heythrop Journal* 36(1), 15–29.

Mortensen, Finn Hauberg (1996) *Kierkegaard Made in Japan* (Odense, Denmark: Odense University Press).

Murdoch, Iris (2001) *The Sovereignty of Good* (London and New York: Routledge).

Nagel, Thomas (1979) *Mortal Questions* (Cambridge: Cambridge University Press).

Nietzsche, Freidrich (1974) *The Gay Science*, trans. Walter Kaufmann (New York: Vintage Books).

Nordentoft, Kresten (1978) *Kierkegaard's Psychology*, trans. Bruce Kirmmse (Pittsburgh: Duquesne University Press).

Nussbaum, Martha (1994) *The Therapy of Desire* (Princeton, NJ: Princeton University Press).

Parfit, Derek (1984) *Reasons and Persons* (Oxford: Oxford University Press).

Pattison, George (1997) ' "Before God" as a Regulative Concept' in Niels Jørgen Cappelørn and Herman Deuser (eds) *Kierkegaard Studies Yearbook 1997* (Berlin and New York: Walter de Gruyter) pp. 70–84.

Pattison, George (2002) *Kierkegaard's Upbuilding Discourses: Philosophy, Literature and Theology* (London and New York: Routledge).

Penner, Myron B. (1999) 'The Normative Resources of Kierkegaard's Subjectivity Principle.' *International Journal of Systematic Theology* 1(1), 73–88.

Perkins, Robert L. (1984) 'Kierkegaard's Critique of the Bourgeois State.' *Inquiry* 27, 207–18.

Piety, Marilyn G. (1993) 'Kierkegaard on Rationality.' *Faith and Philosophy* 10(3), 365–79.

Poole, Roger (1998) 'The Unknown Kierkegaard: Twentieth Century Receptions' in Alastair Hannay and Gordon D. Marino (eds) *The Cambridge Companion to Kierkegaard* (Cambridge: Cambridge University Press) pp. 48–75.

Roberts, Robert C. (1984) 'Passion and Reflection' in Robert L. Perkins (ed.) *International Kierkegaard Commentary: Two Ages* (Macon, GA: Mercer University Press) pp. 87–106.

Roberts, Robert C. (1998) 'Existence, Emotion and Virtue: Classical Themes in Kierkegaard' in Alastair Hannay and Gordon D. Marino (eds) *The Cambridge Companion to Kierkegaard* (Cambridge: Cambridge University Press) pp. 177–206.

Rocca, Ettore (2004) 'Kierkegaards Teologiske Æstetik: Om Troens Perception' *Kierkegaardiana* 23, 76–95.

Rorty, Richard (1989) *Contingency, Irony and Solidarity* (Cambridge: Cambridge University Press).

Ross, William David (2002) *The Right and The Good* (Oxford: Oxford University Press).

Rudd, Anthony (1993) *Kierkegaard and the Limits of the Ethical* (Oxford: Clarendon Press).

Rudd, Anthony (1998) 'Kierkegaard and the Sceptics.' *British Journal of the History of Philosophy* 6(1), 71–88.

Rudd, Anthony (2000) 'Speculation and Despair: Metaphysical and Existential Perspectives on Freedom' in James Giles (ed.) *Kierkegaard and Freedom* (Hampshire: Palgrave) pp. 28–42.

Rudd, Anthony (2001) 'Reason in Ethics: MacIntyre and Kierkegaard' in John J. Davenport and Anthony Rudd (eds) *Kierkegaard After MacIntyre: Essays on Freedom, Narrative, and Virtue* (Chicago and La Salle, IL: Open Court Press) pp. 131–50.

Rudd, Anthony (2005) 'Narrative, Expression and Mental Substance.' *Inquiry* 48(5), 413–35.

Rudd, Anthony (2007) 'Kierkegaard, MacIntyre and Narrative Unity – Reply to Lippitt.' *Inquiry* 50(5), 541–9.

Ryle, Gilbert (1949) *The Concept of Mind* (London: Hutchinson).

Russell, Bertrand (1959) *Wisdom of the West* (London: Macdonald).

Sartre, Jean-Paul (1958) *Being and Nothingness*, trans. Hazel E. Barnes (London: Routledge).

Sagi, Avi (1992) 'The Suspension of the Ethical and the Religious Meaning of Ethics in Kierkegaard's Thought.' *International Journal for Philosophy of Religion* 32(2), 83–103.

Schechtman, Marya (1996) *The Constitution of Selves* (Ithaca and London: Cornell University Press).

Schopenhauer, Arthur (1966) '*The World as Will and Representation*' in two volumes, trans. E.F.J. Payne (New York: Dover).

Schopenhauer, Arthur (1970) *Essays and Aphorisms*, trans. and selected by R.J. Hollingdale (London: Penguin).

Schrag, Calvin O. (1961) *Existence and Freedom: Towards an Ontology of Human Finitude* (Evanston, IL: Northwestern University Press).

Seigel, Jerrold (2005) *The Idea of the Self: Thought and Experience in Western Europe Since the Seventeenth Century* (Cambridge: Cambridge University Press).

Sharpe, Matthew (2003) 'On The Dumb Sublimity of Law: A Critique of The Post-Structuralist Orientation Towards Ethics.' *Minerva: An Internet Journal of Philosophy* 7, 23–43.

Slors, Marc (2004) 'Care For One's Own Future Experiences.' *Philosophical Explorations* 7(2), 183–95.

Strawser, Michael (1994) 'Kierkegaardian Meditations on First Philosophy: A Reading of *Johannes Climacus*.' *Journal of the History of Philosophy* 32(4), 623–43.

Stokes, Patrick (2006) 'The Power of Death: Retroactivity, Narrative, and Interest' in Robert L. Perkins (ed.) *International Kierkegaard Commentary: Prefaces/Writing Sampler and Three Discourses on Imagined Occasions* (Macon GA: Mercer University Press) pp. 387–417.

Stokes, Patrick (2008) 'Locke, Kierkegaard, and the Phenomenology of Personal Identity.' *International Journal of Philosophical Studies* 16(5) (December 2008), 645–72.

Stokes, Patrick (2009) 'Anti-Climacus and Neo-Lockeanism: Towards a Kierkegaardian Theory of Personal Identity' in Niels Jørgen Cappelørn, K. Brian Söderquist and Herman Deuser (eds) *Kierkegaard Studies Yearbook 2009* (Berlin: de Gruyter) pp. 529–57.

Stokes, Patrick (2010, forthcoming) ' "See For Your Self": Contemporaneity, Autopsy and Presence in Kierkegaard's Moral-Religious Psychology.' *British Journal for the History of Philosophy*.

Søltoft, Pia (1998) 'The Presence of the Absent Neighbor in *Works of Love*,' trans. M.G. Piety, in Niels Jørgen Cappelørn and Herman Deuser (eds) *Kierkegaard Studies Yearbook 1998* (Berlin and New York: Walter de Gruyter) pp. 113–28.

Taylor, Mark C. (1974) 'Kierkegaard on the Structure of Selfhood.' *Kierkegaardiana* 9, 84–101.

Taylor, Mark C. (1975) *Kierkegaard's Pseudonymous Authorship: A Study of Time and the Self* (Princeton, NJ: Princeton University Press).

Taylor, Mark C. (1980) *Journeys to Selfhood: Hegel and Kierkegaard* (Berkeley, CA: University of California Press).

Thulstrup, Niels (1984) *Commentary on Kierkegaard's Concluding Unscientific Postscript*, trans. Robert J. Widenmann (Princeton: Princeton University Press).

Turner, Jeffrey S. (2001) 'To Tell a Good Tale: Kierkegaardian Reflections on Moral Narrative and Moral Truth' in John J. Davenport and Anthony Rudd (eds) *Kierkegaard After MacIntyre: Essays on Freedom, Narrative and Virtue* (Chicago and La Salle, IL: Open Court Publishing) pp. 211–32.

Urmson, J.O. (1988) *Aristotle's Ethics* (London: Blackwell).

Velleman, J. David (2006) *Self to Self: Selected Essays* (Cambridge: Cambridge University Press).

Warren, Virginia L. (1982) 'A Kierkegaardian Approach to Moral Philosophy: The Process of Moral Decision Making.' *Journal of Religious Ethics* 10 (Fall 1982), 220–37.

Watkin, Julia (1997) 'The Logic of Søren Kierkegaard's Misogyny, 1854–1855' in Céline Léon, and Sylvia Walsh (eds) *Feminist Interpretations of Søren Kierkegaard* (University Park, PA: Pennsylvania State University Press) pp. 69–82.

Watkin, Julia (2001) *Historical Dictionary of Kierkegaard's Philosophy* (Lanham, Maryland and London: The Scarecrow Press).

Watkin, Julia (2002) 'The Letter from the Lover: Kierkegaard on the Bible and Belief' in Robert L. Perkins (ed.) *International Kierkegaard Commentary: For Self-Examination and Judge for Yourself!* (Macon, GA: Mercer University Press) pp. 287–313.

Watts, Daniel (2007) 'The Paradox of the Beginning: Hegel, Kierkegaard and Philosophical Inquiry.' *Inquiry* 50(1), 5–33.

Weil, Simone (2002) *Gravity and Grace*, trans. Emma Crawford and Mario von der Ruhr (London and New York: Routledge).

Westphal, Merold (1971) 'Kierkegaard and the Logic of Insanity.' *Religious Studies* 7(3), 193–212.

Westphal, Merold (1987a) 'Kierkegaard's Psychology and Unconscious Despair' in Robert L. Perkins (ed.) *International Kierkegaard Commentary: The Sickness Unto Death* (Macon, GA: Mercer University Press) pp. 39–66.

Westphal, Merold (1987b) *Kierkegaard's Critique of Reason and Society* (Macon, GA: Mercer University Press).

Westphal, Merold (1991) 'Kierkegaard's Phenomenology of Faith as Suffering' in Hugh J. Silverman (ed.) *Writing the Politics of Difference* (Albany, New York: State University of New York Press) pp. 55–71.

Westphal, Merold (1996) *Becoming a Self: A Reading of Kierkegaard's Concluding Unscientific Postscript* (West Lafayette, IN: Purdue University Press).

Wiggins, David (1967) *Identity and Spatio-Temporal Continuity* (Oxford: Basil Blackwell).

Williams, Bernard (1973) *Problems of the Self* (Cambridge: Cambridge University Press).

Williams, Bernard (1981) *Moral Luck* (Cambridge: Cambridge University Press).

Wittgenstein, Ludwig (1953) *Philosophical Investigations* (Revised German-English edition), trans. G.E.M. Anscombe (Oxford: Blackwell).

Wood, Allen W. (1990) *Hegel's Ethical Thought* (Cambridge: Cambridge University Press).

Zahavi, Dan (2005) *Subjectivity and Selfhood: Investigating the First-Person Perspective* (Cambridge, MA and London: MIT Press).

Zahavi, Dan (2007) 'Self and Other: The Limits of Narrative Understanding' in Daniel D. Hutto (ed.) *Narrative and Understanding Persons* (Cambridge: Cambridge University Press) pp. 179–201.

Index